THE NINETEENTH-CENTURY CHILD
AND CONSUMER CULTURE

Ashgate Studies in Childhood, 1700 to the Present

Series Editor: Claudia Nelson, Texas A&M University, USA

This series recognizes and supports innovative work on the child and on literature for children and adolescents that informs teaching and engages with current and emerging debates in the field. Proposals are welcome for interdisciplinary and comparative studies by humanities scholars working in a variety of fields, including literature; book history, periodicals history, and print culture and the sociology of texts; theater, film, musicology, and performance studies; history, including the history of education; gender studies; art history and visual culture; cultural studies; and religion.

Topics might include, among other possibilities, how concepts and representations of the child have changed in response to adult concerns; postcolonial and transnational perspectives; "domestic imperialism" and the acculturation of the young within and across class and ethnic lines; the commercialization of childhood and children's bodies; views of young people as consumers and/or originators of culture; the child and religious discourse; children's and adolescents' self-representations; and adults' recollections of childhood.

Also in the series

French Paintings of Childhood and Adolescence, 1848–1886
Anna Green

Fashioning Childhood in the Eighteenth Century
Age and Identity
Edited by Anja Müller

Women and the Shaping of the Nation's Young
Education and Public Doctrine in Britain 1750–1850
Mary Hilton

The Idea of Nature in Disney Animation
David Whitley

The Nineteenth-Century Child and Consumer Culture

DENNIS DENISOFF
Ryerson University, Canada

ASHGATE

Published by
Ashgate Publishing Limited
Gower House
Croft Road
Aldershot
Hampshire GU11 3HR
England

Ashgate Publishing Company
Suite 420
101 Cherry Street
Burlington, VT 05401-4405
USA

Ashgate website: http://www.ashgate.com

British Library Cataloguing in Publication Data
The Nineteenth-Century Child and Consumer Culture. – (Ashgate Studies in Childhood, 1700 to the Present)
    1. Consumption (Economics) – Social aspects – Great Britain – History – 19th century.
    2. Consumer behavior – Great Britain – History – 19th century. 3. Child consumers – Great Britain – History – 19th century. 4. Children's literature, English – History and criticism. 5. Children in literature. 6. English literature – 19th century – History and criticism. 7. Great Britain – Social conditions – 19th century.
    I. Denisoff, Dennis, 1961– .
    306.3'0941'09034

Library of Congress Cataloging-in-Publication Data
The nineteenth-century child and consumer culture / edited by Dennis Denisoff.
        p.   cm. – (Ashgate Studies in Childhood, 1700 to the Present)
    Includes index.
    1. Consumption (Economics) – Social aspects – Great Britain. 2. Consumer behavior – Great Britain – History – 19th century. 3. Child consumers – Great Britain – History – 19th century. 4. Child welfare – Great Britain – History – 19th century. 5. Great Britain – Social conditions – 19th century. I. Denisoff, Dennis, 1961– .
    HC260.C6N55 2007
    306.30941'09034—dc22   2007023674

ISBN 978-0-7546-6156-6

This volume is printed on acid-free paper.

Printed and bound in Great Britain by MPG Books Ltd, Bodmin, Cornwall.

Contents

Figures

Contributors

Patricia Demers, University Professor in the Department of English and Film Studies at the University of Alberta, has just concluded a term as President of the Royal Society of Canada (2005-07). She is the author or editor of 12 books, including *From Instruction to Delight: An Anthology of Children's Literature to 1850* (Oxford UP, 1982; 2nd ed. 2004; 3rd ed. forthcoming 2008).

Dennis Denisoff is Research Chair at Ryerson University, and a member of the Centre for the Interdisciplinary Study of Sexuality and Gender in Europe at the University of Exeter. His recent publications include *Aestheticism and Sexual Parody* (Cambridge UP, 2001) and *Sexual Visuality from Literature to Film* (Palgrave–Macmillan, 2004). He is also the editor of the *Broadview Anthology of Victorian Short Stories* (Broadview, 2004).

Liz Farr was awarded a Wingate Scholarship to complete her Ph.D. at Birkbeck College, University of London, and is now a Lecturer in English and Coordinator of the English Research Group at Plymouth University, UK. She is currently completing a monograph offering a reappraisal of Robert Louis Stevenson in the context of nineteenth-century aestheticism, childhood, masculinity and the periodical press.

Monica Flegel is an Assistant Professor at Lakehead University. Her research focuses on children's literature, on cruelty to children, and on the connections between children and animals in Victorian England. She has published in *Victorian Periodicals Review*, *English Studies in Canada*, and *Victorian Review*. Her monograph, *Conceptualizing Cruelty to Children in Nineteenth-Century England*, is forthcoming from Ashgate.

Marah Gubar is an Assistant Professor at the University of Pittsburgh, where she currently serves as Director of the Children's Literature Program. She is the author of *Artful Dodgers: Reconceiving the Golden Age of Children's Literature* (Oxford UP, forthcoming). She has also published articles on Lewis Carroll, Lucy Maud Montgomery, E. B. White and Jack Gantos in journals such as *Children's Literature* and *Texas Studies in Literature and Language*.

Lorraine Janzen Kooistra is Chair of English at Ryerson University. Her research focuses on Victorian illustrated books and visual culture. Her publications include *Christina Rossetti and Illustration: A Publishing History* (Ohio UP, 2002) and *The Artist as Critic: Bitextuality in Fin-de-Siècle Illustrated Books* (Scolar, 1995).

Richard A. Kaye is an Associate Professor of English at Hunter College, CUNY and on the faculty of CUNY Graduate Center. His scholarly books include *The Flirt's*

Tragedy: Desire without End in Victorian and Edwardian Fiction (U of Virginia P, 2002) and *Voluptuous Immobility: St. Sebastian and the Decadent Imagination* (Columbia UP, forthcoming).

Ymitri Mathison received her Ph.D. from the University of Massachusetts, Amherst and is currently an Associate Professor at Prairie View A&M University. She has published articles in *South Asian Review* and *Non-Western Literature and Christianity* (forthcoming).

Carol Mavor is Professor of Art History and Visual Studies at the University of Manchester. Her publications include *Pleasures Taken: Performances of Sexuality and Loss in Victorian Photographs* (Duke UP, 1995), *Becoming the Photographs of Clementina, Viscountess Hawarden* (Duke UP, 1999) and *Reading Boyishly: J.M. Barrie, Roland Barthes, Jacques Henri Lartigue, Marcel Proust and D.W. Winnicott* (Duke UP, 2007).

Michèle Mendelssohn is Lecturer in English and American Literature at the University of Edinburgh. She is the author of *Henry James, Oscar Wilde and Aesthetic Culture* (Edinburgh UP, 2007).

Teresa Michals received her Ph.D. from Johns Hopkins University and is currently a Term Associate Professor at George Mason University. Her publications focus on Romantic writers and include articles in *Exemplaria*, *Nineteenth-Century Literature* and *Eighteenth-Century Studies*. She is now working on a book entitled *For Adult Audiences: The Child, the Adult, and the English Novel*.

Claudia Nelson is Professor of English and Director of the Women's Studies Program at Texas A&M University. She has published extensively on nineteenth-century children's literature and culture, including *Little Strangers: Portrayals of Adoption in America, 1850-1929* (Indiana UP, 2003), which won the Children's Literature Association's 2005 award for the best scholarly book in the field of children's studies; *Invisible Men: Fatherhood in Victorian Periodicals, 1850-1910* (U of Georgia P, 1995); and *Boys Will Be Girls: The Feminine Ethic and British Children's Fiction, 1857-1917* (Rutgers UP, 1991). Her most recent book is *Family Ties in Victorian England* (Praeger, 2007).

Tamara S. Wagner obtained her Ph.D. from the University of Cambridge in 2002 and is currently Assistant Professor at Nanyang Technological University. She is the author of *Longing: Narratives of Nostalgia in the British Novel, 1740-1890* (2004) and *Occidentalism in Novels of Malaysia and Singapore, 1819-2004* (2005). Wagner's current projects include a book-length study entitled *Speculation in Victorian Fiction: Plotting Money and the Novel Genre, 1815-1901* and a special issue on silver-fork fiction for *Women's Writing*.

Acknowledgements

I wish to thank the essayists not only for allowing me to include their scholarship, but also for proving such wonderfully supportive and invested contributors. Their interest in the collective project and in each other's chapters was inspiring and especially helpful in developing some of the interwoven arguments and mutual interests found here. My editors – Ann Donahue at Ashgate and Claudia Nelson, the series editor for *Ashgate Studies in Childhood, 1700 to the Present* – and the readers for the press also offered important insights and made crucial contributions to the collection's final shape and structure. Their advice, kindness and encouragement throughout the process have been much appreciated. I would also like to thank Morgan Holmes for his assistance and support throughout every stage of this project. Others whom I wish to thank for their help, suggestions and support through discussions of the project and related topics are Liz Farr, Regenia Gagnier, Irene Gammell, Jessica Gardner, David Hanson, Judy Holmes, Ruth Knechtel, Lorraine Janzen Kooistra, Daphne Kutzer, Gail Marshall, Leslie McGrath, Lori McLeod, Andrew O'Malley, John Plunkett, Ann Marie Ross, Christine Roth, Marion Thain and the members of the Nineteenth Century Studies Association.

I am also grateful for the assistance given me by staff at the Ryerson University Library; Robarts Library at the University of Toronto; the Osborne Collection of Early Children's Books at the Toronto Public Library System; and Sir John Betjeman's Library, the Brooks Collection of Victorian Culture and the Bill Douglas Centre at the University of Exeter. I wish also to acknowledge the support of the Social Sciences and Humanities Research Council of Canada for a standard research grant; the School of Arts, Languages and Literatures at the University of Exeter for a Visiting Scholar position at the Centre for Victorian Studies and the Centre for the Interdisciplinary Study of Sexuality and Gender in Europe; and Ryerson University for a Research Chair. Without the time, money and other resources these institutions gave me, this project would not have been possible.

Introduction

Small Change:
The Consumerist Designs of the
Nineteenth-Century Child

Dennis Denisoff

The image on the cover of this collection comes from *New Cries of London; or, Itinerant Trades of the British Metropolis* (1823), which contains a number of visual and verbal depictions of youngsters fulfilling a broad range of consumerist roles. Even the illustration that I have chosen for the cover alone captures this diversity, presenting girls and boys from different classes functioning as both buyers and sellers. One is drawn to infer, moreover, that the girl selling door mats is also probably a producer, helping the older woman in the picture to make the goods that she offers, and that the boy whom the verbal text describes as gluttonous will shortly be a consumer of the hot mutton pie he is buying, if the dog doesn't beat him to it. Meanwhile, the reference to "young" rather than "toy" lambs describing the image in the upper-right corner suggests the illustrator recognized that encouraging girls and boys to buy at an early age entailed selling these young lambs themselves into a habituated commercial lifestyle.

Echoing the range of roles captured by the pages of *New Cries of London*, the essays included in *The Nineteenth-Century Child and Consumer Culture* adopt a variety of approaches, exploring the boundaries of different notions of consumerism and consumption in order to understand more fully the conceptual and real convergences among them. As these essays demonstrate, nineteenth-century concepts of the child took shape through a series of small changes in Western perceptions and attitudes, and one of the most influential trends in this process was the birth of consumer culture in Britain. It arose when the ideology of consumerism – the association of human worth with purchasing power and material possessions – became the basis by which a substantial number of individuals fashioned and identified themselves, others and society. Consumer culture was a large-scale phenomenon that relied for its development on small-scale acts of identity formation, acts that were often most readily fulfilled through the young, who were seen as especially open to and in need of influence, control and shaping. Just as actual youngsters fulfilled key roles in events such as the Industrial Revolution, the solidification of capitalism, and the formation of an economy driven by a consumerist ethos, new notions of the child and childhood helped nourish a society defined by desire and consumption. Considering both the physical realities of the young and the protean communications networks through which their identities were formed, this collection addresses the processes by which youngsters became producers, distributors, purchasers, users and products of consumer culture.

Because consumer culture and the dominant modern concepts of the child arose in Western society at roughly the same time and place, the effects of the young and childhood on this era of consumerism warrant extensive consideration. Scholars in cultural studies, history, literature, sociology and other fields have begun to explore the impact that consumerism has had on childhood. Works such as Karin Lesnik-Oberstein's collection *Children in Culture*, Peter Stoneley's *Consumerism and American Girls' Literature 1860-1940* and Daniel Thomas Cook's *The Commodification of Childhood* make important contributions to this field, albeit focusing primarily on the twentieth century rather than on the era in which consumer culture first arose. Meanwhile, James Kincaid, Jacqueline Rose and Jackie Wullschläger, although not extensively addressing investments in consumerism, do show that pre-twentieth-century adults imbued the child with their own values and desires. In *Men in Wonderland*, Catherine Robson effectively considers the way in which the girl, during the nineteenth century, developed "into a dominant icon both for elite and popular consumption" (5); however, the focus of her book is not the way in which such consumption related to the rise of consumerism. And yet, the formation of the modern child was to a large degree about proffering consumerism to grown-ups. What is the relationship of this development to the formation of consumer culture or, for that matter, the modern notion that the young have an autonomous subjectivity? This collection begins to unravel these multiple lines of influence, including the effects young people had on the rise of consumer culture.

The first two sections of my introduction consider nineteenth-century conceptions of the child and consumer culture in relation to the image of the young as particularly open to, and in need of, shaping and direction. I then turn to examples from history, visual culture, literature and science in order to consider some of the ways in which youngsters and the concept of the child influenced nineteenth-century British consumerism. In order to suggest the diverse scholarly avenues that can contribute to a more complete understanding of the plasticity of the child at this time, this portion of my introduction is divided into the four categories around which the collection's chapters are also organized: "Play Things: Toys and Theater," "Consuming Desires," "Adulthood and Nationhood" and "Children and the Terrors of Cultural Consumption." This approach has allowed me to make use of the contributors' research and insights, while also noting some of the conceptual connections among the essays.

The Child Open to Influence

In nineteenth-century Britain, the young came in a variety of packages. They were presented as the embodiment of the artistic imagination and as the most profound product of creation; a source of labor and a lightning rod for labor regulation; a spiritual ideal and a biological stage in human development. The child and childhood also fulfilled a range of important roles in abetting consumerism's saturation of the social framework. They functioned, for example, as proof that middle-class materialist ventures were assisting in the formation of a more ethical society. Meanwhile, the cultish veneration of girls and boys also reflected a growing recognition that their bodies supplied the tools, labor and even goods that society's monetary aspirations demanded. As Monica Flegel notes in her contribution to the collection, parents went so far as to murder their own offspring in order to take advantage of burial-society insurance.[1]

Nor were girls and boys unaware of such abuse. In "Something About Toys" (1870), which appeared in the periodical *Chatterbox*, W. Baird instructs his young readers to recognize the oppression and mistreatment required to satiate their own desires for toys. "Some of those things are made by children little older than yourselves," he asserts, "If you could see the pinched faces of the little doll-makers and doll-dressers, I am sure you would be sorry for them. A brass button is to them a perfect luxury, in the way of a toy. The people who supply you with these toys are mostly very old people or very young ones" (327). What is perhaps most surprising about Baird's piece is the mature responsibility he demands of his audience. He goes on to suggest that they even donate money to the poor in compensation for contributing to the modern market system. One might begin to wonder whether these instructions are directed less at the young than at their parents and guardians. But while the material in the *Chatterbox* is generally the sort of healthy, instructive fare that parents and guardians would encourage, it seems unlikely that they would have read all the various contributions that it contained. Moreover, as Baird makes clear, even if the young did not recognize themselves as functioning as an audience for and potential supplier of the imperialist, nationalist, middle-class, heteronormative family values from which an increasing number of them benefited, they were aware of their complicity in the process of their own commodification.

Youngsters realized that the identity or image that they were given or that they adopted often depended on adults' preferences, expressed within particular social, economic and cultural contexts. This does not mean that adults' constructions of childhood – perhaps better expressed as "childhoods" – were utterly self-serving. Such conceptualizations, however, risked dehumanizing the young by over-emphasizing idealist models or theoretical paradigms that devalued or erased individual subjectivity. The concern with such dehumanization has extended into contemporary academic scholarship as well, especially in historical research.[2] Just as academic discussions do not produce physical youths but images of them created by and, usually, for adults, the subject of historical study inevitably remains not actual young people but recorded perceptions of them. Even earnest efforts to address this epistemological gap – such as Hugh Cunningham's *Children of the Poor* and Carolyn Steedman's *Strange Dislocations* – remain entangled in it. As Steedman declares, "it is helpful to make an analytic separation between real children, living

---

1   For a recent extensive analysis of various views of child murder in nineteenth-century Britain, see Josephine McDonagh's *Child Murder and British Culture, 1720-1900*.

2   James Allison and Alan Prout's collection *Constructing and Reconstructing Childhood* offers an effective exploration of the relations between, on the one hand, constructionist theoretical approaches to the history of childhood and, on the other, the effect of cultural constructions on the young themselves.

in the time and space of particular societies, and the ideational and figurative force of their existence. However, this is a cognitive dislocation that is extremely difficult to perform" (5). Indeed, such a dislocation would seem to be neither possible nor perhaps especially useful either. After all, actual young humans and the concepts of the child and childhood are so heavily invested in each other that such a separation would present us with something that never actually existed – a type of being devoid of the culture that not only sustained its changing identities but also brought it into existence in the first place.

Although the young cannot be separated from such influences, it is important to recognize that John Locke's infant with its blank character slate ready for inscription existed alongside other young people who, in various ways, helped write the text of consumerism. In addition to existing *within* an already articulated cultural context, they also participated in its formation. Even though the vast majority of them had minimal access to money, they nevertheless held formative roles as agents defining demand, swaying market forces and challenging older people's conceptions, not only of children and consumerism, but also of adults as well. The complexity of these interactions is effectively highlighted by recognizing that, in nineteenth-century Britain, adulthood and childhood were far from distinct – let alone oppositional – subject positions, with individuals often fulfilling both roles simultaneously. Even the age demarcating childhood from later life was not stable. Childhood had the potential of extending anywhere from birth to the age of twenty or even higher, depending on who one was, who was doing the categorizing, and when in the century the categorizing was taking place. Further complications arose from issues of gender, race, ethnicity and class. As Sally Shuttleworth points out, "the lower class child, as worker, inhabited the social space reserved in middle class life for the adult" (108). Meanwhile, ongoing changes in legislation and medico-scientific definitions of childhood, as well as the influence of things such as rural versus urban roles, proximity to work, and technological innovations, further complicated the situation.

While various issues affected age-based and other definitions of childhood, there remained a relatively persistent view throughout the nineteenth century that a person's early years were the most formative. Indeed, many saw high receptiveness to external influences as a key distinguishing feature of childhood. This perception followed Locke and Jean-Jacques Rousseau in conceptualizing people as blank slates that became decreasingly open to inscription as they grew older. And most people also held the belief that the young needed adult assistance in the process. Robson has noted that even the Evangelical movement's conception of the child, which was distinct in character from the Romantic image that dominated the first half of the century, held the view that children needed adult protection and education. The same logic can be found in *London Labour and the London Poor* (1861-62), in which Henry Mayhew contends that "if we neglect to train them to virtue," the young "will form their own characters – developing habits of dissipation, and educing all the grossest passions of their natures" (1:35-36). The young were seen as born innocent and yet nevertheless in need of character-molding if they were to become virtuous adults.

In his discussion "Of the Children Street-Sellers of London," Mayhew turns to criminology to support his conclusion that people who are pre-pubescent (generally under 15 years of age) can be categorized as children because, "as our prison statistics and other returns show," those just beyond that age take greater charge of their own identities – exerting "self-will," becoming more headstrong and (if their propensity lay in that direction) developing "criminal dispositions" (1:468). Mayhew describes people who are under 15, however, as less recognizable as individuals, and as lacking any notable agency. While they might have "vagrant dispositions and tastes," they are primarily absorbent beings – regardless of whether they are poor, working-class or otherwise – who are available to be molded by others. With roughly one third of all the people in Victorian England and Wales being fourteen or younger,[3] Mayhew was demarcating an immense population pool within which a cultural development such as consumerism had its greatest potential for influence.

In *Seven Curses of London* (1869), James Greenwood demonstrates a similarly strong concern regarding the poor and working-class youths' vulnerability to persuasion, offering "Neglected Children" as the first of the city's curses. Greenwood also echoes Mayhew's decision to define "the child" not simply by age but by susceptibility to influence, presenting a rough correlation between being a child and being dependent on others (which he sees as ending when one turns 16). He is worried that the young who are not closely monitored and controlled by middle-class parents or, if necessary, the state will fall into the vices of wicked individuals who will use them for personal gain within the capitalist system. One might argue that these people's commercial purposes are simply more explicit than those of many middle-class parents; for Greenwood, however, non-parental influences of nearly any sort are in themselves dangerous.

He contends, for example, that "the boy who has been sent to school and knows how to read has this advantage over his poor brother of the gutter": he is made vulnerable to the criminal influence of proprietors and promoters of penny fiction (99). Notably, here the danger lies among a narrower pool, demarcated as literate male youths with some disposable income and inadequate supervision. More specifically, the market is public schoolboys, youths who were generally boarded away from their parents and therefore exposed to the influence of older boys within a culture of contest, daring and abuse.[4] As Ymitri Mathison notes in her chapter included here, boys' public-school culture was of particular concern in this regard, because it was intended to extend into imperialist commercial exploits. Other influences such as pulp fiction that celebrated a life of independence and crime were a threat not only to the health and identity of a youth, but also to that of the nation.

---

3   Pamela Horn calculates the percentage of people in England and Wales who were under the age of 15 in 1841, 1851, 1861, 1871, 1881 and 1891 to have been just above one third, while in 1901 it was just below that proportion (211).

4   In England, the term "public school" refers to a school funded not by the state but by private resources, technically making it available to any member of the public who can pay. For useful considerations of how not only consumerism, but also, and especially, the notion of the ruling class and imperialism molded the nineteenth-century public schoolboy, see T. W. Bamford's *The Rise of the Public Schools*, John Chandos's *Boys Together* and Rupert Wilkinson's *Gentlemanly Power*.

Greenwood's overarching concern appears to be with the impact on undiscerning youngsters of cheap, sensationalist goods. However, he also describes a far broader sphere of manipulation, the impact that children's participation in the circulation of cheap wares has on their parents (104-05). Associating one youth's reading of a penny dreadful with the instigation of a plague, Greenwood declares that such consumption of seductive fiction results in the "fright and bewilderment" of adults. In a curious reversal of the Romantic trope of the guiltless infant, it is youths and their insatiable desire for private pleasures that function as immoral agents, and bourgeois adults (and those aspiring to enter that socio-economic category) who are depicted as innocent victims.

As Greenwood suggests, by the mid-nineteenth century the British were well aware that the young, despite lacking actual money, played a crucial role in the production, consumption and distribution of consumerism. This was in large part because, as both he and Mayhew claim, boys' and girls' identities – the models through which they understood themselves as human individuals – were particularly open to influence and formation. They were recognized as the most accessible context through which consumerism – whether seen as a seductive "vampire" (Greenwood 168), a stimulating reinforcement of healthy middle-class aspirations, or something else – could become the driving force of cultural identity. To establish and maintain its position as a broad social ideology, consumer culture had to develop not simply in step with the new model of childhood, but *through* it.

The Rise of Consumer Culture

Aspects of consumerism existed before the eighteenth century and, as historians have argued, were partial catalysts for the rise of industrialization. Early hints of the traits that would define consumer *culture* specifically can be found in the eighteenth century among the British middle class. By the later nineteenth century, that culture had influenced the larger population of the working classes, and had developed roots in France, Germany, the United States and elsewhere. Don Slater has argued effectively that even early in the nineteenth century in Britain some form of consumer culture can be said to have existed "as a problem for social critics, an ideology for the population and a reality for the bourgeoisie" (14). It became the dominant culture later on, when identities, relations and ideologies began to be defined through it more often than through any other social paradigm.

Various developments have been seen as marking this shift from a society that has consumers to one defined by something called a consumer culture. Building on the claims of Rachel Bowlby and Kim Humphery, Jane Kenway and Elizabeth Bullen conclude that the culture arose with industrialism's shift from a productionist to a consumerist ethos reliant on the creation of new desires. Thomas Richards similarly proposes that the key stage occurred in the second half of the nineteenth century, with the development of the commodity as the "one subject of mass culture, the centerpiece of everyday life, the focal point of all representation" (1). For Mike Featherstone, a consumer culture first existed when the variety of commodities and services offered for consumption did not simply fulfill needs and desires, but also created them: "consumer culture through advertising, the media, and techniques of display of goods, is able to destabilize the original notion of use or meaning of goods and attach to them new images and signs which can summon up a whole range of associated feelings and desires" (114).[5] This stimulation was encouraged through new strategies of presentation, spectacle and conspicuous consumption. The commercialized visual discourse was the result of an increase in product exhibitions, department store displays and promotional techniques aimed at both young and old, as well as an increase in individuals' self-displays, in which people assumed the role of signboard for products that were seen to signify attributes such as health, taste and success.[6]

It was only a matter of time, as Jean Baudrillard argues, before the significatory function of the commodity disengaged from any real role as a good or service, with people's consumerist decisions coming to be based on an aestheticized view of the world in which simulation, fantasy and wish-fulfillment are the only relevant considerations. As Christoph Lindner proposes, one can mark the appearance of consumer culture in Britain as occurring when "the discourse of economic exchange became *the* discourse of social exchange; and the commodity, as the prime organizer of the capitalist economic system, lent itself to nineteenth-century society as *its* prime organizer" (7). Two key factors in the production of consumer culture were, first, the stimulation of desires that fostered the purchase of goods and, second, the impact of these fabricated desires on the formation of human subjectivities. For the culture of consumerism to affect the identities of young people, it was not actually necessary that they should have the money to operate as consciously autonomous agents within it. At the same time, however, the establishment of consumer culture in nineteenth-century Britain did not mean that all its inhabitants were fully inscribed within it, or that those who fashioned and identified themselves through consumerism at one moment might not invest in an alternative identity at another. This very fluidity contributed to the inchoate status of the child, and of childhood, through much of the period.

Characterized by its cult of the child and its "golden age" of children's literature, the nineteenth century was also marked in Britain by an economic migration of the majority of youngsters to towns and cities (Horn 4). This abetted the transmission of commercial data among a larger portion of the populace, which helped give rise to what Karl Marx termed the commodity fetish, with the result that goods and services exerted an influence on more people's processes of identity formation. A growing number of the young – especially from the middle classes, who were better off financially than most – were both being objectified and were also objectifying themselves as what was coming to be recognized as the unique phenomenon of the

---

5   On the invention of desire as an element of nineteenth-century consumerism, see Andrew H. Miller's *Novels Behind Glass: Commodity Culture and Victorian Narrative* and Thomas Richards's *The Commodity Culture of Victorian England*.

6   Useful historical considerations of shifts in retail structures during the nineteenth century include David Alexander's *Retailing in England During the Industrial Revolution*, John Benson and Gareth Shaw's collection *The Evolution of Retail Systems, c. 1800-1914* and James B. Jefferys's *Retail Trading in Britain, 1850-1950*.

modern child. And just as they began fulfilling stronger symbolic roles in day-to-day consumerism, their influence within its culture also grew.

British society nurtured a Romantic idealization of childhood, shying away from economic and monetary discourses when describing children as precious vessels of virtue and promise. Nevertheless, the young did function as possessions with currency within a system of cultural exchange, and the image of the pure infant was used to sell consumerism itself. These were not contradictory developments. As Colin Campbell argues, "the romantic ideal of character, together with its associated theory of moral renewal through art, functioned to stimulate and legitimate that form of autonomous, self-illusory hedonism which underlies modern consumer behaviour" (201). The desires and fantasies encouraged by consumer culture found reinforcement in the Romantic notion that the imagination – especially the child's imagination – is connected to an otherworldly realm that was also the source and affirmation of the dominant moral order.

As Teresa Michals argues in her chapter in this collection, during the Romantic era the fact that ethical ideals and commercial aspirations were mutually reinforcing was not comfortably acknowledged. Nevertheless, by the end of the century, the Romantic/consumerist model of the pleasure-seeking child had worked its way even into the scientific study of the young, a field that actually arose partly as a result of growing concerns during the nineteenth century about child labor (Valentine xlvi). The late-Victorian psychologist James Sully declares that, based on extensive observations of the very young, "the grace of childhood may almost be said to have been discovered by the modern poet" (2), with William Blake and William Wordsworth among the first to manage this articulation. But Sully also recognized that Wordsworth's "Child among his new-born blisses" swaddled in an image of passive innocence had, by the end of the century, begun quite ungracefully kicking the blankets off the less-than-altruistic aspirations covered by the ideal. A professor at University College, London, and a member (and for a time vice-president) of the British Child Study Association, Sully observes in his 1895 *Studies in Childhood* that a very young human's impulses are hedonistic:

> What is better marked, for example, than the boundless greed of the child, his keen desire to appropriate and enjoy whatever presents itself, and to resent others' participation in such enjoyment? For some time after birth the child is little more than an incarnation of appetite which knows no restraint. (231)

While this description foreshadows Freud's notion of the id, with further echoes arising in Sully's descriptions of cognitive development, it also holds important parallels with the consumerist discourse Campbell ascribes to Romanticism.[7]

For Sully, infants' recognition of subjectivity seems only to enhance the pleasure-seeking greed with which they were born, with a youngster "apt not only to make free with another child's toys, but to show the strongest objection to any imitation of this freedom, often displaying a dog-in-the-manger spirit by refusing to lend what

---

7   Susan Sugarman offers a cogent comparison of Sully's and Freud's views on children. For a discussion of Freud in relation to consumerism, see Richard A. Kaye's chapter in this collection.

he himself does not want" (232). If Sully characterizes the young as unrestrained appetite incarnate, he then constitutes this self-satisfying drive specifically in relation to others' acts of consumption. He describes the actions as reflective of a Hobbesian community, explicitly acknowledging a culture of discrimination driven by ownership, comparison and competition. Even the psychologist's most basic infants appear to recognize that their consumption operates within a social order in which individuals are differentiated by acquisitiveness. The pain and anger experienced through the competition for and display of goods are the principal catalysts for the maturing of moral awareness. "This consciousness," Sully claims, "reaches a higher phase when the opposing force is distinctly apprehended as another will. Self-feeling, a germ of the feeling of 'my worth,' enters into this early passionateness and differentiates it from a mere animal rage" (235). Thus, in Sully's account, the same competitive negotiations, acquisitions and consumptions that an infant uses to define self-worth introduce the infant to a moral world order.

In his study of the way in which the "wee amorphous thing takes shape and bulk, both physically and mentally" (4), Sully roots the observed actions of babies in an egotism that then also naturalizes a consumerist social model. Meanwhile, others had already begun to expose as an inhumane façade the highly influential image of the middle-class familial space as free of commercial taint. There arose, for example, an exacerbated and increasingly publicized discrepancy between bourgeois ideology and the widespread reliance on the labor of working-class girls and boys. In this regard, Regenia Gagnier points out that, during much of the era, both the marketplace and the young themselves failed to differentiate between child and adult labor (68-69). The first effective legislation to address child-labor abuse in factories appeared in the 1840s, with additional regulations in the 1860s and 1870s extending some degree of protection to youngsters employed in various trades. But while working-class youths physically toiled, the image the ruling class wished to envision of British society required that this fact be less readily recognized as part of the standard model of childhood – a category therefore reserved predominantly for the middle and upper classes. As Steven Mintz argues in his history of American childhood, class was "the most significant determinant of children's well-being" (ix), a position Eric Hopkins supports in his study of nineteenth-century working-class children in England. The economic desperation of the poor often denied them the privilege of embodying the category of childhood. The formulation of child poverty, not only as a necessary contribution to the economy, but also as the threat that justified society's own inhumane practices, offers an especially poignant example of the conflicts within nineteenth-century consumer culture.

Such abuses became more obvious as increasing regulation of mandatory schooling exposed areas of employment that had been covertly accessing child labor. In 1857, the state attained the right to send any non-criminals between the ages of 7 and 14 seen as vagrants to industrial schools, for vocational and moral direction. To assist with the growing need for educated workers, in 1861 the Education Department put in place a "payment by results" system of grant distribution, awarding funds to schools dependent on attendance and examination results in reading, writing and arithmetic. Such institutional acknowledgements of the economy's reliance on the young for its own well-being helped conjoin the identity of youth with that of industry. At the same time, it also enhanced people's awareness that there were at least as many forms of childhood as there were functions within the consumerist system.

During the nineteenth century, the main purpose of education became the development of responsible contributors to economic growth and progress. Anne Digby and Peter Searby's view that schools fulfilled the role of an ideological state apparatus in England (29-31) is supported by Troy Boone's assertion that education permitted a streamlining of working-class children toward employment and self-identification with the state and nation (see also Cunningham 217). By the end of the century, some argued that a lack of appropriate training fostered drunkenness, urban misery and economic depression (Digby and Searby 147). One of the most effective means of ensuring that the energies of the young supported adult values and visions was through directing their desires. Developments in industrial, legal and pedagogical institutions proved crucial to the process, helping the young escape forced labor by shaping them into people who would *choose* to contribute to consumerism.

The identities of the young ultimately became inseparable from the confirmation of consumerism's newborn blisses. Robust middle-class children in particular became walking advertisements for the larger economic model. In a discussion of the Victorian social fabric, John Sloan points out that "the promotion of new goods as embodiments of wholesome traditional values was to be a favorite technique of slick, successful advertising" (59). The modern child was one such new good, with society developing an identity for the young that was intended to support established emotional and spiritual ideals without undermining the potential for future prosperity. At the same time, however, the process also made self-commodification a viable means of empowerment for young and old alike.

Play Things: Toys and Theater

The presence of consumerism within even the seemingly private lives of girls and boys is perhaps most readily established through a consideration of their playthings. From early on in the century, not only were the young invested in their roles as consumers, but consumerism relied on their fulfillment of those roles. Conversely, their function as vendors disrupted the child's persona. Like the boy on the cover of this book with the medley of toys balanced on his head, and the girl helping her mother sell door mats through the windows of the bourgeoisie, vending youngsters were at the low end of the working classes. In 1851, Mayhew estimated that approximately 10,000 youths were earning a living on the London streets (1:479) selling a wide range of items including toys, toy-pottery and cakes (1:470-71).[8] Other children worked as entertainers or sold services, sometimes even helping in the propagation of consumerism by distributing advertising and selling playbills.

---

8   Notably, in this section of his study, Mayhew comments that he does not actually recall the street-sellers vending toys that they themselves would enjoy. In *Growing Up Poor*, Anna Davin offers a number of useful insights into poor children's playthings, many of which were handmade or merely found.

Often, the young worked for other people, although many also bought cheap stock and then kept whatever profit they could make by reselling it.

If childhood was associated with dependence and openness to influence, there is a strong sense that any freedom a person gained through the role of vendor came with a reduced sense of one's self as a child. Mayhew offers the example of the costermonger who, "although only eight years of age, had entirely lost all childish ways, and was, indeed, in thoughts and manner, a woman" (1:151). As Caroline Arscott notes, Mayhew often portrays the young as blameless, but not as Romantic innocents (99). Focusing on poor and street-working youths, Mayhew faults the parents and the state; this does not mean, however, that he regards the young as naïve, fragile and utterly free of sin. Life on the streets diminishes the relevance of biological age on a person's identity, thereby shifting the individual more readily into a more ambiguous status that disallows fragility or naïveté. "At first I treated her as a child," Mayhew writes, "speaking on childish subjects. [. . .] I asked her about her toys and her games with her companions; but the look of amazement that answered me soon put an end to any attempt at fun on my part" (1:151). Here, Mayhew actually does see the person as a child; it is the vendor who fails to self-identify as such because of the hardship associated with her class position, poverty and occupation. The young who had the privilege of being on the purchasing end of commercial exchanges, meanwhile, saw things quite differently.

Lynda Nead and others have noted that the visual culture of public amusements such as penny gaffs, as well as the display of toys, sensationalist periodicals and advertising in general, offered free entertainment to those who could not afford to buy, including most of the poor and the young. In addition, the century saw an increase in goods and advertising directed at boys and girls. Products made specifically for them were readily displayed at toy emporia such as the Lowther Arcade, the Soho Bazaar and Cremer's of Regent Street (Horn 162). Thomas Crane and Ellen Houghton's poem "The Lowther Arcade" (1883) effectively recreates this bounty: "Toys are hanging up on strings, / Toys are laid in tempting rows, / And each shop with pretty things / Is so crammed it overflows" (52). "Do you love a fine new toy?" the narrator goes on to ask, "Yes, you say, of course you do." Intended for the young, Crane and Houghton's poem first tantalizes its readers, and then basically coerces them into conforming to a consumerist agenda. Rather than warn against the dangers of materialist greed, as many nineteenth-century works aimed at youngsters did, "The Lowther Arcade" instructs its readers to obtain the items that they "of course" desire by letting their mothers know.

"The Lowther Arcade" appeared later in the century, but even works as early as Maria Edgeworth's 1796 story "The Purple Jar" reflect an awareness of the position held by girls and boys within a society invested in consumerism. This well-known children's tale is heavy-handed in its instruction to the young to give purchasing preference to practical necessities and objects of use rather than those of pleasure. But it also informs parents of their duty to instruct offspring in how to be responsible shoppers who recognize value and direct their purchases accordingly. In the story, Rosamund is attracted to a shop window displaying a beautiful jar that proves to have been altered to arouse a desire it cannot fulfill. The young heroine's focus on the object's superficial image blinds her to its actual worth. Edgeworth's lesson on the difference between appearance and intrinsic value foreshadows Oscar Wilde's interrogation – in tales such as "The Happy Prince" (1888) and "The Young King" (1891) – of the relations between, on the one hand, conspicuous consumption and, on the other, the theory that morals and individual identity are innate yet teachable.

An equally informative element of Edgeworth's story is the comfort with which the middle-class mother and daughter participate in the shared shopping experience, so many decades before the consumerist ethos overtook the Industrial Revolution's productionism. The rise of consumerism at this time was assisted by a conceptualization of toys as symbols of a lifestyle not influenced by commercial elements.[9] Yet the mother in "The Purple Jar" does not discourage her daughter's entry into the marketplace. Rather, she works to re-direct Rosamund's agency toward adopting a need-based purchasing pattern, rather than the desire-based one that the girl has somehow already developed. As Michals argues in her chapter published here, Edgeworth often similarly intended her non-fiction to educate parents in the use of toys to direct youngsters toward fulfilling responsibilities within a market economy. Thus, even before the nineteenth century, toys were being conceptualized not only as lures for young shoppers, but also as tools for constructing them as consuming subjects.

Michals demonstrates that toys, and their use for instruction to the young, were used to reinforce industry, commercial prosperity and a supporting domestic family model. But the social dynamic around playthings also reflected adults' wishes to maintain a connection to their own early years, a desire that actually questioned the boundaries of family roles. In her chapter on gender formation in relation to the popularity of toy theaters among men such as Charles Dickens, G. K. Chesterton and Robert Louis Stevenson, Liz Farr notes that these miniature worlds addressed a highly influential nostalgic longing in adults. At the same time, they introduced the young to the contemporary aesthetic marketplace, configuring as childish a mature visual aesthetic and model of masculine desire. In the process, toy theaters prepared people – especially males – early on for a life in which desires could not all be fulfilled. The commercial dream that Edgeworth's toys were to help propagate had, by the end of the century, been reconceived by many as a perpetual dissatisfaction inherent in consumer culture.

Farr argues that the discontent lurking within playtime was more than just adults' melancholic remembrances of the past. This fact becomes especially apparent when one considers the young themselves as the goods intended for consumption, whether by their peers or by adults. Such was the case, for example, with children's theater performances. Marah Gubar demonstrates in her contribution here that, when it came to this particularly popular product, the consumption practices of the young and older audience members were informatively distinct. Although the fact that the plays were to a notable degree produced, distributed and consumed by girls and boys suggests a potential circumvention of adults in the system of commoditization, adults managed the productions, controlled the finances and joined the young in watching the plays; therefore, their interests were always also addressed. Gubar observes that,

---

9   On the nineteenth-century British industry in child-centered commodities other than toys and clothing, see Adrian Forty's *Objects of Desire*.

while the few records of boys' and girls' responses to child performances suggest a general exuberance, adults such as Lewis Carroll often commented not on the actors' boisterous vivacity or their innocence and purity (as one might expect), but on their professionalism, adaptability and, especially, eager and easy performance of adult identities. One finds in such language a sense that mid-century adults were becoming aware that their control of the relationship of the young to consumerism was not as strong as somebody like Edgeworth might have previously been able to assume. This was, Gubar notes, because youngsters succeeded so well in performing within a consumerist environment characterized as an adult sphere. These suggestions of maturity and independent agency helped construe the young not simply as things to objectify as distant idols, but also as people with whom to interact. This blurring of childhood and adulthood introduced young and old to new goods and services, and to new forms of capital and agency, ones that often involved sexualized consumption.

Consuming Desires

Although set at roughly the same time as Edgeworth's "Purple Jar," Elizabeth Gaskell's novel *Sylvia's Lovers* was published over half a century later, in 1863, and explores more fully the macro-economic repercussions of youths' consumerist agency. Set in and around the small English town of Monkshaven during the French Revolutionary wars of the 1790s, the novel traces the life of the country girl Sylvia Robson. Emphasizing the mismatch between Sylvia's "character as undeveloped as a child's" (24) and her 17 years, Gaskell's narrator emphasizes that the farmer's daughter is childlike (76, 94), a girl (11) reminiscent of Little Red Riding Hood (87). And as with Little Red, the ambiguities around Sylvia's level of maturity prove dangerous, especially as she gradually recognizes not only her own value as a sexual object, but also her desire for others – most notably the dashing sailor Charley Kinraid.

In order to establish a frame for the novel's complex negotiations around Sylvia's identities as idyllic innocent and desiring woman, Gaskell turns to commercial discourse. In light of her youth, lower working-class status, existence outside of any major urban center and lack of money, it might appear surprising that the heroine is first presented to us as a vendor and a shopper, going into town with her friend Molly to sell butter and eggs and to buy material for a cloak. Gaskell is not offering a fully fledged member of consumer culture here; she emphasizes that it is rare for the girl to shop with "not even an elder authority to curb her as to price, only Molly to give her admiring counsel, and as much sympathy as was consistent with a little patient envy" (11). Notably, the poorer Molly proves more experienced both as seller and purchaser. Unlike Edgeworth's Rosamund, Molly's shopping is all for necessities and none of her purchases exercises individual desire: "not a single thing was for herself, nor, indeed, for any one individual of her numerous family. There was neither much thought nor much money to spend for any but collective wants in the Corney family" (11). Similarly, in the anonymous "Mother's Right Hand" (1878), published by the Religious Tract Society, the middle-class Lucy demonstrates her maturity by successfully doing the family shopping at the butchers, greengrocers, tea-dealers and elsewhere, all with her two younger brothers in tow. In this children's story, the ten-year-old heroine is complemented specifically for being a responsible adult, the result, we are informed, of her fully obeying her parents. Although it is generally argued that youngsters' purchasing power grows as their class and wealth increase, in the case of Gaskell's Molly it is because of the character's greater poverty that adult responsibilities, including shopping, have been transferred onto her shoulders sooner than they have onto Sylvia's. Similarly, Molly proves to be better prepared to take part in the sexual and marriage markets. She readily participates in flirtation and marital speculation, and eventually proceeds open-eyed, even calculatingly, into a marriage with an established merchant with whom she proves content.

The commercial language of *Sylvia's Lovers* is more than just a metaphor for issues of sexuality, desire and marriage. Gaskell notes more than once in the opening three chapters that Molly is, in all practicality, less likely to be courted precisely because her family cannot supply her with a dowry. Conversely, Sylvia's cousin Philip (an up-and-coming shop clerk) makes a distinct correlation between the heroine's naïveté and her being "sadly spoilt" (26), with even her slight and tenuous financial security allowing her a dangerous freedom in the selection of a partner. In accord with this equation of a young person's purchasing power with a broader sense of individual agency, Sylvia ultimately decides to buy the showy red material for her cloak rather than the gray (against her mother's wishes), and eight yards rather than nine (against the advice of the vendor, Philip). More than a minor rebellious streak, Sylvia's selection of the more daring cloth for the cloak foreshadows her ultimate devotion to Charley and her disregard for the gray, secure Philip. The immature shopping choice establishes early on the pattern for the tragedy that leaves Sylvia and Philip damaged, while the wolfish Charley quickly forgets the heroine and finds himself a wealthy beauty from another town.

Despite the story's late-eighteenth-century context, Gaskell's novel weaves a tight connection between the consumerist values of the young and their approach to the fulfillment of other desires. Notably, by the end of the century, as Michèle Mendelssohn shows in her contribution to the collection, everyday consumerist and sexual discourses had become so enmeshed that the former took over much of the task of the latter. The model of mutual influence between child and adult, discussed by Farr in her consideration of toy theaters, thus also operates in the desires and consumption of sex. Emphasizing Henry James's fiction, together with contemporary views on child prostitution, Mendelssohn establishes that the influences characterized by Gaskell as molding the young consumer grew more powerful by the end of the nineteenth century. More specifically, interwoven legal and commercial discourses now underwrote the articulation of a parent's or guardian's responsibility regarding the raising of female children. Through the logic of consumer culture, this responsibility was constituted as an investment in which girls were prepared as products within the marketplace, as much as they were being sold an ideal version of adult sexuality.

Mendelssohn's scholarship focuses on females in the marriage market, but the analytical model she develops extends effectively to the ways in which the young in general were not just being seduced by the value system of their elders, but being seduced *into* it. By addressing Lewis Carroll's constructions of girls in writing and photography, Carol Mavor demonstrates just how crucial sensuality and physicality are to this thicker conception of the young within consumer culture. The commodification of the Alice character, and the delight readers find in her stories and images, are shown also to be celebrations of adults' consumption of the young. Ultimately, Carroll's writings and photographs reflect a key logistic impasse in the rise of consumer culture. If this culture is constructed through the young, how can it be kept from asserting, if not privileging, their own longings? Moreover, how is it possible to commercialize adults' desires without acknowledging greater agency in the young who are inseparable from them?

What is actually at stake in this development is effectively dramatized through one of the most daring nineteenth-century images of a youth taking production and consumption out of adult hands – that of Salome. The second half of the century saw various visual, verbal and musical representations of the girl, using the sexuality adults had transposed onto her body, to undermine the authority of the adults themselves. This plethora of depictions reflects a growing anxiety over children's adept participation in a consumerist society that promised the fulfillment of their passions. In his contribution to this collection, Richard A. Kaye argues that the mass production of Salomes as a running commentary (extending to the present day) demonized the fulfillment of desire as an end in itself. Tracking the equation of Salome's non-productive sexuality with homosexuality, Kaye demonstrates that the youth was deemed dangerous not simply because of her consuming passion, but also because of what he refers to as her "obdurate, spoiled girlishness." Salome's willful disregard for others in her quest for self-gratification reflects middle-class anxiety that consumer culture was a self-motivating process, no longer reliant on actual goods and services, or their producers and consumers. Peaking at the end of the nineteenth century – just as Western nations' imperialist and capitalist materialism was facing its greatest scrutiny and criticism from within – the swarm of Salomes evokes an image of consumerism as no longer just the innocent, healthy babe of which adults could not get enough. Instead, it was being recognized as an uncontrollable, spoiled brat who would sacrifice all for the opportunity to satiate its desires – the very identity that would become the twentieth century's key target market.

Adulthood and Nationhood

Like Salome, nineteenth-century Britons and the nation at large came across to more and more of its members as rather gluttonous in their adoption of the consumerist ethos. No other event captured the early pride in this appetite better than London's Great Exhibition of 1851; by then, the commercial rhetoric through which people were forming their values and identities was woven, as Queen Victoria's own journal suggests, into the most innocuous of practices and customs. The Queen describes 1 May 1851 as "one of the greatest and most glorious days of our lives" (qtd. in Gibbs-Smith 16), apparently, as the next sentence suggests, because it is her son's first birthday:

> We began the day with tenderest greetings and congratulations on the birth of our dear little Arthur. He was brought in at breakfast and looked beautiful with blue ribbon on his

frock. Mama and Victor were there, as well as all the children and our dear guests. Our
little gifts of toys were added to by ones from the Pce and Pcess [of Prussia]. (16)

But after this momentary reflection on the charming domestic celebration, Britain's
matriarch turns to another event that took place later the same day – the opening of
the Great Exhibition of Works of Industry of All Nations. Fondly recalling "the flags
of every nation," "the myriads of people filling the galleries and seats around," and
"the flourish of trumpets as we entered the building," she records her reaction:

> The tremendous cheering, the joy expressed in every face, the vastness of the building,
> with all its decoration and exhibits, the sound of the organ (with 200 instruments and 600
> voices, which seemed nothing) and my beloved husband, the creator of this peace festival
> "uniting the industry and art of all nations of the earth," all this was indeed moving, and a
> day to live for ever. God bless my dearest Albert, and my dear Country, which has shown
> itself so great today. (17)

Queen Victoria offers a more detailed description of the event than she had of the
breakfast gathering, and a reader soon realizes that she saw 1 May 1851 as "most
glorious" not because of Arthur's birthday but because of the opening of a trade show
that presented Britain and the empire in all its globalizing commercial splendor.

Citing Rosalind Williams, Don Slater notes that, while the London Exhibition
emphasized new developments in industry and technology, less than forty years later
the Paris Exhibition of 1889 emphasized the consumerist element of the event by
putting price tags on the items on display. In this shift, Slater recognizes no less
than the "transformation of modernity itself into a commodity, [. . .] and of the
commodity into the goal of modernity" (14). The author of the 1851 *Palace of
Glass and the Gathering of People*, however, saw the London Exhibition as also
rooted in commodities, declaring, perhaps with a touch of pride, that the "spirit of
industrial activity and commercial competition creates all these scenes, and as we
trace them to their source we cannot help noticing the desire of acquisition, one of
the original principles of human nature" (qtd. in Miller 63). As Andrew H. Miller
points out, the exhibition's organizers had initially intended to affix price tags to
various wares on display (63). Although the idea was ultimately rejected, the fact
that it was considered demonstrates that the commodification of modernity was well
on its way by mid-century.

As the Queen's journal entry reveals, the Great Exhibition displayed not only
products, but also their admirers. As such, it helped popularize both the identity of the
consumer and the semiotics of modern shopping, signaling what Lindner proposes
was "the emergence of commodity culture in the most public and sensational of
ways" (5). The international participation in the Exhibition made it clear that many
nations besides Britain had also begun to use commodities as markers of their vitality
and self-image. An 1851 *Punch* cartoon by John Tenniel entitled "The Happy Family
in Hyde Park" (fig. 0.1) shows a cluster of children, men and women of various
nationalities (as well as Punch himself) gathered around Prince Albert, who is
pointing instructively at another group of people of various nationalities performing
for yet another audience. The self-referentiality of the illustration of the world's
citizens consuming an image of themselves suggests an imperialist wish that they

accept Albert's claim that all of humanity is part of one order based on display and consumption. The anonymous accompanying column, also entitled "The Happy Family in Hyde Park," describes "that magnanimous quadruped, the British Lion, [. . .] feelin' perfectly satisfied in his own mind that he is 'monarch of all he surveys.'" "Walk in, walk in, ladies and gentlemen," the narrator encourages, "and see the Happy and United Family of All Nations, under the immediate patronage of Her Most Gracious Majesty and the Royal Family."

Anne McClintock has noted the way in which a standardized bourgeois family model came to "constitute the organizing trope for marshaling a bewildering array of cultures into a single, global narrative ordered and managed by Europeans" (45). Just as the *Punch* cartoon both points to and reinforces this organizing ideology, Queen Victoria's journal entry moves beyond an image of Albert and herself as figurative parents of the nation by conflating the family's celebration of her son's health and prosperity with the crowning of the United Kingdom as the world's fatherly leader in industrial production and consumerist growth. The description of the Great Exhibition even parallels that of the birthday party: the joy and pride the Queen derives from her son's charming frock and ribbons, the guests' congratulations and the array of gifts are all echoed in the Exhibition's pomp and decorations, congratulations from international dignitaries and over 13,000 exhibits of goods. The correlation between youngsters' toys and parents' business, located by Michals in Edgeworth's earlier writings, is now extended by the Queen to the nation's welfare. Meanwhile, books such as *Fireside Facts from the Great Exhibition* (by S. Prout Newcombe) and *Little Henry's Holiday at the Great Exhibition* (by Newcombe, William Dickes and Edward Whymper) helped turn the event into a tool for selling the adventure of international commerce to the young. While such works make it clear that consumerist values were inscribed into children's literature, this was not purely the result of adult wishes to manipulate the young. In English-speaking nations during the nineteenth century, there was a boom in the consumption of children's literature by adults themselves, as Claudia Nelson argues in her contribution to this collection. Men and women were drawn to works depicting children as guidance for a purer adult approach to life, and as confirmation that their own desires and aspirations were sanctioned by the supposed innocent. Within the logic of this idealizing rhetoric, the perfect adult becomes one who most coherently performs values embodied by the celebrated image of the child.

The packaging of children for middle-class adult self-adulation, discussed by Nelson, reached its peak with the ornate Christmas gift books. As Lorraine Janzen Kooistra argues in her chapter, collections such as the Dalziel Brothers' *Home Thoughts and Home Scenes* (1864) presented images of childhood that functioned for parents as a form of self-flattery, the paterfamilias giving the gift to his wife as a signifier of their success. The young acted neither as the objects nor participants of such exchanges, but as the symbolic medium through which the messages were transmitted from adult to adult. At the same time, the images in the gift books naturalized the fabricated parental roles that supported middle-class prosperity by confirming the adult consumers' success in living up to the identities they had, literally, bought into.

Works such as *Fireside Facts* and *Little Henry's Holiday* demonstrate that Victorians were well aware of the value of literacy in the formation of consumer culture. Legal and other institutional developments that contributed to the rapid growth of literacy among the young during the nineteenth century were intended in large part to consolidate further Britain's large-scale industrial and economic operations.[10] Although dubbed the "golden age" of children's literature because of the talents of authors such as Lewis Carroll and George MacDonald, the second half of the century was especially lucrative in the realm of pulp fiction, which appeared in cheap periodical publications that were affordable even for to many youngsters. Advanced techniques in advertising, reduced production costs (the result of developments in tax laws and in print technology), and the rise in literacy all combined to make the market for children's literature increasingly lucrative in Europe, North America and elsewhere. *The Boys of England* in 1866 proved that British writing designed to entertain the young could prove immensely successful. Patriotic adventure stories, often deprecating other nationalities and races, were mingled with sensational scenes of violence and gory stories of dashing, dastardly criminals and pirates with a penchant for torture – narratives that, as Sally Mitchell has argued, appealed to many girls as well as to boys. Such thematic emphases lead James Greenwood, Margaret Oliphant and others to question the benefits of literacy in general. These texts were seen to develop immoral desires and to lure shoppers away from more sensible purchases. Even though, from a practical standpoint, the success of the market reinforced a rising consumerist ethos, it did so only by celebrating lifestyles and values that seemed to revel in its inhumane potential.

A key crisis of the situation, as far as the middle class was concerned, arose from the fact that, while working-class youths had been central to industrial development, pulp fiction held the potential not only for imaginative escapism but also for generating discontent among the young with their position in the economy. Ymitri Mathison's "Maps, Pirates and Treasure," included here, reveals the dangerous game that was played out in selling economic development and imperial growth to the young as part and parcel of the spirit captured in juvenile literature. Establishing the connection between education, literacy and the promotion of industry, Mathison demonstrates that adventure fiction extended the public-school ethos into the world of international relations. The move objectified other nations and cultures, portraying them as goods for British purchase. However, it also packaged and sold the act of economic exploitation, not only as a continuation of the escapades of youth, but also as the all-consuming framework of a modern subjectivity that had been memorably displayed – and even reified – during London's Great Exhibition.

Children and the Terrors of Cultural Consumption

Consumerist extrapolations of childhood identity, such as those discussed by Nelson, Janzen Kooistra and Mathison, often taxed the traditional depth model of subjectivity

---

10   Sally Mitchell, Richard Ohmann and David Vincent have insightfully analyzed child literacy in Britain during the nineteenth century.

and its moral foundation. The complexity of this conflict is suggested in George Du Maurier's 1875 cartoon "True Distinction" (fig. 0.2), in which a middle-class mother and son broach the relationship between identity, conspicuous consumption and ethics. The mother words her advice to the boy implicitly, suggesting that she expects him already to know the elements of moral character essential to the identity, not of males in general, but more specifically of modern gentlemen. The lack of any diminutive language in her discussion with Gerald reflects the intended gravity of her message. The boy's response, however, reveals him to be unprepared to recognize his mother's wish that he view certain ethical values as essential elements of his identity. He instead pays more attention to sartorial self-awareness, reflecting the strong consumerist element in the fashioning of middle-class youthful identity.

Du Maurier's cartoon lends credence to the view that consumerism encouraged an objectification of the child that also worked to subordinate the young as passive and in need of adult support and guidance. But the economy's sustained reliance on girls and boys as a labor source, and on idealized images of the child throughout the nineteenth century, brought a growing sensitivity to the position that young people – including members of the middle class such as Gerald – were in fact more than merely little creatures whose sole destiny was that of being used by their elders, and/ or shaped into appropriate adults. The familiarity of the consumerist youth in British society at the time fostered legal, pedagogical and other institutional developments that identified and categorized boys and girls as people with individual worth and rights. Even if the young were hugely invested in the broader cultural network, they were, as Patricia Demers reminds us in her contribution to this collection, also always recognized as sentient beings. Indeed, while young people's physicality was at times ignored, it was perhaps the one characteristic that was never denied outright. Demers's chapter focuses on Lucy Clifford's stories which, though aimed at young readers, sustain a complex, often sensual meditation on the place of desire within the subjectivity of the young. The modern economic processes that defined late-Victorian culture fostered not only yearning for the unattained and the forbidden, but also terror of a system that threatened to dehumanize and alienate the individual.

In Clifford's story "Wooden Tony," the titular character's transmutation into part of a clock would not be so horrific if he did not actually want the process to occur. After all, the conception of girls and boys as machinery, products and resources had been taking place in nineteenth-century Britain for some time, as Elizabeth Barrett Browning suggests in her 1841 poem "The Cry of the Children." "[H]ow long, O cruel nation," lament the young in the poem, "Will you stand, to move the world, on a child's heart— / Stifle down with a mailèd heel its palpitation, / And tread onward to your throne amid the mart?" (184).[11] Many people in the nineteenth century accepted using the young as a labor force, in part because, as Chris Jenks puts it, childhood was reconfigured as a "form of human capital which, through modernity, has been dedicated to futures" (100). Consumerism prospered on the backs of boys and girls through tactics of duplicity and subterfuge, erasing the sentimental concept

---

11   Caroline Levine offers an insightful reading of Browning's "The Cry of the Children" in relation to how the trope of the normative family hierarchy may be extended to include forms of international economic organization, such as those supported by the Great Exhibition.

of childhood from certain aspects of its operation, even as it elsewhere implied its centrality. Tamara Sylvia Wagner demonstrates in her chapter here that this deception involved a "double investment in the fiscal and the sentimental" that avoided the responsibilities of humanism by conveniently conceiving of orphans as distinct from other children. Some people regarded these unclaimed souls as not only more akin to produce ripe for the picking than other youths, but as having greater exchange value than children on which families had staked a claim. As Wagner shows, this view also infiltrated the mass market, with authors such as Ellen Wood, Mary Elizabeth Braddon and Charles Dickens running the sentimental model of the orphan through the mill of the sensation novel for their own gain, thus themselves profiting from the orphan's commercial status.

By focusing on the subcategory of the orphan, Wagner illuminates how crucial wealth and class were in establishing whether a young person was readily visualized as a child or not. As Monica Flegel argues, the denial of a person's youth in fact extended even into altruistic rhetoric intended to aid the poor. The youngster in need of sustenance, she demonstrates in her contribution to the collection, was often the first to be cannibalized – in some cases perhaps literally. Through the process of consumption, children seen as a draw on funds were reconceived as natural resources to be exploited. While various discourses contributed to this notion of the young as consumable, Flegel focuses on the role that The National Society for the Prevention of Cruelty to Children (NSPCC) played, despite itself, in developing this infanticidal economics. The organization tried to emphasize not the difficulties poor parents faced, but the exploitative nature of the commercial ventures industry. Despite these efforts on the part of the NSPCC to shift discussion to the larger economic machinations that encouraged adults to use, abuse and profit from their offspring, Flegel exposes a contradictory bias in the society's rhetoric – one that re-inscribed the tendency to chastise poor parents as ignorant incompetents who, despite being adults, still needed to be taught virtue.

In "True Distinction," Du Maurier's young male is neither orphaned nor poor; he is a member of the prosperous middle class. And even as the cartoonist gently mocks Gerald's pleasure in performing the role of self-objectifying consumer, both the boy's enjoyment in his part and the conspicuous consumption of clothing in general are depicted as acknowledging – and even celebrating – the cultural authority of the individual. The youth, his mother and the cartoonist all suggest a respect for anybody who is able to display monetary autonomy, regardless of its source. Du Maurier is making a joke when he has Gerald voice the view that consumerism is intrinsic to his subjectivity; however, the deflationary gesture also acknowledges that some saw it as such. The ubiquity of consumer culture is only all the more confirmed by the cartoonist's situating of the subjectivity within a seemingly naïve youngster.

This fusion of consumerism and childhood echoes Queen Victoria's earlier conflation of her joy at her son's birthday party with her delight at the opening of the Great Exhibition. Many other members of nineteenth-century British society similarly developed the concept of childhood in part to celebrate their own, their classes' and their nation's roles as consumers. But at the same time, the consumption of girls and boys as labor and tasty treats became less easy to ignore or justify. Meanwhile, the young were being increasingly recognized as separate agents within the domestic economy. The important contributions they made to the diffusion of consumerism begot anxieties among adults regarding a decrease of their own authority and control within a system on which they had come to rely for their sense of self-worth. As the essays in this collection demonstrate, during the nineteenth century, consumer culture, which arose as a key source of pleasure, vitality and identity, was characterized and sustained by youth. The result, however, was a complex and often conflicting series of negotiations among people young and old who wanted to have their cakes and eat them too.

Works Cited

Alexander, David. *Retailing in England During the Industrial Revolution*. London: Atholone, 1970.

Allison, James, and Alan Prout, eds. *Constructing and Reconstructing Childhood: Contemporary Issues in the Sociological Study of Childhood*. London: Falmer, 1990.

Arscott, Caroline. "Childhood in Victorian Art." *Journal of Victorian Culture* 9 (2004): 96-107.

Baird, W. "Something About Toys." *Chatterbox* 31 Aug. 1870: 327-28.

Bamford, T. W. *The Rise of the Public Schools: A Study of Boys' Public Boarding Schools in England and Wales from 1837 to the Present Day*. London: Thomas Nelson, 1967.

Barrett Browning, Elizabeth. *Elizabeth Barrett Browning: Selected Poems*. Ed. Margaret Forster. Baltimore: Johns Hopkins UP, 1988.

Baudrillard, Jean. *The Consumer Society: Myths and Structures*. 1970. Trans. Chris Turner. London: Sage, 1998.

Benson, John, and Gareth Shaw, eds. *The Evolution of Retail Systems, c. 1800-1914*. London: Leicester UP, 1992.

Boone, Troy. *Youth of Darkest England: Working-Class Children at the Heart of Victorian Empire*. New York: Routledge, 2005.

Bowlby, Rachel. *Just Looking: Consumer Culture in Dreiser, Gissing and Zola*. New York: Methuen, 1985.

Campell, Colin. *The Romantic Ethic and the Spirit of Modern Consumerism*. Oxford: Blackwell, 1989.

Chandos, John. *Boys Together: English Public Schools 1800-1864*. Oxford: Oxford UP, 1985.

Cook, Daniel Thomas. *The Commodification of Childhood: The Children's Clothing Industry and the Rise of the Child Consumer*. Durham: Duke UP, 2004.

Crane, Thomas, and Ellen Houghton. "The Lowther Arcade." *London Town*. London: Marcus Ward, 1883. 53.

Cunningham, Hugh. *The Children of the Poor: Representations of Childhood since the Seventeenth Century*. Oxford: Basil Blackwell, 1991.

Davin, Anna. *Growing Up Poor: Home, School and Street in London 1870-1914*. London: Rivers Oram, 1996.

Digby, Anne, and Peter Searby. *Children, School and Society in Nineteenth-Century England*, London: Macmillan, 1981.

Du Maurier, George. "True Distinction." *Punch* 31 July 1875: 43.

Edgeworth, Maria. *The Parent's Assistant, or Stories for Children*. 1796. London: Macmillan, 1903.

Featherstone, Mike. *Consumer Culture and Postmodernism*. 1991. London: Sage, 1992.

Forty, Adrian. *Objects of Desire: Design and Society since 1750*. London: Thames and Hudson, 1986.

Gagnier, Regenia. *Subjectivities: A History of Self-Representation in Britain, 1832-1920*. New York: Oxford UP, 1991.

Gaskell, Elizabeth. *Sylvia's Lovers*. 1863. Ed. Andrew Sanders. Oxford: Oxford UP, 1982.

Gibbs-Smith, C. H., ed. *The Great Exhibition of 1851: A Commemorative Album*. London: Her Majesty's Stationery Office, 1950.

Greenwood, James. *Seven Curses of London*. Boston: Fields, Osgood, 1869.

"The Happy Family in Hyde Park." *Punch* 19 July1851: 36.

Hopkins, Eric. *Childhood Transformed: Working-Class Children in Nineteenth-Century England*. Manchester: Manchester UP, 1994.

Horn, Pamela. *The Victorian Town Child*. New York: New York UP, 1997.

Humphery, Kim. *Shelf Life: Supermarkets and the Changing Cultures of Consumption*. Cambridge: Cambridge UP, 1998.

Jefferys, James B. *Retail Trading in Britain, 1850-1950*. Cambridge: Cambridge UP, 1954.

Jenks, Chris. *Childhood*. London: Routledge, 1996.

Kenway, Jane, and Elizabeth Bullen. *Consuming Children: Education – Entertainment – Advertising*. Buckingham, UK: Open UP, 2001.

Kincaid, James. *Child-Loving: The Erotic Child and Victorian Culture*. New York: Routledge, 1992.

Lesnik-Oberstein, Karin, ed. *Children in Culture: Approaches to Childhood*. London: Palgrave-Macmillan, 1998.

Levine, Caroline. "Strategic Formalism: Toward a New Method in Cultural Studies." *Victorian Studies* 48.4 (2006): 625-57.

Lindner, Christoph. *Fictions of Commodity Culture: From the Victorian to the Postmodern*. Burlington, VT: Ashgate, 2003.

Mayhew, Henry. *London Labour and the London Poor*. 1861-1862. 4 vols. New York: Dover, 1968.

McClintock, Anne. *Imperial Leather: Race, Gender, and Sexuality in the Colonial Context*. New York: Routledge, 1995.

McDonagh, Josephine. *Child Murder and British Culture, 1720-1900*. Cambridge: Cambridge UP, 2003.

Miller, Andrew H. *Novels Behind Glass: Commodity Culture and Victorian Narrative*. Cambridge: Cambridge UP, 1995.

Mintz, Steven. *Huck's Raft: A History of American Childhood*. Cambridge: Harvard UP, 2004.

"Mother's Right Hand." *The Town and Country Toy Book*. London: The Religious Tract Society, 1878: n. pag.

Mitchell, Sally. *The New Girl: Girls' Culture in England 1890-1915*. New York: Columbia UP, 1995.

Nead, Lynda. *Victorian Babylon: People, Streets and Images in Nineteenth-Century London*. New Haven: Yale UP, 2000.

Newcombe, S. Prout. *Fireside Facts from the Great Exhibition. Object Lesson on the Food and Clothing [of] All Nations. Object Lessons from the Exhibition of the Industry of All Nations*. London: Houlston and Stoneman, 1851.

Newcombe, S. Prout, William Dickes, and Edward Whymper. *Little Henry's Holiday at the Great Exhibition*. London: Houlston and Stoneman, 1851.

Ohmann, Richard. *Selling Culture: Magazines, Markets, and Class at the Turn of the Century*. London: Verso, 1996.

Oliphant, Margaret. "The Byways of Literature: Reading for the Million." *Blackwood's Magazine* August 1858: 200-16.

Richards, Thomas. *The Commodity Culture of Victorian England: Advertising and Spectacle, 1851-1914*. Stanford: Stanford UP, 1990.

Robson, Catherine. *Men in Wonderland: The Lost Girlhood of the Victorian Gentleman*. Princeton: Princeton UP, 2001.

Rose, Jacqueline. *The Case of Peter Pan: or, The Impossibility of Children's Fiction*. Basingstoke, UK: Macmillan, 1984.

Shuttleworth, Sally. "Victorian Childhood" *Journal of Victorian Culture* 9 (2004): 107-13.

Slater, Don. *Consumer Culture and Modernity*. 1997. Cambridge, UK: Polity, 2000.

Sloan, John. *Oscar Wilde*. Oxford: Oxford UP, 2003.

Steedman, Carolyn. *Strange Dislocations: Childhood and the Idea of Human Interiority, 1780-1830*. Cambridge, MA: Harvard UP, 1995.

Stoneley, Peter. *Consumerism and American Girls' Literature 1860-1940*. New York: Cambridge UP, 2003.

Sugarman, Susan. "Introduction." Sully vii-xli.

Sully, James. *Studies of Childhood*. 1895. London: Free Association Books, 2000.

Tenniel, John. "The Happy Family in Hyde Park." *Punch* 19 July 1851: 38.

Untitled Illustration. *The New Cries of London; or, Itinerant Trades of the British Metropolis*. London: Harvey and Darton, 1823: 36.

Valentine, Elizabeth. "Biographical Introduction." Sully xlii-liii.

Vincent, David. *Literacy and Popular Culture: England 1750-1914*. Cambridge: Cambridge UP, 1989.

Wilkinson, Rupert. *Gentlemanly Power: British Leadership and the Public Schoolboy Tradition*. Oxford: Oxford UP, 1964.

Williams, Rosalind. *Dream Worlds: Mass Consumption in Late Nineteenth-Century France*. Berkeley: U of California P, 1982.

Wordsworth, William. *William Wordsworth: Selected Poems*. Ed. Stephen Gill. London: Penguin, 2004.

Wullschlager, Jackie. *Inventing Wonderland*. New York: Simon & Schuster, 1995.

Fig. 0.1　　　John Tenniel, "The Happy Family in Hyde Park."

TRUE DISTINCTION.

Mamma (improving the occasion). "I LIKE YOUR NEW SUIT IMMENSELY, GERALD! BUT YOU MUST RECOLLECT THAT IT'S NOT THE *COAT* THAT MAKES THE GENTLEMAN!"

Gerald. "No, MAMMA! I KNOW IT'S THE *HAT!*"

Fig. 0.2   George Du Maurier, "True Distinction."

PART 1
Play Things: Toys and Theater

Chapter 1

Experiments before Breakfast: Toys, Education and Middle-Class Childhood

Teresa Michals

Toys stand for play, and play stands for childhood. In one respect, this equation is an old one. In the early sixteenth century, Sir Thomas More drew on it in the first of his verses describing the stages of human life:

> I am called Chyldhod, in play is all my mynde,
> To cast a coyte, a cokstele, and a ball.
> A toppe can I set, and dryue it in his kynde.
> But would to god these hateful bookes all,
> Were in a fyre brent to pouder small.
> Than myght I lede my lyfe always in play. (3)

With his tops, balls and wistful demand to "lede my lyfe always in play," the allegorical figure Chyldhod appears familiar even today. Indeed, medieval and early modern historians point to archeological finds of manufactured lead-tin alloy rattles, miniature knights-on-horseback, wooden poppets, tops, hobby horses and coksteles as proof that childhood in the pre-industrial West was basically the same as childhood now. Despite Philippe Ariès's claims to the contrary, these playthings suggest to several historians that medieval and early modern adults possessed a conception of childhood as a distinct and special stage of life, one that deserved its unique objects and culture. Their toys seem to support the claim that these children "are ourselves, five hundred or a thousand years ago" (Orme 10).

I believe that looking closely at toys reveals a more complicated story. There was an idea of childhood before the eighteenth and nineteenth centuries; however, this earlier conception was in many ways less separate from adulthood than is our own. Medieval and early modern children largely inhabited the social world of adults, which prominently included work, violence, sex and death. These are realities that later eighteenth- and nineteenth-century parents increasingly tried to fence out of child-safe spaces, the physical and cultural spaces in which children were encouraged to play. Ironically, as this idea of a separate children's world grew in importance, one aspect of adult life proved more and more difficult to exclude: consumerism. In the eighteenth and nineteenth centuries, children's toys and education became deeply entwined with buying and selling. They also reflect the middle class's anxiety over its commercial consumption.

The open violence of earlier children's play is perhaps its most dramatic difference from later ideals. Familiar as More's Chyldhod might seem, there is something disconcerting about the figure's delight in throwing coksteles. Medieval and early modern children played this popular game by burying a rooster up to its neck in the dirt, then hurling sticks and arrows at its head until they killed it – not exactly a scene likely to be featured on toy commercials today.

More fundamentally, however, earlier childhood play is most foreign in its stark opposition to work. Both medieval and early modern moral authorities tended to assume that people of all ages shared the desire for play, and that play was idleness. At best, play was a waste of time, or a communal release of social tension; at worst, a damnable sin (Thomas 63; Orme, 197). In contrast, today we are more likely to assume that play, when accompanied by proper supervision and appropriate playthings, is the central work of childhood, fostering key physical, social, intellectual and emotional developments.[1]

The items in More's catalogue of toys (quoits, cokstele, ball, top) all facilitate active physical play, but what matters most about them is the fact that they are not "hateful bookes," that they offer a child who naturally dislikes learning an alternative. Notably, in this passage More does not differentiate between one toy and another. In contrast, I want to look at Maria Edgeworth's writing on education as one starting point for the nineteenth-century preoccupation with distinguishing between the Good Toy – the symbol and instrument of childhood innocence, freedom, intellectual and emotional development, and ultimate professional success – and its evil twin, the corrupting, commercial Bad Toy. A perceptive observer of both children and the developing consumer culture, Edgeworth illuminates the contradictory idea of children's toys as both symbols of non-commercial innocence and as major market forces. She invites us to reflect on how our own educational playthings not only help children to learn the concepts and skills they need to become mature women and men, but also help adults to conceive of the children playing with these toys as removed from the adult world and the marketplace.

Edgeworth wrote *Practical Education* (1798; Rev ed. 1801) in collaboration with her father, Richard Lovell Edgeworth. Her habit of beginning her published works with prefatory notes written by her father, thereby stamping them with his approval, also suggests the depth of her continuing sense of intellectual and emotional indebtedness. *Practical Education*'s preface states, however, that the younger Edgeworth alone wrote the book's chapter on toys, the section most central to my discussion:

---

1   Early modern humanists did imagine that play could help aristocratic boys learn. Erasmus, for example, commended a father who taught his son Greek and Latin letters by having him shoot alphabetically decorated arrows at targets made of Greek and Latin alphabets. This anecdote and the ideal for which it stands, however, have the feel of wishful near-fantasy. Real schools, Erasmus remarks bleakly, are "torture-chambers" in which unhappy masters flog a rote knowledge of Greek and Latin into unhappy boys (339). The humanist interest in learning through play had a greater impact when it reappeared in John Locke's *Some Thoughts Concerning Education* (1693).

When a book appears under the name of two authors, it is natural to inquire what share belongs to each of them. All that relates to the art of teaching to read in the chapter on Tasks, the chapters on Grammar and Classical Literature, Geography, Chronology, Arithmetic, Geometry, and Mechanics, were written by Mr. Edgeworth, and the rest by Miss Edgeworth. (ix)[2]

The daughter's analysis of toys reflects lines of thought that remain constant in works she wrote both with and without her father. In this chapter, I refer to "the Edgeworths" when discussing material co-authored by father and daughter, and "Edgeworth" when discussing work written by Maria on her own.

In the eighteenth century, a transformation began which changed children from producers to consumers. Their toys, and the meaning of their toys, changed with them. Earlier children belonged overwhelmingly to the world of work. In eighteenth-century Britain, however, a different world, defined by the sometimes uneasy marriage of two new imperatives, education and commercial consumption, began to claim children. It was not until the end of the nineteenth century, however, that the adoption of compulsory universal education in Britain and the United States finally gave cultural dominance to this middle-class, minority view of the young as students and consumers, rather than as producers (Cunningham 189).

As Neil McKendrick, John Brewer and J. H. Plumb declare in the title of their seminal study, eighteenth-century England saw *The Birth of a Consumer Society* in which discretionary spending on mass-produced luxury goods became a major occupation of a larger proportion of people than ever before. Increasing affluence encouraged parents to intervene in their children's development in a number of new ways. Even Linda Pollock, one of the strongest and most influential advocates for continuity rather than change in the history of childhood, feels that something important altered in the eighteenth century. A secular, labor-intensive, developmental model of childrearing emerged, one that began in the middle classes as a militantly progressive ideal, and that came, by the late-nineteenth century, to be a widely accepted orthodoxy:

> the amount of parental interference in a child's development would appear to increase during the eighteenth century. [...] It is not till the eighteenth century that some parents became concerned not with forming a child so as to ensure his salvation but with forming a child who would be accepted by society. (123)

This increasing "parental interference" focused intensively on the development of both mind and body, employing everything from breast-feeding and alphabet blocks to attractive books and catchy songs in order to draw out children's talents and to teach the skills the middle classes believed to be most important for a respectable, happy and prosperous life.

Here I want to focus on one sign of the new affluence of eighteenth-century England, the manufactured toy. As Brewer observes, this period invented a new

---

2   The Edgeworths are scrupulous in attributing authorship, also noting that "the first hint of a chapter on Toys was received" from Maria's brother-in-law, Dr. Thomas Beddoes ("Preface" ix).

meaning for the word "toy" (33). For the influential lexicographer Samuel Johnson, "toy" had no essential connection to childhood. Rather, it was "a petty commodity; a trifle; a thing of no value; a plaything or a bauble": any small, cheap object such as a bangle, buckle, or bauble sold by a traveling peddler or "toyman" to both children and adults (n. pag.). In contrast, by the nineteenth century, "toy" was well on its way to becoming a synecdoche for childhood. The one thing that had not changed about such toys, however, was the fact that they were produced as commodities.

Unlike the homemade toys given to children by adults, or the much wider category of toys improvised by children themselves through the ages, manufactured toys were bought and sold – usually by adults, albeit on behalf of children. Whatever other values they embodied, the possession of manufactured toys conveyed to children the pleasure of luxury goods. In treating their children as occasions for conspicuous consumption, parents also taught their children a new set of relations to consumer culture. Plumb observes that, by the early nineteenth century, middle-class parents had become consumers on a newly grand scale: "Children, in a sense, had become luxury objects upon which their mothers and fathers were willing to spend larger and larger sums of money [...] children had become a trade, a field of commercial enterprise" (310).[3] The enormous increase of manufactured toys made the pleasure of commercial consumption a key element of children's play, which itself was becoming more central to the lives of children and their parents.

Manufactured toys linked consuming to learning in two ways. Toys were bought for the specific purpose of teaching children skills and concepts. Less intentionally, however, the buying of toys for children taught them about the pleasures of ownership. At first, the new wealth of manufactured toys, marketed primarily in England and Germany, but also much-admired in North America, were, Brewer notes, "almost all remorselessly didactic" (37). Locke's influential *Some Thoughts Concerning Education* (1693) had associated learning with carefully designed playthings. He celebrates, for example, a father who replaced the beatings and scoldings of his children's early education with a set of alphabet blocks:

> by pasting on the six Vowels [...] on the six sides of a Die, and the remaining eighteen Consonants on the sides of the three other Dice, [he] has made this a Play for his Children, that he shall win, who at one cast throws most Words on these four Dice; whereby his eldest Son, yet in Coats, has *played* himself *into Spelling* with great eagerness, and without once having been chid for it, or forced to do it. (21)

Jean-Jacques Rousseau's *Émile* (1762) also champions the child's right to play, but as one part of a broader defense of natural childish pleasure. Moreover, Rousseau offers nothing as marketable as these "Locke blocks," which progressive middle-class parents bought in great quantities (Brewer 33).

Educational toys helped to teach middle-class children not only letters, but also cultural values. Examining early nineteenth-century American autobiographies,

---

3   Plumb outlines the rise of the children's toy market in eighteenth- and nineteenth-century England. Focusing on London in particular, he states that "In 1730 there were no specialized toyshops of any kind whereas by 1780 toyshops everywhere abounded, and by 1820 the trade in toys, as in children's literature, had become very large indeed" (310).

for example, Bernard Mergan sees a new emphasis on competitive strategy in childhood play. An "achievement game culture", characterized by board games that emphasized strategy and decision-making, replaced an "old ascriptive game culture", characterized by the imitation of adults by groups of children, who assigned to a central person the role of boss or scapegoat, and maintained these roles by physical force (9, 22). Brewer points not only to the explicit promises made by manufacturers of eighteenth-century board games to teach industry and competition, but also to the new status of such toys as children's personal possessions:

> These toys and games – educational or otherwise – also helped children develop a sense of private property. Previously most children's playthings had not belonged to them; they had been everyday objects whose use was often shared with the rest of the family. Toys – objects given by parents or adults to children to play with – were for a child's exclusive use. He or she *owned* toys, whereas they had formerly *shared* playthings. (38)

For Brewer, eighteenth-century toys were only too effective at reproducing the professed values of capitalism: "The new toys and games [...] epitomised the bourgeois attributes necessary for commercial, industrial and social success in adult life. They were not only puzzles and problems but the concrete expression of a strict morality" (38). Maria Edgeworth, however, revealed a puzzling problem within this bourgeois morality and its concrete expression in toys: the place of consumer desire.

From *Practical Education*, and throughout her long and prolific career, Edgeworth was recognized as a serious, empirically minded, progressive thinker about childhood development. Together, she and her father elaborated Locke's influential but relatively brief remarks on education, through their own first-hand observation of how children play and learn, producing a detailed program that progressive, book-buying parents could follow in their own homes. For about four decades after its publication, *Practical Education* was widely read as a child-rearing manual, appearing in a number of European translations and American editions.

Edgeworth has received particular criticism, in her time and our own, for seeing children's toys as being all about the work of education rather than the joy of play. The pleasure Edgeworth attacks in *Practical Education* and in her other writings for and about children, however, is not the pastoral frolicking of a Romantic child, or the sinful idleness of an early modern one, but the more equivocal joy of conspicuous consumption in commercial society. The increase in manufactured toys for children in the late eighteenth and early nineteenth centuries conditioned in complex ways Edgeworth's advice on how to construct and defend a middle-class identity in one's children. For example, although she acknowledges that dolls are supported both by Rousseau's authority and by "the prescriptive right of ancient usage" (3) Edgeworth suspects them of teaching little girls "a love of finery and fashion" (*Practical Education* 4). In her account, two of the greatest dangers to the middle-class family are also two of its defining features: manufactured toys and live-in servants. Edgeworth's advice on both subjects reflects eighteenth- and early-nineteenth-century anxiety about the relation between middle-class identity and commercial consumption.

In her fiction for adults and in her writing for and about children, Edgeworth wanted to teach people how to navigate their way through a new consumer culture. As Dennis Denisoff discusses in the introduction to this collection, Edgeworth's well-known children's story, "The Purple Jar," which appeared in *The Parent's Assistant, or Stories for Children* (1796), focuses on little Rosamund learning how to shop with her mother. Trial and error teach Rosamund to reject the beautiful and useless commodities that beckon through London's appealing shop windows, in favor of sensible shoes. As simple as learning how to shop might appear, many full-grown characters in Edgeworth's novels and tales for adults approach or cross the brink of absolute ruin before learning to manage it properly.[4]

In the context of the era's new commercialism, the child contemplating a toy became a particularly complex figure. For Edgeworth, as for the economist Adam Smith, economic rationality distinguished the modern middle class from both the aristocrats of the past and the working class of the present. And economic rationality consisted of being *unlike* a child – of being able to resist the allure of flashy, worthless toys.

As early as 1776, Smith pointed to the surprising centrality of toys to a founding condition of mercantile commerce – the break up of feudal authority. The market itself depended not only on the praiseworthy industry of merchants, but also on the ridiculous folly of landed aristocrats oblivious to what should have been their key interests. Despite being armed to the teeth and backed by hordes of warrior retainers, feudal overlords were vanquished by toys. "To gratify the most childish vanity was the sole motive of the great proprietors" in abandoning their feudal obligations, Smith fumes. They renounced "the whole weight and authority" gained by supporting a thousand men on their land "for a pair of diamond buckles perhaps, or for something as frivolous and useless" (439). The old pleasures of paternalism were no match for the emerging pleasures of commercial consumption, for the new luxury goods that aristocrats "could consume themselves without sharing […] with either tenants or retainers" (437).

In Smith's scheme of historical development, these "childish" feudal lords, dazzled by diamond buckles, inadvertently cleared the way for a better economic system; their folly was in the end a good thing for all who followed. But Edgeworth was concerned with how the life of each middle-class child must recapitulate this historical narrative. A firm believer in the importance of early habits – in "the ease and rapidity [with which] the early associations of ideas are formed, on which the future taste, character, and happiness depend" (*Parent's Assistant* iii) – she was anxious to get children's diamond-buckle stage over with as quickly as possible before it became an enduring and deadly habit.

For Edgeworth and the wider educational reform movement she represented, middle-class family life was not about leisure, but about work – the toil of educating children. As Mitzi Myers states, "Home is now imagined as a happy educational

---

4   See, for example, *The Absentee*'s spendthrift Lady Clonbrony, *Belinda*'s spendthrift Lady Delacour, and Mr. and Mrs. Ludgate of "Out of Debt, Out of Danger," whose incorrigible extravagance brings them, respectively, to the gallows and to "the lowest state of imbecile despair" (*Novels and Tales* II.157).

enclave, crowded with youngsters busied in every variety of learning activity and chatty with instructive parent-child interaction" (54). Parents were to resist the old habit of delegating this work to the ubiquitous, tempting, but treacherous servant: "If children pass one hour in a day with servants, it will be in vain to attempt their education" (*Practical Education* 126), Edgeworth insists, echoing, in extreme form, the common maxim that other progressive educators chanted throughout the century following Locke's *Thoughts Concerning Education*. In early-nineteenth-century progressive writing on education, servants are the equivalent of television or the Internet in educational writing today – the alien influence in the heart of the middle-class home, teaching idleness and extravagance instead of diligence and intellectual ambition, the original Bad Toy.

Flashy, flattering servants undermine the very social prestige that they represent, encouraging expensive displays on the part of their employers' families: "servants love show and prodigality in their masters [...] if children are suffered to hear them, they will quickly catch the same tastes," the Edgeworths warn (*Practical Education* 121-22). In their view, servants embody the evils of the social classes above the middle class, as well as those below. While the Edgeworths echoes standard warnings about servants as purveyors of peasant superstitions, their greatest worry is not that the children who live with them will hear about fairy tales and bogeymen, but rather that these children will hear about the spending habits of aristocrats – "The luxuries and follies of fashionable life [that servants] mistake for happiness" (121). A child's prattling about fine coaches, phaetons and expensive gigs is a sure sign that it has been left alone with servants, in some corner of the house that is conveniently removed from the parents' social life (121).[5]

Maria Edgeworth insists that well-brought-up children, in contrast, had to be both seen and heard by their parents and by all the other intelligent and well-educated adults of their parents' social class, who should eagerly nurture every hint of intellectual curiosity or sound judgment in them. The kind of supervision that Edgeworth recommended would have been a stretch for even the most affluent and most ferociously child-centered home. Edgeworth was the first to admit that the regime she described in her educational writing was, generally speaking, impossible. In particular, she knew that she would draw hostile disbelief for her description of little Harry's father's enthusiasm for explaining the adhesive properties of water, as his children blew soap bubbles in his shaving basin before he was well out of bed. Edgeworth anticipated readers' protests that her educational theory assumed a world of limitless personal resources, both economic and emotional, that could be exclusively devoted to two small children:

> The poor father and mother never had anything to do, or never did anything, but attend to these children, answer their questions, and provide for their instruction or amusement. [...] Be it therefore hereby declared [...] that no father is expected, like Harry's father, to devote an hour before breakfast to the trying of experiments for his children; that no mother is required to suspend her toilet – no father to delay shaving – while their children

---

5   For a discussion of Edgeworth's ambivalence about preserving the subordination of servants in the middle-class home while improving their education, see Julia Nash's "'Standing in Distress Between Tragedy and Comedy': Servants in Maria Edgeworth's *Belinda*."

blow bubbles, or inquire into the construction of bellows, windmill, barometer, or pump. ("A Few Words to Parents" xi)

Despite this disclaimer, Edgeworth's educational writing does create exactly this expectation that the combination of two parents – poised to seize every teachable moment in their child's day, and armed with an expensive array of books, hand tools, scientific instruments and domestic spaces where fragile experiments might lay undisturbed for days – is the sole domestic arrangement that can hope to produce a well-educated child. The Romantic child's upbringing might (at least in theory) have been confidently left to the benign forces inherent in mountains, cataracts, green valleys and the infant's own poetic nature, but Edgeworth's rational child was a resource-intensive project.

It is important to note the historical novelty of this kind of parental attention. One index of the expansion of parents' sense of both power and responsibility to interfere in their children's destiny is provided by changes in attitudes toward fatal childhood accidents. Ever since Ariès questioned it in the mid-twentieth century, decades of medieval and early modern historians have indignantly documented the deep attachment felt by earlier parents for their children, an attachment often apparent in the written records of childhood death. Medieval and early modern parents noticed that unsupervised children tended to fall into fires, ponds and streams, and under the wheels of carts. But the parental love that reveals itself in these records did not manifest itself in the enclosure of the young within child-safe, intensively supervised spaces. This ideal appeared, and increased in authority, in the eighteenth and nineteenth centuries, in writing by and for middle-class parents. Although accidental childhood injuries and deaths still occurred in Victorian middle-class nurseries, the assumption that parents are responsible for anticipating and preventing these occurrences became newly central to discussions of childrearing

In contrast, in earlier written records parental anguish over the death of particular children more routinely mingles with a sense that death is often the unavoidable fate of careless children who insist on playing in the midst of an adult, working world, naturally full of dangers. While Keith Thomas emphasizes continuity between early modern and contemporary ideas of childhood, his discussion of medieval and early modern coroners' inquests describing childhood deaths by fire, drowning and scalding, as well as injuries inflicted by farm animals and equipment, reveals an outlook that would have been increasingly foreign to a growing number of nineteenth-century readers. Thomas acknowledges that "for the children themselves this kind of unsupervised life had obvious hazards," but that "the most common adult reaction" to these continual "misfortunes" was the sense that "children were tiresome creatures who played in the wrong way, at the wrong time, and in the wrong places" (52). What is missing is not deep grief at the accidental death of a child, but rather the sense of adult culpability, the assumption that such easily predicted accidents could and should have been prevented by the watchful attention of a parent or other guardian.

Perhaps the relative poverty of the early modern period offers one explanation for this apparent fatalism; these earlier parents may have assumed that close supervision of children was not an option in households that were often also workplaces, often struggling for mere subsistence. To some extent, whenever we examine two of the hallmarks of modern childhood – the manufactured toys and the parental attention increasingly lavished on middle-class children – we simply examine the rise of affluence. But ideas about childhood itself have an effect too. For example, well into the nineteenth century, the view that children, or at least the sons of gentlemen, could not, or should not be supervised out of mortal danger lingered on in a place far removed from the constraints of scarce resources and manual labor – England's great public schools: "boys at public schools from 1800 to approximately 1860 were free of adult authority to a degree which might seem bizarre to the modern eye. […] Little short of death seems to have been taken much notice of, and not always that" (Chandos 116, 70). John Chandos argues that only the invasion of these traditionally and deeply aristocratic strongholds by growing hordes of middle-class boys eventually made them child-safe. There is a remarkable contrast between the public schools' traditional commitment to unsupervised boyhood, often defended as freedom necessary for the development of more privileged young males' leadership skills, and the middle class's insistence on intensive supervision.

At home, even middle-class parents did not always watch their children as closely as educational theorists recommended. Edgeworth's writing found a wide transatlantic audience through much of the nineteenth century, but her readers were often quick to point out that there was nothing practical about the resource-intensive educational regime these books describe in such enthusiastic detail. Other domestic manuals confirm this impression. Isabella Beeton's best-selling *The Book of Household Management* (1861) contains the matter-of-fact remark that "every woman is not gifted with the same physical ability for the harassing duties of a mother," and that there are numerous occasions at which "the mother is either physically or socially incapacitated from undertaking those most pleasing duties herself" (1025). Supervising the preparation and presentation of the socially ambitious, multi-course dinners that Beeton describes through 56 very closely worded pages would have drawn any parent away from the nursery. Beeton assumed the likelihood of such limited contact, stressing the importance of securing a nurse observant enough to notice the early symptoms of serious childhood illnesses whenever "the nurse has the entire charge of the nursery, and the mother is too much occupied to do more than pay a daily visit to it" (1014). Despite its ringing claims for domesticity, Sarah Ellis's *The Women of England* (1838) is similarly pragmatic about the actual number of hours in a day that England's middle-class mothers and children are likely to spend together.

Both Maria Edgeworth's fiction, and handbooks such as *Practical Education* and *Early Lessons* (1801), detail the transformation into an educational instrument of not just the mother, but both middle-class parents and their household in general. Other times and other systems of value imagined the home otherwise, as a little commonwealth, a little church, a productive workshop, or a political salon. Edgeworth's ideal family home was a school – but a kind of school that did not yet exist anywhere but in the middle-class home itself. We are more familiar than were Edgeworth's own contemporaries with this bright, well-demarcated space filled with small groups of children busy playing in developmentally progressive ways with sturdy, carefully designed educational toys, under the vigilant supervision of well-educated and superhumanly responsive adults. It looks more like our own ideal of pre-school, kindergarten and early grade school, than a nineteenth-century public school, charity school, dame school, or even the most progressive, non-conforming academy. This normative idea of early childhood education appeared first in middle-class homes, not in schools themselves.

Friedrich Froebel (1782-1852), the inventor of kindergarten, made schools for young children more like child-centered homes that fostered learning through carefully supervised play with educational toys (Shapiro 22). Moreover, Froebel saw the school and the home as so continuous, that he was committed to training nurses, mothers and teachers, in kindergarten methods of supervised play (25). Professionalized early childhood education might have moved from the home to the school, but the widespread nineteenth-century interest in the reform and expansion of schooling reflected the continued strength of the principle of large-scale involvement in children's development. The ideal of middle-class children living with their parents rather than with their parents' servants might have seemed quixotic in the nineteenth-century heyday of the separate world of the nursery, but it remained a respectable minority position.

Edgeworthian parents' passion for childhood development led, however, not just to the self-disciplined labor of education, but to the pleasure of commercial consumption as well. Maria Edgeworth's ideal mother and father bought a great many things for their children. She was concerned that in doing so, they avoid turning their children into eager consumers.[6] Plumb also notes Edgeworth's sensitivity to the newly available variety of children's toys, and to the issues this raised for parents (311). Even while they devoted enormous effort to preventing their servants from initiating their children into the pleasures of spending, Edgeworth's progressive parents were in danger of doing it themselves.

Edgeworth meets this challenge head-on. *Practical Education*'s first chapter is called simply "Toys." It opens on a scene of thoroughly unhappy consumption, extravagance, idleness and destruction:

> "Why don't you play with your playthings, my dear? I am sure that I have bought toys enough for you; why can't you divert yourself with them, instead of breaking them to pieces?" says a mother to her child, who stands idle and miserable, surrounded by disjointed dolls, maimed horses, coaches and one-horse chairs without wheels, and a nameless wreck of gilded lumber. (1)

Breaking such toys to pieces, Edgeworth argues, is in fact the very best thing any child could do to them. The real danger lies in cherishing these expensive, fragile, brightly painted, gilt-covered "fashionable toys" as versions of the objects consumed by "fine" adults:

---

6 We might more fully appreciate the paradoxes of this project today, standing as we do at a much later moment in the commercialization of childhood. As Patricia Crain remarks, "consumption appears to have become, without anyone's quite willing it, the central acculturation technique of our own [time]" (548).

as long as the child has sense and courage to destroy his toys, there is no great harm done; but in general, he is taught to set a value upon them totally independent of all feelings of utility, or of any regard to his own feelings. Either he is conjured to take particular care of them, because they cost a great deal of money; or else he is taught to admire them as miniatures of some of the fine things on which fine people pride themselves. (3)

The ultimate reward won by John Newbery's character Little Goody Two-Shoes, for example, is the privilege of *being seen* to drive in a coach-and-six. Newbery, and the chapbook tradition on which his children's books drew, offered conspicuous consumption as a perfectly valid pleasure enjoyed by the wealthy, similar to charity to the poor. Edgeworth, however, and her fellow educational reformers, departed from this tradition.

In contrast to Newbery, Edgeworth suggests, as a most urgent example of the Bad Toy (after the servant), a little gilt coach – expensive, fragile, and useless to children, except for its almost magical ability to excite a life-long appetite for aristocratic excess manifested in real coaches, real horses and bankruptcy. No boy "untainted with prejudice" could feel much enthusiasm for "the finest frail coach-and-six that ever came out of a toyshop," Edgeworth argues (2). He can do nothing with this coach "after having admired, and sucked the paint, but drag it cautiously along the carpet of the drawing-room, watching the wheels, which will not turn," and "sympathizing" with "the lady and gentleman within." The only pleasure this toy offers the boy is that of imagining himself riding inside it, and of conforming to adult opinion that sees the coach as the "prettiest" possible toy (2). The boy learns to value this toy because he sees that others value it, and will grow up wasting his substance buying other, more expensive things with an agreed-upon social value. "Shall we wonder if the same principle afterwards governs him in the choice of 'the toys of age'," Edgeworth ominously questions (3).

The Good Toy, meanwhile, is an educational tool. Like the good servant, it is an inconspicuous means to an end. It is a useful tool that draws no attention to itself, not a flashy status symbol. Rather than useless toys, Edgeworth's rational children are surrounded by a multitude of quite different playthings: child-sized "strong little carts," carpentry and gardening tools, wooden blocks, pulleys, pumps, prints of familiar objects and animals, microscopes, pencils, paper, chemistry kits, modeling clay and paste-board construction sets, to name just a few. She favors most enthusiastically toys that foster scientific inquiry, although toys that encourage strength and coordination are also well worth buying: "tops, kites, hoops, balls, battle-dores and shuttlecocks, ninepins, and cup and ball, are excellent" (17). Focusing on children's carpentry, Edgeworth imagines the future success of the high-end marketing of educational playthings. She envisions a new kind of store, a "rational toy-shop," and the eagerness with which parents will enter and buy:

A rational toy-shop should be provided with all manner of carpenter's tools, with wood properly prepared for the young workman, with screws, nails, glue, and emery paper, and a variety of articles which it would be tedious to enumerate; but of which, if parents could readily meet with a convenient assemblage, they would willingly purchase for their children. (22)

In willingly buying properly prepared wood, screws and glue for their young carpenters, model parents built not only their child's skills, but also a new market segment.

Edgeworth's discussion of children's toys foregrounds a tension between the self-denial of economic rationality and the self-indulgence of commercial consumption. Even the simplest books intended for very young children can still reflect this tension today. As Perry Nodelman points out, contemporary books for babies and toddlers usually present an ideal world, one typically "quite unlike the world as young children experience it" (35). These books not only "depict bright, colorful objects in full light, objects that are clean and undamaged," but also offer a particularly nostalgic selection of objects:

> *A First Book Open and Say* depicts decidedly old-fashioned toys like a top, a toy soldier dressed in a busby, and a train engine. […] in fact, objects like tops and toy trains appear again and again in children's books despite their absence from the lives of most contemporary children. The Transformers and Cabbage Patch dolls that children actually own rarely appear in books except as commercial tie-ins, perhaps because of problems of copyright. (34)

This principle of selection avoids more than simple problems of copyright. These books exclude toys that allude to the most conspicuous aspect of contemporary children's status as consumers – the role of television in constituting children as a market.[7] Ironically, the comfortably old-fashioned toy train engines and toy soldiers in busbies pictured in these books allude instead to the eighteenth and nineteenth centuries and the very genesis of children as a consumer market.

There is great continuity in the history of childhood, but history also shapes ideas of childhood and children's experiences. A brief consideration of the history of manufactured toys suggests that a more nuanced sense of children's place in contemporary culture can be gained by historically contextualizing the Romantic ideal of the child as untouched by the complexities of the adult world. Like eighteenth- and nineteenth-century observers, we can see in children playing with their toys all the pleasures and all the anxieties of commercial consumption.

For their helpful responses to an earlier version of this chapter, I would like to thank Cara Baylus, Elaine Hadley, Robert Matz, Amelia Rutledge and Kristin Samuelian.

Works Cited

Ariès, Philippe. *Centuries of Childhood: a Social History of Family Life*. Trans. Robert Baldick. New York: Vintage, 1962.
Beeton, Isabella. *The Book of Household Management*. 1861. New York: Farrar, Straus and Giroux, 1969.
Brewer, John. "The Genesis of the Modern Toy." *History Today* 30 (1980): 32-39.

---

7   On television's role in integrating children into the marketplace, see Cunningham (183) as well as Neil Postman's *The Disappearance of Childhood*.

Chandos, John. *Boys Together: English Public Schools, 1800-1864*. New Haven: Yale UP, 1984.

Crain, Patricia. "Childhood as Spectacle." *American Literary History* 11 (1999): 545-53.

Cunningham, Hugh. *Children and Childhood in Western Society Since 1500*. New York: Longman, 1995.

Davidoff, Leonore and Catherine Hall. *Family Fortunes: Men and Women of the English Middle Class, 1780-1850*. Chicago: U of Chicago P, 1987.

Edgeworth, Maria. "A Few Words to Parents." Preface. *Early Lessons*. 1801. London: George Routledge & Sons. n.d. ix-xii.

---. *Early Lessons*. 1801. London: George Routledge & Sons. n.d.

---. *The Parent's Assistant, or Stories for Children*. 1796. London: George Routledge & Sons. n.d.

---. *Novels and Tales by Maria Edgeworth*. New York: Harper and Brothers, 1850.

Edgeworth, Maria and Richard Lovell Edgeworth. *Practical Education*. London: J. Johnson,   1798.

Ellis, Sarah Stickney. *The Women of England: Their Social Duties and Domestic Habits*. Philadelphia: E. L. Carey & A. Hart, 1839.

Erasmus, Desiderius. *Collected Works of Erasmus*. Trans. R. A.B. Mynors and D. F. S. Thompson. Ed. R. S. Schoeck. Vol. 26. Toronto: U of Toronto P, 1974.

Hamlin, David. "The Structure of Toy Consumption: Bourgeois Domesticity and Demand for Toys in Nineteenth-Century Germany." *Journal of Social History* 36.4 (2003): 857-69.

Johnson, Samuel. *A Dictionary of the English Language*. Ed. Robert W. Burchfield. New York: Arno, 1979.

Locke, John. Some thoughts concerning education. Ed. John W. and Jean S. Yolton. Oxford : Clarendon Press, 1989.

Mergen, Bernard. *Play and Playthings: A Reference Guide*. Westport, CT: Greenwood, 1982.

McKendrick, Neil, John Brewer and J. H. Plumb. *The Birth of a Consumer Society: The Commercialization of Eighteenth-Century England*. Bloomington: Indiana UP, 1982.

More, Thomas. *The Complete Works of St. Thomas More*. Ed. Robert W. Burchfield. Vol. 1. Eds. Anthony S. G. Edwards, Katherine Gardiner Rodgers and Clarence H. Miller. New Haven: Yale UP, 1997.

Myers, Mitzi. "Servants as They Are Now Educated: Women Writers and Georgian Pedagogy." *Essays in Literature* 16.1 (1989): 51-69.

Nash, Julie. "'Standing in Distress Between Tragedy and Comedy'; Servants in Maria Edgeworth's *Belinda*." *New Essays on Maria Edgeworth*. Ed. Julie Nash. Aldershot, UK: Ashgate, 2006.

Newbery, John. *The History of Goody Two-Shoes. A Facsimile Reproduction of the 1776 Edition*. London: Griffith & Farrar, 1881.

Nodelman, Perry. *Words About Pictures: The Narrative Art of Children's Picture Books*. Athens: U of Georgia P, 1988.

Orme, Nicholas. *Medieval Children*. New Haven: Yale UP, 2001.

Plumb, J. H. "The New World of Children in Eighteenth-Century England." *The Birth of a Consumer Society: The Commercialization of Eighteenth-Century England*, by Neil McKendrick, John Brewer and J. H. Plumb. Bloomington: Indiana UP, 1982. 286-315.

Pollock, Linda. *Forgotten Children: Parent-Child Relations from 1500 to 1900*. Cambridge: Cambridge UP, 1983.

Postman, Neil. *The Disappearance of Childhood*. New York: Vintage, 1994.

Shapiro, Michael Steven. *Child's Garden: The Kindergarten Movement from Froebel to Dewey*. University Park: Pennsylvania UP, 1983.

Smith, Adam. *An Inquiry into the Nature and Causes of The Wealth of Nations*. Ed. Edwin Cannan. Chicago: Chicago UP, 1976.

Thomas, Keith. "Children in Early Modern England" *Children and Their Books: A Celebration of the Work of Iona and Peter Opie*. Eds. Gillian Avery and Julia Briggs. Oxford: Clarendon, 1989. 45-77.

Chapter 2

Paper Dreams and Romantic Projections: The Nineteenth-Century Toy Theater, Boyhood and Aesthetic Play

Liz Farr

The very first thing I can ever remember seeing with my own eyes was a young man walking across a bridge. He had a curly moustache and an attitude of confidence verging on swagger. He carried in his hand a disproportionately large key of a shining yellow metal and wore a large golden or gilded crown. The bridge he was crossing sprang on the one side from the edge of a highly perilous mountain chasm, the peaks of the range rising fantastically in the distance; and at the other end it joined the upper part of the tower of an almost excessively castellated castle. In the castle tower there was one window, out of which a young lady was looking. I cannot remember in the least what she looked like; but I will do battle with anyone who denies her superlative good looks.

To those who may object that such a scene is rare in the home life of house-agents living immediately to the north of Kensington High Street, in the late seventies of the last century, I shall be compelled to admit, not that the scene was unreal, but that I saw it through a window more wonderful than the window in the tower; through the proscenium of a toy theatre constructed by my father. (31)

G. K. Chesterton

Recalling this earliest memory of his childhood, G. K. Chesterton conjures up a speculative fantasy of cardboard and paste. Rather than impressions of maternal care or his Kensington home, he details a miniature artificial tableau glimpsed through the proscenium arch of a toy theater. While alert to the faintly ludicrous charms of the scene, he is nonetheless at pains to stress the psychic importance of this encounter as "something at the back of all my thoughts: very like the back-scene in the theatre of things" (32). Chesterton was not the only nineteenth-century boy to be seduced by the visual charms and imaginative potential of diminutive figures such as swaggering young men brandishing disproportionately large golden keys whilst being watched by inconsequential young ladies. Throughout the nineteenth century, a number of writers and critics cited their childhood experiences of this recreational toy as a formative influence on their mature aesthetic practice. Aubrey Beardsley, Charles Dickens, John Everett Millais, Robert Louis Stevenson, Ellen Terry and Jack B. Yeats were all juvenile theatrical producers, a recreation that many of them continued to indulge into adult life. The influential drama critic and Ibsen translator, William Archer, for example, used no uncertain terms when he declared in the *Art Journal* in 1887 that the only source of an adult appreciation of art lay in childhood, and that a child who had never possessed a toy theater would "never be a poet or true lover of poetry" (105). For Archer, childhood play involved a seriously strenuous psychological workout, the toy theater acting as "a very gymnasium for the imagination."

While girls such as Terry played with toy theaters, they appear to have done so less often than boys, often occupying subsidiary roles in aiding their brothers. In this chapter, I wish to focus on the ways in which this ubiquitous middle-class toy helped shape the aesthetic sensibilities and desires of at least two generations of young men, thus occupying a significant place in a shared cultural imagination. Not only did budding dramatists acquire a range of popular narratives and recognizable stylistic conventions from juvenile dramas; many adults also retained fond memories of this paper toy, identifying it as symptomatic of a psychological stage on the developmental path to a mature aesthetic practice. Read in this context, writings on the toy theater shed light on the late-nineteenth-century investment in boyishness less as a form of nostalgic escapism than as the site for the realization of a profoundly visual model of aesthetic practice involving the production and consumption of spectacular fantasies. Together with magic lanterns and illustrated penny papers, toy theaters shaped middle-class men's desires in the process of juvenile play.

From its beginnings in the late-eighteenth century, juvenile drama demonstrates the ways in which art and commerce were mutually imbricated through a spectatorial relationship of desire. Moreover, its genesis complicates passive models of consumption, because its early consumers, despite their youth, were not merely submissive recipients of market products, but active agents who helped shape the materials through which they could explore their playful fantasies. Although its invention cannot be securely attributed to any one publisher or source, George Speaight traces the toy's emergence from a range of sources intended for adults and children, including late-eighteenth-century children's paintings and cut-out character story books, theatrical portraits, and printed sheets depicting principal characters from contemporary plays (52-88). The last of these objects featured engravings of celebrated actors such as Edmund Kean, John Kemble, Mrs. Siddons and Madame Vestris in the poses and costumes of specific productions and served as advertisements and souvenirs for adult theater enthusiasts (40). Sketched from life by artists who attended performances in both the legitimate theaters of Covent Garden and Drury Lane, and their popular "illegitimate" counterparts such as Astley's and the Surrey Theatre on the South Bank of the Thames, these printed sheets recorded an eclectic mix of theatrical entertainments, including pantomimes, melodramas, tragedies and spectacles (15-29).

More recently, critical attention has been given to Henry Mayhew's *Morning Chronicle* interview with William West (1850), which suggests that the toy theater grew more directly from contemporary theatrical illustrations and children's lottery prints, a game involving the matching of a series of illustrations to initial letters of the alphabet or captions (Powell 8-22). An early and prolific publisher of toy theaters, West ran a shop in Exeter Street alongside the Lyceum Theatre, close to

Covent Garden and Drury Lane.[1] In the interview, he describes how the runaway success of his lottery print based on the contemporary pantomime *Mother Goose* (1811), which "sold like wildfire among the young folks," encouraged him to produce more juvenile prints derived from theatrical productions. David Powell has recently suggested that, once cut out, the characters on these sheets were taken up by older boys, who subsequently demanded that West produce accompanying stage fronts, scenery and wooden stages, thus leading to the birth of the toy theater (10) (fig. 2.1). Powell emphasizes West's passive and reactive response to requests from his young consumers, as he found himself "hobligated" to make scenery and sets, grudgingly giving way to their specific demands (13). As a result of this dialogue between the producer and his customers, the early juvenile drama, without scripts, came into being in 1812, with complete plays becoming available in approximately 1835 (Speaight 88).

Like many of the theatrical productions it represented, the toy theater was concerned less with high art than with spectacular forms of entertainment that could be replicated in miniature at home. To this end, putative dramatists were not only invited to cut out and color in the characters; they could also purchase footlights fuelled by foul-smelling colza oil, and visual effects including tinsel, "red and blue fire," and the means to create minor drawing-room explosions. During its heyday in the first half of the nineteenth century, juvenile drama became a popular pastime, especially for middle-class boys. A general lack of leisure time, and the cost of the sheets required for a full production, put the toy beyond the reach of poorer children. Meanwhile, the rise of the public schools was symptomatic of a lengthening period of middle-class boyhood, a stage in the onward progression from early childhood, during which toy theatres served as a shared recreational activity of this particular gender and class, marking a stage on the road to a particular conception of manliness.

The nineteenth-century fascination with all things theatrical is well documented. Descriptions of amateur theatricals in novels such as *Villette* (1853) and *Little Women* (1868), and in Dickens's satirical sketch "Private Theatres" (1835), are merely the most obvious evidence of a widespread enthusiasm for amateur productions. However, although the toy theater may be read as a further extension of this general passion for the stage, Speaight convincingly argues that, from the outset, it provided a recreational pursuit for older middle-class boys, a major constituent of the early-nineteenth-century "theater craze" that, together with visits to the theater, served both as a harmless pastime and as an educational instrument for burgeoning young gentlemen (89-91). While girls also took part in the performance of these miniature plays, they normally held subsidiary positions under the direction of a youthful

---

1   In this interview with Mayhew, West claimed to be the originator of the juvenile drama, selling children's theaters and penny theatrical characters from his shop in Exeter Street. Speaight notes that, like many publishers of the time, West also ran a circulating library and sold pornography from under the counter (his shop was located close to Holywell Street, the center of London's pornographic book trade) (41). While she does not discuss toy-theater displays, Lynda Nead provides an account of the window displays in Holywell Street in the nineteenth century, and refers to the ways in which Radical pamphlets and pornography were sold side by side (189-203). David Powell gives more detail on West's production of "bawdy songsters" (23), which were smutty music-hall ditties.

"stage manager," who would have been a brother or an older boy. Recalling his own youthful productions some 45 years earlier, John Oxenford was emphatic about the relationships of gender and power played out in the course of juvenile productions:

> This little stage was regarded as something above a mere toy: its management was deemed neither a childish nor effeminate pursuit. The young ladies of the family might assist with their scissors or their camel's hair pencil, and the children might gape, as the growing wonder matured to perfection before their eyes; but in a well-regulated household the manager and proprietor was always a boy, beginning to think himself a man. One of the great advantages of the Toy Theatre was the quantity of time which it occupied. A boy with his bare wooden stage yet unprovided with proscenium and curtain, with his sheets of scenery and characters yet uncoloured was supplied with ample enjoyment for all the spare hours of his winter holidays. (67)

Although a commercial product, juvenile drama could be categorized as a "good toy", in the sense that Teresa Michals describes elsewhere in this volume, because it combined the pleasures of consumption with an opportunity for creative industry and quiet occupation. Transforming the black-and-white engravings of the "penny plain" uncolored sheets into a finished production involved hours of coloring in, pasting and assembling. For Oxenford, this effort was a sign of virility.[2] He described as "effeminate" the lazy boys who circumvented this laborious process by purchasing the ready-colored sheets (67).

William Makepeace Thackeray's satirical account, in *Vanity Fair* (1847-8), of Master George Osborne's youthful "education" illustrates the ways in which toy theaters became an approved recreation for middle-class boys. He describes the boy's habit of inflicting West's pasteboard productions on the Todd family, which – interspersed with visits to real theaters and the coloring in of theatrical portraits – were recognizable ingredients in the making of "a young gentleman" (712-15).

Another youthful aficionado of the toy theater, Charles Dickens, as a schoolboy at Wellington House Academy, staged a miniature production of *The Miller and his Men* (Forster 41-42). It was an aesthetic activity that he, like several Victorian men, continued to indulge. Charles Culliford Dickens recalled how his father, together with the celebrated scenery painter Clarkson Stanfield R.A., was once intensely preoccupied for days in customizing the popular juvenile drama *The Elephant of Siam* as a family entertainment (Baldwin 148). A further indication of Dickens's continued investment in this toy can be found in his *Household Words* story "A Christmas Tree" (1850). This work also sheds light on the ways in which, for many men of the time, this ubiquitous toy was not merely an abandoned relic of childhood, but a model that described the workings of the imagination as they continued to resonate in later years.

---

2   Oxenford was at pains to stress the sophistication of these larger theaters over the smaller, cheaper models that were "toys for children only" (68). The larger, more expensive juvenile dramas are the ones that the writers discussed here recalled from their youth and early manhood and that continued to fuel their adult minds as significant aesthetic objects and psychological models of the imagination.

The first of Dickens's Christmas stories, the tale is a flight of fancy induced by the scene of excited children gathered around a tree festooned with toys. Later that night, an act of Wordsworthian recollection leads the narrator to conjure up an image of another tree, a composite of familiar toys and tales – the traces of past festive pleasures – "by which we climbed to real life" (127). Still rooted in the earth, this fantasy tree illustrates the way in which an expanding commodity culture provided increasingly specialized toys attuned to particular stages of a child's psychological development. In Dickens's story, the youth envisions his path to manhood as a series of increments marked by the ever-widening branches of the tree, each adorned with an array of progressively sophisticated toys that chart the gradual refinement of the child's playful imagination. A cornucopia of wooden animals, masks, dolls' houses, pantomimes and storybooks culminates in a branch holding a toy theater. For the narrator, this particular object provokes "a teeming world of fancies so suggestive and all-embracing, that, far below it on my Christmas Tree, I see the dark, dirty, real Theatres in day-time, adorned with these associations as with fresh garlands of the rarest flowers and charming me yet" (134). Rather than remaining a second-order representation, this stylized world in miniature becomes the primary template by which Dickens, an avid theatergoer, came to view real theatrical productions.

Audrey Jaffe has also observed the circular relationship between spectacular forms of cultural representation and the larger society of spectacle in the Victorian period. Discussing the similar collapse between illusion and reality in the form of spectacles in Dickens's *A Christmas Carol*, Jaffe suggests that, by the nineteenth century, this spectacularized reality, "images of images," became the exemplary form of culture in which "nothing exists – at least nothing worth looking at – outside those images" (33). Jaffe demonstrates the ways in which literary texts such as *A Christmas Carol* participate in an ideological process reliant on spectacle, through framing devices, lighting, a preoccupation with surfaces, and attention to detail. The gap between vision and participation constructs desire, with alienated observers seeking to recapture a lost or "best" self that they can never fully atttain (29).

In Dickens's case, this idealized self was encapsulated in a conception of boyhood as a time of unalienated labor, in the form of play epitomized by the toy theater. Later Victorian critics saw the traces of theatricality in Dickens's own literary productions as stylistic weaknesses: his use of melodrama, tableaux and pantomime patter; however, these characteristics can also be viewed as symptomatic of theater's mediating influence (Vlock 1-7). In addition, as "A Christmas Tree" makes clear, Dickens's continuing investment in the toy theater went beyond the lexicon of styles and genres that it offered. These were merely the surface manifestations of a model of adult aesthetic production envisaged according to a childhood model of work and play, school and home – a model in which a shared boyish imagination offered respite from an increasingly competitive, calculating world: "And I *do* come home at Christmas. We all do, or we all should. We all come home, or ought to come home for a short holiday – the longer the better – from the great boarding-school, where we are forever working at our arithmetical slates, to take, and give a rest" (135). For Dickens, the enduring ability to "come home" to the toy theater is a crucial component of adult life, a psychic structure of arrested development that he later clearly articulated in his essay "Where We Stopped Growing" (1853).

Rather than accept, in Wordsworthian fashion, the unrecoverability of youth and the compensations of the mature philosophic mind, he insists here on the adult's ability to retain a juvenile capacity for "fancy" and an admiration for "perfect illusions" that "we never have outgrown and never shall outgrow" (387). Deborah Thomas argues that, although he repeatedly used the term "fancy," for him it was a less clearly defined concept of the imagination than it was for Wordsworth or Coleridge, serving more simply "as an infallible panacea for a debilitating overdose of fact" (13).

Dickens was not alone in declaring an enduring fondness for the stylized artifice of juvenile drama that, for him, epitomized a means of recapturing unalienated youthfulness. Some three decades later, in "A Penny Plain, Two Pence Coloured" (1884), Robert Louis Stevenson similarly recollected how his boyhood walks in Leith often took him past a stationer's shop, where he would stop in his tracks to stare in wonder and delight at the window displays of *Skelt's Juvenile Drama* toy theater sets. While enticed by scenes such as "robbers carousing" and "the forest set," what really attracted Stevenson's eye were the engraved sheets of cardboard characters lying partially obscured in a heap (104) (fig. 2.2). To the often-penniless boy and his peers, the contents of these piles caused the shop to exert the pull of "a lodestone rock," an attraction halted only by the barrier of the window glass, and by the surveillance of the owner, rightly suspicious that the boys may not be *bona fide* purchasers.

This is not the only reference Stevenson made to the power of the window displays in the Leith stationer's shop. For him, boyhood visits to that store supplied memories that became significant both as a source of wonder and as a provider of fictions for play. In "Popular Authors" (1888), he described the seductive delights provided, by glimpses in the window, of the titles of and illustrations from fiction serialized in the penny papers.[3] In this manner, Stevenson expressed the genesis of his selective method of reading, a pre-eminently pictorial process by which the middle-class boy, like the semi-literate lower classes, pieced together displayed snatches of popular stories, woodcuts and engravings as the materials for imaginative constructions of his own. Lacking economic agency, on account of a shortage of pence, both classes of readers, by using their imaginations, transformed these financial barriers to their awakened desires into a mode of aesthetic autonomy.[4] Stevenson explained these speculative daydreams as a common process by which "we act as our own artists"

---

3   In this essay Stevenson recounts that his nurse, Alison Cunningham (aka Cummy), introduced him to the delights of popular fiction. However, although innocently exposing him to such reading matter, she soon became alert to its potential moral dangers, and banned it. Thereafter, young Stevenson was reduced to snatching glimpses of the latest installments through shop windows. This simultaneously erected a barrier to gratification and heightened his desire (26).

4   As the title of Stevenson's essay indicates, the normal price of the original sheets was a penny for an uncolored engraving and twopence for the colored version, although Hodgson and Co.'s extra large sheets were priced at sixpence each. As Speaight argues, the cost of all the sheets required for a whole production amounted to a considerable sum, often well over £1, which was beyond the means of many juvenile enthusiasts. Cheaper paper and cruder coloring enabled printers such as Green and Skelt to produce popular editions in halfpenny sheets (65-66).

(26), an illustration of the way in which individuals were inducted into imaginative play – a form of modern autonomous hedonism.

Colin Campbell identifies this mode of post-Romantic speculation as an aesthetic sensibility that gradually shaped modes of consumption from the late-eighteenth century onward (77-95). As Campbell argues, people increasingly learned to use cultural objects as the material for daydreams, a form of projected illusory enjoyment from which one derives a greater pleasure than from the ownership of the objects themselves. Novels, plays, paintings and other cultural objects, selected according to each window-gazer's particular tastes, constituted psychological resources that could be brought to mind in the future, and repeatedly reused and adapted, as Dickens had found, as the basis for personal fantasies. In common with most consumers, the boyhood Stevenson lacked the resources to obtain every novelty thrown up by the market. He therefore learned to operate within a mode of desire between art and life, and between the perfected pleasures of his dreams and the imperfect joys of reality. In his juvenile response to particular articles in the shop window, Stevenson demonstrated that the modes of aesthetic and economic consumption had become inextricably intertwined.

For middle-class boys, the occasional possession of money removes these barriers to consumption, enabling them to enter shops and acquire the goods on offer. Nothing, Stevenson maintained, could compare with these illustrated sheets of characters and tableaux, and with his childish desire "to breathlessly devour these pages of gesticulating villains, epileptic combats, bosky forests, palaces and warships, frowning fortresses and prison vaults," which are the "raw stuff of story books" ("Penny Plain" 104). Although readily available in Dickens's lifetime, by the late-nineteenth century many of these productions were out of print. Notably, while toy theaters gradually declined as a pastime for boys, they simultaneously became a focus for adults, who viewed them as desirable aesthetic objects. The archaic style of their engraving, picturesque landscapes and artificially posed figures from an earlier age appealed not just to those who were nostalgic for a lost childhood, but also to aesthetes and serious collectors of art (fig 2.2).[5] Many of the engraved sheets were found to have been initialed by the artists, including George Cruikshank, who had also provided illustrations for *Oliver Twist* (1838) and *Punch* magazine (Turner 177-82). These relics from a bygone era helped to feed an increasing interest in artificiality that was to crystallize into the *fin-de-siècle* decadence of artists such as Aubrey Beardsley, who had designed his own sets and characters while at school in Brighton (Wilson 8).[6]

Stevenson's own collection of toy theaters existed in the form of memories from his youth, as a creative psychological resource of kaleidoscopic images: "changing

---

5   Archer describes a set of juvenile drama prints that Sidney Colvin, Stevenson's mentor and a Slade Professor of Art, had shown him in the British Museum (105).

6   This double appeal of toy theater sets at the end of the nineteenth century helps to explain Stevenson's own attraction to a readership comprising both boys and aesthetes, including Oscar Wilde, who demanded that copies of *Kidnapped* and *The Master of Ballantrae* be sent to him while he was on remand in Holloway Prison. He later requested that yet more of Stevenson's novels be dispatched to Reading Gaol (Wilde 789).

pictures, echoes from the past" ("Penny Plain" 103); "a gallery of scenes and characters with which, in the silent theatre of the brain, I might enact all novels and romances" (109). It was not the scripts of these juvenile dramas, too full of practical stage instructions, that were the source of their attraction, but the ways in which the scenery and characters appealed to the visual sense and fueled imaginative projections. Having selected and paid for his purchases, Stevenson recalls running home in exultation, only to discover that his projected pleasure was short-lived, lasting barely half an hour. While the coloring of the black-and-white reproductions of characters and scenery helped to stall this anti-climax, he soon found that true pleasure came only from the speculative process rather than the finished object. Not only did it seem "sacrilege" to cut out the sheets, but by this point they were all spoiled, leaving the boy to undertake only "the long-drawn disenchantment of the actual performance" (106).

Stevenson was not the only middle-class writer to recall this sense of desire and anti-climax in relation to toy theaters. An anonymous contributor to *All The Year Round* (1869) had earlier described the similar responses of city dwellers to spectacles in shop windows (fig. 2.3). He recollected the boyhood attractions of the stationer's shop, with its cheap illustrated papers and *Skelt's Juvenile Dramas*. Once again it seems that the pleasure of this particular toy did not survive long after the act of purchase, as he recorded a similar – if slightly longer – cycle of pleasurable anticipation, disenchantment and renewed anticipation: "We had weeks of joyous preparation, followed by a few days of unceasing performance, until we thirsted for fresh managerial triumphs, and would repair once more to Fairy-Street to gaze with covetous eyes on fresh Skelt's and dramas anew" ("Looking" 28). The visual style of these productions, which Stevenson labeled "stagey and piratic" ("Penny Plain" 107), reproduced the artificially posed tableaux and forms of acting that were common in the early decades of the century. Like many boys of the period, he was particularly drawn to the range of masculine heroes and villains, such as Regency dandies, or pirates and banditti often armed to the teeth, rather than to "the extreme hard favour" of the more passive female characters (107).[7] Once the figures were colored in, cut out and pasted onto cardboard, the boy would be equipped with a number of colorful characters with which to people a stage, against an illustrated backdrop and wings that drew heavily upon the early-nineteenth-century vogue for the picturesque. Over 50 years later, this archaic stylization appeared pre-eminently artificial, creating a faintly ludicrous world that Stevenson dubbed "the kingdom of Transpontus" (107), recognizably shaped by the popular productions of the illegitimate theaters across the bridge on the South Bank of the Thames. Although outdated, this theatricality was nonetheless, for both Stevenson and William Archer, the source of its familiar charm.

---

7   Speaight argues that the depictions of actresses from the early-nineteenth century did not accord with later Victorian ideas of womanliness as childlike and angelic. Consequently, they were often deemed ugly and insipid. He also suggests that the boys were not yet of an age to appreciate their allure, and that, from a practical point of view, their costumes were less suitable for tinseling (135; see also Wilson 106).

Stevenson saw this version of the world as "domestically British," and characterized by "an old, insular home-bred staginess" ("Penny Plain" 107). In its Orientalist mode, this insularity was manifested in scenes of deserts tamed by the inclusion of hollyhocks. Meanwhile, the Occidental sets, which he described as "a sort of indigestion of England," drew upon the full lexicon of the picturesque, including wandering roads, windmills, a castle on a hill and the sun irradiating the scene from behind a cloud. Such was the influence of this characteristically English scenery upon the Scottish boy that, when Stevenson finally crossed the border from Edinburgh, he felt he had "come home to Skelt" as he confronted the physical landscape that he, like Dickens, viewed through the template of his childhood games and fantasies. Emphasizing the power of the toy on his imagination, Stevenson declared that, from the age of 14 onwards, he had become "but a puppet in the hands of Skelt": "What am I? What are life, art, letters, the word, but what my Skelt has made them? He stamped himself upon my immaturity. The world was plain before I knew him, a poor penny world; but soon it was all coloured with romance" (108). By providing a range of picturesque backdrops and tableaux, the toy theater offered juvenile dramatists a series of templates by which the world could be "colored in" or read from a particular point of view.

As Susan Stewart has argued in relation to the tableau, this miniature world of clearly limited frozen space, shut off from history and surrounding reality, was both particularized and generalized in time (48). The cardboard sheets of characters, scenery and wings, depicting moments in a specific production, could also be recycled or customized to construct a number of other scenes, thus providing a series of templates by which new fantasies could be represented and read. For Stevenson, this flexibility provided an imaginative psychological resource, the basis for subsequent literary endeavors:

> Those who try to be artists use, time after time, the matter of their recollections[,] setting and resetting little coloured memories of men and scenes, rigging up (it may be) some especial friend in the attire of the buccaneer, and decreeing armies to manoeuvre, or murder to be done, on the playground of their youth. But memories are a fairy gift which cannot be worn out by using. After a dozen services in various tales, the little sunbright pictures of the past still shine in the mind's eye with not a lineament defaced, not a tint impaired. ("Memoirs" 59)

Through its adaptability, the toy theater was a vehicle for a particular cultural education. It extended beyond stylistic and formal features by introducing versions of an eclectic range of literary texts. These included *Robinson Crusoe*, novels by Walter Scott, plays by Shakespeare, Romantic folk tales such as *Der Freischutz*, pantomime favorites such as *The Miller and his Men*, stories from *The Arabian Nights,* and historical battles and crimes. This array of seemingly disparate materials was funneled through a product aimed at juvenile consumption, and came to occupy the shared imagination of roughly two generations of grown men.

Like Dickens, Stevenson continued his boyhood games in adult life. He and his stepson Lloyd Osbourne not only spent time together playing with such things as toy soldiers and a miniature printing press, but also constructed their own toy theater (Osbourne 26–27). At the same time, Stevenson became a successful author of poetry for children, boys' stories and romances, which he described as making "paper people to please myself, and Skelt and God Almighty, and with no ulterior purpose" (*Letters* 4: 217). While both writers looked to the toy theater as a means to unlock the imagination through spectacle and play, which Dickens defined loosely according to a Romantic conception of "fancy" (Thomas13), Stevenson situated his understanding of the process according to late-Victorian psychological models of aesthetics pioneered by Herbert Spencer and Grant Allen.

Less concerned with high art than evolutionary development, Spencer and Allen claimed that an aesthetic capacity, albeit unrefined, is nascent in all humans, including children, primitive populations and the less educated classes. In his *Principles of Psychology* (1855), Spencer biologized Friedrich von Schiller's earlier conception of aesthetic play in order to account for aesthetic development as a psychological process that allowed civilized men to release desires that were no longer required for survival in modern life (627-28). A great admirer of Spencer, Stevenson incorporated his ideas into a number of essays on childhood and boyhood that he illustrated with memories of his own.

In "Child's Play" (1878), Stevenson describes the solipsistic world of early childhood as akin to that of the aesthete. Lacking moral sense, and oblivious to the concerns of daily life, young children are amoral hedonists licensed to spend their days solely preoccupied with pleasure, creating and acting out fantasies of their own making. Conversely, mature art is the end product of a philosophical, moral and social education, and it demands that adults gradually substitute self-interested pleasures with impersonal, abstract representations – the sign of a civilization that can distinguish between fantasy and reality. As a result, the ability to act out personal desires in the form of play becomes increasingly circumscribed, indulged only impotently in the privacy of the mind:

> Our daydreams can no longer lie all in the air like a story from the *Arabian Nights*, [...] the child['s] play breathes him, and he no sooner assumes a passion than he gives it vent. Alas! When we betake ourselves quietly by the fire or lying prone in bed, we rouse many hot feelings for which we can find no outlet. Substitutes are not acceptable for the mature mind, which desires the thing in itself, and even to rehearse a triumphant dialogue with one's enemy, although it is perhaps the most satisfying piece of play still left within our reach, is not entirely satisfying, and it is even apt to lead to a visit and interview which may be the reverse of triumphant after all. (111-12)

Despite Spencer's faith in art as a form of release, for Stevenson the necessary distinction between art and life required that violent desires and passions remain unexorcised. If acted upon, they would fail to conform to the projections of fantasy. Actual encounters thus threaten to humiliate and destroy any pretensions to heroism.

Stevenson refused to relinquish the pleasures of childhood that the toy theater offered. In "A Chapter on Dreams" (1888), juvenile drama provides a psychological model for figuring the workings of his dream life. For Stevenson, dreams were a site of aesthetic spectacle: not only were they a means of recapturing the pleasures of a past boyishness, they might also be adapted as the basis for his mature literary productions. Recounting the process by which the dreams of his infancy gave way to historical romances of the Georgian period in which he "masqueraded in a three-cornered hat" (43), Stevenson, by early adulthood, had shifted from being the performer. The amoral hedonism of his childhood play had been displaced onto miniature surrogates, in the form of "the little people who manage man's internal theatre" (46). "Like children," they escaped the full force of adult censorship, as Stevenson "dozed off in his box seat" while they acted out amoral fantasies for the dreamer's delectation. On waking, the author recounted how he revised his recollections of these unstructured scenes and fragmentary plots as the basis for his future literary productions.

These nineteenth-century testaments speak to the powerful effect of juvenile drama on youthful imaginations. More broadly, they show that a growing culture of spectacle reached deep into childhood, such that these capitalist subjects, only partially interpellated and therefore immature, gradually learned to structure their relations to the world through mass-produced fantasies of financial success and emotional fulfillment. And yet, juvenile dramas, together with the real theatrical productions they represented, were not simply streamlined vehicles for conveying ideological messages to a passive audience. Rather, they were sites of cultural ambivalence, a means to test reality against its representations. This was part of their appeal.

In her study of the flourishing minor theaters of the early-nineteenth century, Jane Moody demonstrates the ways in which the need for alternatives to the rhetorically based tragedies and comedies, restricted to the licensed theaters of Covent Garden and Drury Lane, encouraged the development of a theater of spectacle and bodily gesture (79-117). Never respectful of social and aesthetic distinctions, or of cultural ownership, these "illegitimate" theaters borrowed plots and characters piecemeal from disparate sources, ranging from European dramas to accounts of criminals and highwaymen in the periodical press. Stories were adapted to allude to topical events, such as mutinies, Luddite insurrections and Radical politics. The inclusion of wild men, monsters and criminals, all of whom sometimes elicited pity, similarly thwarted moral clarity. This disregard for boundaries was further borne out in the style of the productions, which drew on a pastiche of melodrama, burlesque, burletta and pantomime. Melodramas were also often undercut by the humor of the burlesque, resulting in morally dubious messages. The authority of reason and state were further undermined by a reliance on spectacular effects and body language, together with the melodramatic reduction of plots to a Manichean opposition of good and evil, a duality often resolved in the form of physical explosions.

Although only one of Dickens's novels, *Oliver Twist* (1838), was adapted for the Surrey Theatre, and subsequently became a juvenile drama, the author drew upon popular theatrical techniques throughout his literary career. Using melodramatic plots, pantomime and patter, he created a series of miniature worlds, reliant less on description than on characters that could be made to speak and act in ways easily understood by a middle-class readership well versed in the shared experience of such conventions (Vlock 1-7). An early appraisal of Dickens's work in the *Edinburgh Review* (1838) describes the effect of reading his characters in a way that echoes the process of coloring black-and-white characters for the juvenile drama: "They are, however, not complete and finished delineations, but rather outlines, very clearly and sharply traced, which the reader may fill up for himself; and they are calculated not so much to present the actual truth as to suggest it" ("Dickens' Tales" 85). Drawing upon *dramatis personae* that included long-lost relations, stricken heroines, desolate orphans, and villains such as Fagin and Uriah Heep, Dickens used melodrama to expose the workings of vicious systems such as the Poor Laws and factory legislation.[8] In this manner, as Sally Ledger has recently argued, he was able to tread a fine line between high and popular culture, as well as between popular culture and Radical politics (595-96)

Later in the century, Stevenson likewise employed, in his fiction, characters and plots drawn from juvenile drama. *Treasure Island* (1883), for example, echoes a number of earlier pirate dramas in its depiction of an eighteenth-century world inhabited by a boy hero and an unpredictable mutinous tar, Long John Silver, who challenges the authority of his "betters," in the form of a magistrate, a doctor and a squire. The influence of juvenile drama is not confined to Stevenson's boys' stories, but can also be found in his adult romances. Perhaps the most overt example of the latter is *Prince Otto* (1885), which displays its theatrical origins as self-consciously mannered artifice. The vaguely eighteenth-century "bygone state" of Grünewald, in which the novel is set, is depicted as a wooded, hilly country of pine forests, mills and streams. Peopled by a cast of charcoal burners and mountain sawyers, the setting invites associations with miniature versions of German Romantic dramas. The focus of the story is Otto, the last prince of Grünewald, who traces his line of descent to Perdita, the only daughter of King Florizel of Bohemia. This detail both establishes Otto's mixed lineage and hints at the hybrid genealogy of the text, invoking playful associations with both Shakespeare's late romance, *The Winter's Tale*, and the central character of Stevenson's own early series of short stories, *New Arabian Nights* (1882).

Some readers later viewed these intertextual borrowings as a sign of Stevenson's artistic weakness, a series of poses suggesting a lack of originality. I would argue, however, that they are symptomatic of a more general strategy, employed by Stevenson in many of his fictions, to encourage his readers to draw upon a familiar stock of shared cultural references. Stevenson's borrowings from other sources, many of which had been produced in versions for the toy theater, also included details taken from German Romantic dramas and European operas, with characters and scenes drawn from Jacques Offenbach's *La Grande Duchesse de Gerolstein*, Carl Maria von Weber's *Der Freischütz* and George Frederick Handel's *Rinaldo*. The dramatic origins of *Prince Otto* are further foregrounded by its division into three books, which function as a series of acts, subdivided into a series of chapters or "scenes." The resolution of the plot, a play within a play, charted through three consecutive chapters numbered as "acts," is accomplished by the manipulations of a courtesan, the Countess Von Rosen. She functions as a human *deus ex machina*, whom Stevenson christens "Providence" to indicate the way she moves between the characters, setting them on their rightful paths and thwarting the machinations of Gondremark, an East Prussian villain. The tale concludes in the manner of *The*

---

8   For an extensive analysis of Dickens's use of the character of the orphan, see Tamara Sylvia Wagner's chapter in this collection.

Tempest, with a "bibliographical postscript" that playfully invents a series of sources as the basis for the story, while simultaneously exposing its framed artifice.

In addition to these structural devices, the descriptive passages and tableaux in *Prince Otto* deploy a spatial flatness and verticality akin to the wings and backdrops of a toy theater set, and against which are arranged a series of stock characters, including woodsmen, huntsmen, dandies and their ladies. The anti-realism of the novel's opening description conforms to the principles of picturesque scenery painting, including details such as trees, rocks, cottages with smoking chimneys, and the ubiquitous windmill, all harmonized into a single aesthetic vision by the momentary effect of light from the setting sun (4–5). The flatness of the novel's scenes and tableaux, together with its obvious intertextuality, has led Alan Sandison to locate Stevenson as a putative modernist or postmodernist in the manner of Gertrude Stein (152). Less anachronistically, I suggest that these effects are the product of a late-nineteenth-century aestheticist interest in the imaginative potential of more lowly contemporary materials intended for boyhood play.

From *Prince Otto*'s first chapter to the book's end, readers encounter a world of courtly romance in which a crisis of political authority is played out. A thinly disguised account of Bismarck's rise to power, the transition of Grünewald from a feudal monarchy to a democratic state is simultaneously rendered as a crisis of gender relations. Evincing all the limpness of an effeminate Regency dandy, Prince Otto is both an impotent husband and an idle ruler who would rather play at life than concern himself with affairs of state. His neglect of both his wife and his kingdom has inverted the gender balance in his marriage, allowing the Princess Seraphina to take on "man's work" and meddle in politics (81). Her inexperience, however, leaves her ripe for manipulation by the ambitious prime minister, Gondremark.

The 36-year-old Otto, "Prince Puppet" in his "toy kingdom," provides a particularly recalcitrant example of a Stevensonian "boy" who resists both modern life and maturity in favor of short-term amateurism, involving hunting, playing chess and writing execrable verse (53). In his juvenile recreations, it would seem that Otto has failed to grow up, which he acknowledges as a shortcoming. As the ruler of a feudal state, he is able to indulge in the cycles of aesthetic consumption and spectatorship that Stevenson so enjoyed, a stage of boyish pleasure to which mature men can return only in their dreams. Although normative gender alignments are eventually restored when Seraphina realizes her wifely duties, the couple is forced into exile when Grünewald is declared a republic. As anachronistic outcasts from this modern democratic state, Otto and Seraphina are banished to her father's kingdom to live out a life of idle pleasure and dependency.

Stevenson undoubtedly identified with Otto's refusal to grow up. The author defended him against charges of "unmanliness" in his pursuit of self-interested pleasure, while simultaneously depicting his artificial stage-play world as a social and political anachronism.[9] The immature realm of fantasy could not, it would seem, be

---

9   In a reply to the American poet Harriet Monroe, who had criticized Otto's weakness, Stevenson defended his character by suggesting he was not different from any other man (*Letters* 5: 257). Although earlier refuting any connection between Stevenson and his fictional prince, in a prefatory note to *The Strange Case of Dr. Jekyll and Mr. Hyde* Stevenson's wife

sustained within late-nineteenth-century capitalism, which demanded that men grow up and assume practical roles as full producers and consumers. For some Victorians, however, the toy theater had opened up a private, if impotent, world of reverie that could not be accessed either through the social spaces of the playground, or through later professional life. Understood in this context, it is perhaps not surprising that a number of Victorian men clung to the form of non-productive amateurism epitomized by juvenile drama. Chesterton, with whose reminiscences I opened this chapter, offers an especially poignant characterization of his father as one such adherent to this secret life of aesthetic enjoyment. While "known to the world, even his next-door neighbours, as a very reliable and capable though unambitious business man" (41), his study testified to a hidden aesthetic life involving toy theaters, fretwork and medieval illumination. His father's "private career," which, he insisted, was not merely a reaction to a practical profession, taught Chesterton "the first and last lesson of life; that in everything that matters, the inside is much larger than the outside" (41). This was a less popular model of mature masculinity that his son sought to emulate – even when he had become a successful author – by undertaking "serious, solid and constructive work like cutting out cardboard figures and pasting coloured tinsel upon them," whenever he did not have to "fritter" his time on "frivolous things" such as producing lectures or literary works (45).

I would particularly like to thank Alan Powers of the Pollock's Toy Museum Trust; thanks are also due to David Powell. Both have provided invaluable help with details of toy theater history, and permission to use suitable illustrations.

Fanny expressed surprise that portrait painters did not depict Stevenson as Otto, "whom he did resemble to a degree" (xviii).

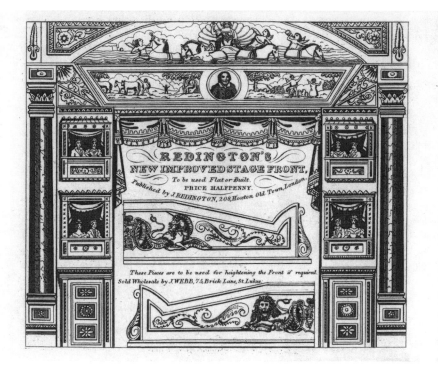

Fig. 2.1   "Redington's New Improved Stage Front," c.1850. 7 × 8 ¾ inches.

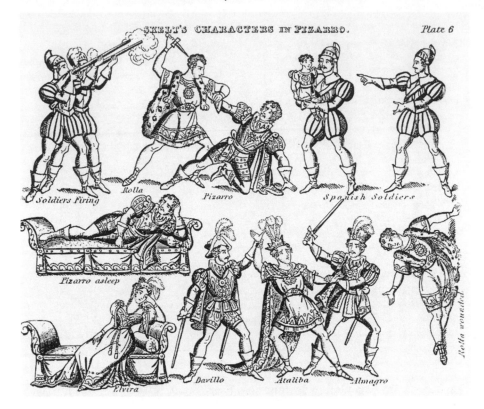

Fig. 2.2   "Skelt's Characters in Pizarro." While this sheet is undated, the Skelt family produced such halfpenny sheets between 1835 and 1872. According to George Speaight, the first production of *Pizarro* illustrated by this sheet was performed in Drury Lane in 1799.

Fig. 2.3   "[J. K.] Green's Scene in *Harlequin and Oliver Cromwell*," Scene 12, 1852 (depicting the shop of his retailer, John Redington, at 208 Hoxton Old Town). 6 ¾ × 8 ½ inches.

Works Cited

Archer, William. "The Drama in Pasteboard." *Art Journal* (April and May 1887): 105-08, 140-44.

Baldwin, Peter. *Toy Theatres of the World*. London: A. Zwemmer, 1992.

Campbell, Colin. *The Romantic Ethic and the Spirit of Modern Consumerism*. Oxford: Blackwell, 1987.

Chesterton, G. K. *Autobiography*. London: Hutchinson University Library, 1936.

Davis, Philip. *The Victorians*. Oxford: Oxford UP, 2002. Vol. 8 of *The Oxford English Literary History*. 13 vols.

Dickens, Charles. "A Christmas Tree." *Selected Short Fiction*. Ed. Deborah A. Thomas. Harmondsworth, UK: Penguin, 1985. 126-41.

---. "Private Theatres." *Sketches by Boz*. Ed. Dennis Walder. Harmondsworth, UK: Penguin, 1995. 145-52.

---. "Where We Stopped Growing." *Miscellaneous Papers* and *The Mystery of Edwin Drood*. London: Hazell, Watson and Viney, n.d. 385-90.

"Dickens' Tales." *Edinburgh Review* (Oct. 1838): 75-97.

Forster, John. *The Life of Charles Dickens*. Vol. 1. London: Dent, 1969.

Jaffe, Audrey. *Scenes of Sympathy: Identity and Representation in Victorian Fiction*. Ithaca, NY: Cornell UP, 2000.

Ledger, Sally. "From Queen Caroline to Lady Dedlock: Dickens and the Popular Radical Imagination." *Victorian Literature and Culture* 32 (2004): 575-600.

"Looking in Shop Windows." *All The Year Round* (12 June 1869): 37-43.

Moody, Jane. *Illegitimate Theatre in London, 1770-1840*. Cambridge: Cambridge UP, 2000.

Nead, Lynda, *Victorian Babylon: People, Streets and Images in Nineteenth-Century London*. New Haven: Yale UP, 2000.

Osbourne, Lloyd. *An Intimate Portrait of R. L. S.* New York: Charles Scribner's Sons, 1924.

Oxenford, John. "The Toy Theatre." *The Era Almanack* (1871): 67-68.

Powell, David. "William West and the Development of the Toy Theatre." *William West and the Regency Toy Theatre*. London: Sir John Soane's Museum, 2004: 8-16.

Sandison, Alan. *Robert Louis Stevenson and the Appearance of Modernism*. Basingstoke, UK: Macmillan, 1996.

Speaight, George. *The History of the English Toy Theatre*. 2nd ed. London: Studio Vista, 1969.

Spencer, Herbert. *Principles of Psychology*. 3rd ed. New York: Appleton, 1880.

Stevenson, Robert Louis. "A Chapter on Dreams." *The Works of Robert Louis Stevenson*. Tusitala ed. Vol. 30. London: Heinemann, 1924. 41-53

---. "A Penny Plain, Two Pence Coloured." *The Works of Robert Louis Stevenson*. Tusitala ed. Vol. 29. London: Heinemann, 1924. 103-09.

---. "Child's Play." *The Works of Robert Louis Stevenson*. Tusitala ed. Vol. 25. London: Heinemann, 1924. 106-16.

---. *Letters of Robert Louis Stevenson*. Eds. Bradford A. Booth and Ernest Mehew. Vol. 4. New Haven: Yale UP, 1995.

---. *Letters of Robert Louis Stevenson*. Eds. Bradford A. Booth and Ernest Mehew. Vol. 5. New Haven: Yale UP, 1995.

---. "Memoirs of an Islet." *The Works of Robert Louis Stevenson*. Tusitala ed. Vol.29. London: Heinemann, 1924. 59-64.

---. *New Arabian Nights. The Works of Robert Louis Stevenson*. Tusitala ed. Vol. 1. London: Heinemann, 1924.

---. "Popular Authors." *The Works of Robert Louis Stevenson*. Tusitala ed. Vol. 28. London: Heinemann, 1924. 20-32.

---. *Prince Otto. The Works of Robert Louis Stevenson*. Tusitala ed. Vol. 4. London: Heinemann, 1924.

---. *The Strange Case of Dr. Jekyll and Mr. Hyde. The Works of Robert Louis Stevenson*. Tusitala ed. Vol. 5. London: Heinemann, 1924. 1-74.

---. *Treasure Island.* The *Works of Robert Louis Stevenson*. Tusitala ed. Vol. 2. London: Heinemann, 1924.

Stewart, Susan. *On Longing: Narratives of the Miniature, the Gigantic, the Souvenir and the Collection*. Durham: Duke UP, 1993.

Thackeray, William Makepeace. *Vanity Fair*. Ed. John Sutherland. Oxford: Oxford UP, 1998.

Thomas, Deborah A. Introduction. *Selected Short Fiction*. By Charles Dickens. Ed. Deborah A. Thomas. Harmondsworth, UK: Penguin, 1985. 11-30.

Turner, Godfrey. "A Penny Plain: Twopence Coloured." *The Theatre* (Oct. 1886): 177-82.

Vlock, Deborah. *Dickens, Novel Reading and the Victorian Popular Theatre*. Cambridge: Cambridge UP, 1998.

Wilde, Oscar. *The Complete Letters of Oscar Wilde*. Eds. Merlin Holland and Rupert Harte-Davis. London: Fourth Estate, 2000.

Wilson, A. E. *Penny Plain, Two Pence Coloured: A History of Juvenile Drama*. London: George B. Harrap, 1932.

Chapter 3

The Drama of Precocity:
Child Performers on the Victorian Stage

Marah Gubar

The most famous child actor of the Victorian era is not a real performer at all but a fictional construct: Charles Dickens's pathetic "infant phenomenon," Miss Ninetta Crummles, who staggers through a few scenes in *Nicholas Nickleby* (1839). Neither an infant nor a phenomenon, Miss Crummles is instead a victim of the adult desire to freeze the child in place as the personification of youthful innocence: "she had been kept up late every night, and put upon an unlimited allowance of gin-and-water from infancy, to prevent her growing tall" (365). Her "aged countenance" (365) reveals that Miss Crummles is much older than her advertised ten years, and her utter lack of talent ensures that she can never make up for this discrepancy by acting. Although her parents and fellow actors in the company wax eloquent onstage and off, Miss Crummles barely says a word. The only performance of hers that Dickens describes at length is an absurd "little ballet interlude" about a maiden's encounter with an "Indian Savage" (364). Her father proudly declares that children in particular adore his daughter's performances, but Dickens quickly reveals that "the offending infant" (384) is foisted on child viewers against their will: mingling with her young audience members after the show, the hapless Miss Crummles finds herself in danger of "being torn limb from limb" (388).

While this particular infant phenomenon never existed beyond the pages of literature, it can be argued that she has had more impact on critical accounts of the theatrical cult of the child than any actual performer, since commentators frequently echo many aspects of Dickens's characterization in their efforts to explain the appeal of child actors to the nineteenth-century public. For example, after surveying a few of the pantomimes and plays that featured young people during this period, Jacqueline Rose declares, "Children are not the cause of this literature. They are not the group for whom it [was] created" (102). Both she and Carolyn Steedman suggest that children were thrust onto the stage for adults' viewing pleasure; child performers were valued not for their skills, but for the opportunity they gave adults to ogle their bodies while simultaneously enthusing about their innocence. Fixed in place as the passive objects of the adult gaze, the majority of stage children, Steedman contends, functioned as "animated stage props who [...] swelled processional scenes or decorated landscapes. Some were asked to speak a line or two, and their voices were added to the chorus; but for the main part they were mute" (143-44). In other words, talent was not an important part of their appeal; what adults wanted to see was the artless child "up there, on display[, ...] just being – a child" (134).

Such claims are in keeping with our current critical story about the cult of the child, which insists that the Victorians were obsessed with freezing young people in place as icons of innocence.[1] But this characterization of the stage child ignores the tremendous range of roles that young performers took on during the era. Many did remain in the background as ensemble members, and, because the choruses were often enormous (in some cases numbering into the hundreds), this group naturally constituted a majority.[2] But child stars were a much more visible presence on the nineteenth-century stage than recent critics recognize. To begin with, there was the thriving tradition of child prodigies that stretched from the triumphant London debut in 1804 of Master William Betty (1791-1874) – the "Infant Roscius" – through the closing decades of the century. Moreover, children frequently acted major roles, alongside adults, in plays and pantomimes. Then, too, there were numerous all-child productions in which young actors played every part. Disgusted by the fascination that theatrical consumers felt for featured child performers, many contemporary commentators campaigned against this trend, insisting – as Dickens did – that stage children were talentless victims of adult voyeurism. However, a close examination of the kinds of roles children played and the reviews they received reveals that we should not simply accept this partisan characterization as fair and accurate. Far from functioning as voiceless embodiments of purity, child performers appealed to diverse audiences by exhibiting extreme precocity. Their prematurely developed skills and much-vaunted versatility enabled them to blur the line between child and adult, innocence and experience.

Prodigies such as Betty were therefore celebrated for their ability to slip seamlessly into a variety of roles and to demonstrate a broad range of artistic abilities. A typical performance by Master Joseph Burke (1817?-1902) illustrates this point. Billed as the 11-year-old "Irish Roscius," Burke would not only take on adult roles such as Shylock, Richard III or Sir Peter Teazle, but also would conduct the orchestra in the playing of an elaborate overture, and perform a violin solo. Burke would wind up an evening by playing five or six radically different roles in virtuoso showpieces such as *Whirligig Hall* and *The March of Intellect*. In the latter, he played Master Socrates Chameleon, justifying his name by shifting "from Mister Terrence O' Leary (from Killarney) with a new Irish song by W. West, to Signor Sordini, from Italy, with an Italian air with variations, on the violin; thereafter, he was Bluster Bubble,

---

1   Among others, Rose, James Kincaid and Catherine Robson argue that the Victorians set up the child as "a pure point of origin," and that this investment in childhood innocence is essentially a "demand made by the adult on the child [...] which fixes the child and then holds it in place" (Rose 8, 3-4). This characterization of the cult of the child undergirds much recent work on Charles Dodgson as well. Critics such as U. C. Knoepflmacher, Jackie Wullschläger and Douglas R. Nickel contend that Dodgson conceived of children as categorically different from – and superior to – adults, and used his camera and his children's fiction to freeze them in place as emblems of "childish innocence" (Nickel 65). For a complication of such a reading of Dodgson's intent, see Carol Mavor's chapter in this collection.

2   Tracy C. Davis notes that in the 1880s Drury Lane "engaged between 150 and 200 youngsters for each pantomime" ("Employment" 118). Similarly, the Avenue Theatre bragged in its advertisement for *Dick Whittington and His Cat* (1882) that the show was "Supported by 100 Talented Children."

from the Moon, Jack Ratline, a sailor, with a hornpipe, and Napoleon Buonapart, from Elysium" (Odell 490). Performances by female prodigies such as Clara Fisher (1811-98?), Jean Davenport (1829-1903) and Lydia Howard (dates unknown, but she performed as a child prodigy in the early 1870s) followed a similar pattern. They sang, danced, and impersonated a wide range of characters – tragic and comic, male and female, old and young, English and foreign – often in vehicles such as *An Actress of All Work* and *The Manager's Daughter,* which were specially designed to showcase their versatility.

Talent and dramatic flexibility were also required for child actors who tackled major roles in pantomimes such as *Babes in the Wood* and *Dick Whittington,* as well as featured parts in classical dramas and contemporary plays. For instance, when Kate Terry (1844-1924) joined Charles Kean's company at the Princess's Theatre at the age of eight, she played Prince Arthur in *King John* (1852), Piccolo in the burlesque *Wittikind and His Brothers* (1852), the Duke of York in *Richard III* (1857) and several starring roles in the Christmas pantomimes, including the good fairy Preciosa in *Harlequin and Bluebeard* (1854) and the fairy queen Paradisa in *Harlequin and the Maid and the Magpie* (1855). At 13, she played Ariel in *The Tempest*; at 14, Cordelia in *King Lear*. Kate's more famous sister Ellen also made her official debut with Kean's company, playing Mamillius in *The Winter's Tale* when she was nine. A year later, she performed the role of Puck in *A Midsummer Night's Dream*, and the Fairy Goldenstar in *Harlequin and the White Cat*.[3] Contemporary admirers, such as Dutton Cook, marveled that such young actresses "could impart sentiment to their speeches, could identify themselves with the characters they played, could personate and portray, could weep themselves that they might surely make others weep, could sway the emotions of crowded audiences" (341).

The Terry sisters were exceptionally talented, but they were certainly not alone in playing featured roles at a young age. The Victorian stage was crowded with families of young siblings with similar résumés, including the Batemans, the Grattans, the Lloyds, the Vokeses, the Cootes, the Bowmans, the Vallis, the Vaynes and the Harrises. Particularly in the 1880s and 1890s, a startling number of new plays featured child characters. According to Brian Crozier, 22 dramas with "major child roles" debuted on the London stage during the five-year period from 1887 to 1891 – and this total does not include melodramas or pantomimes (266). Vera Beringer (1879-1964) and Kate and Ellen's niece Minnie Terry (1882-1964) were perhaps the most famous child actresses from this period, and they starred in many of these plays, including *Partners* (1888), *Bootles's Baby* (1888), *The Prince and the Pauper* (1890), *That Girl* (1890) and *The Holly Tree Inn* (1891). Beringer also played the demanding title role in Frances Hodgson Burnett's *Little Lord Fauntleroy* (1888), which was a commercial and critical smash hit. Its tremendous success attests to the public's fascination with precocity, since young Fauntleroy's charm arises directly from his uncanny emotional maturity, which allows him to relate to his mother and

---

3   As Nina Auerbach notes, by the time Ellen Terry was thirteen, she had also appeared as William Waddilove in *To Parents and Guardians*, as Jacob Earwig in *Boots at the Swan*, as Karl in *Faust and Marguerite*, as Prince Arthur in *King John*, as Fleance in *Macbeth*, as Genie of the Jewels in *The King of the Castle*, and as Tiger Tim in *If the Cap Fits* (50).

other characters as an adult. As Crozier notes, critics such as Clement Scott picked up on this quality, describing Fauntleroy as "a strange child with an old head on young shoulders" (qtd. in Crozier 174).

The public's fascination with precocity manifested itself in a variety of other ways as well. Gifted classical musicians such as the young piano prodigies Josef Hofmann and Pauline Ellice took London by storm in the 1880s. Describing one of Hofmann's performances, *The Theatre* observed that it was "attended by the usual phenomena – the walls of the room lined with triple rows of standing listeners, and hundreds of applicants for places, money in hand, turned from the doors for lack of room" (Clavichord 91). Music hall performers such as Vesta Tilley (1864-1952), Connie Gilchrist (1865-1946) and Dot Hetherington (dates unknown) also began performing star turns at an early age, often singing provocative songs that had been popularized by adults. Meanwhile, theatrical newspapers such as *The Era* continued to feature advertisements for assorted infant phenomena, including Master John Manley, "the Australian Infant Comedian (Six Years Old)" and nine-year-old Little Teddy Barber, "England's Bicycle Wonder" (Master John 14; Little Teddy 15).

All this activity helps refute Allardyce Nicoll's claim, in his magisterial *History of English Drama*, that the fad for child performers died away early in the nineteenth century.[4] Indeed, child stars remained so visible that an 1878 issue of *The Theatre* includes a lengthy editorial calling for their banishment from the stage. After acknowledging that child actors are necessary to the plot of certain Shakespeare plays, and of dramatized novels such as *East Lynne* and *Uncle Tom's Cabin*, the anonymous author of "Children on the Stage" objects to contemporary playwrights' propensity for inserting youngsters into domestic dramas, pantomimes and melodramas as well. Worst of all, fulminates this disgruntled critic, are the new all-child productions, "whole entertainments given on the stage at Christmas-time" entirely by children, featuring "child heroes and child heroines, child lovers and child heavy-fathers, child clowns and child columbines" (187).

This tradition of all-child productions, which thrived from the late 1860s to the late 1890s, has received no sustained critical attention. Yet contemporary descriptions and reviews of these shows constitute a rich resource for cultural historians hoping to gain a better understanding of the cult of the child actor. As we will see, they reveal that young performers were enthusiastically received not only by child-loving men such as Charles Dodgson and Ernest Dowson, but by many women and children as well.[5] And once again, the evidence suggests that child actors were valued not for

---

4   Nicoll suggests that "the infant frenzy [had] died away" by 1822, but, as Hazel Waters notes, many famous child prodigies emerged well after that date, garnering enthusiastic praise from some reviewers and impassioned attacks from others (21). Nicoll bases his claim on the comments of one such critic, neglecting to notice that those who disapproved of this theatrical trend often declared, as Gilbert à Beckett did in August of 1832, that "The days for prodigies are over", apparently in the hope that saying so would make it so (152).

5   Hugues Lebailly and Richard Foulkes emphasize that Dodgson was merely one of "thousands of enthusiasts" who embraced the fad for child prodigies, and this essay aims to bolster their point (Lebailly 27).

their innocent artlessness, but for their prematurely developed talents, and personal and professional "knowingness."[6]

If anyone could be expected to enthuse about the purity and natural spontaneity of child actors, it would be Dodgson, who often voiced his allegiance to the ideal of childhood innocence in letters to the parents of his child friends. But his public and private descriptions of child actors suggest that he was transfixed above all by child actors' "clever[ness]" and canny professionalism (*Diaries* 1.98). In January 1867, Dodgson took two of George MacDonald's children to the Haymarket Theatre to see the Living Miniatures, a troupe of 27 children "varying in height from 30 to 50 inches," who were performing a double bill of the comedy *Littletop's Christmas Party* and the burlesque *Sylvius* "during the daytime for the benefit of juveniles just now 'home for the holydays'" ("Haymarket" 7). Dodgson was so impressed with this all-child production that he wrote to Thomas Coe, the Haymarket's manager, who invited him to return for a peep behind the scenes, an experience Dodgson described in a lengthy diary entry as well as in a letter to his brother Edwin.

Dodgson certainly admired the "picturesqueness" of these Lilliputian performers (*Letters* 1.101), but what emerges most clearly from these accounts is his amazement at their autonomy and intelligence as actors. For instance, he marveled at the fact that the children did not need a prompt, nor anyone "to send [them] on at the right time: they seemed to do it all for themselves, as regularly as clockwork" (*Diaries* 1.251). He was particularly impressed by the "very remarkable" acting of a five-and-a-half-year-old boy named Solomon, who, just before the curtain went up, rehearsed a new comic song to be introduced that night (*Diaries* 1.251). Dodgson was also intrigued by the unexpected ambition of Solomon's four-year-old sister, Annette, whom he overheard declaring her desire to take over one of the larger roles in the production; afterwards, Mrs. Coe confirmed Annette's claim that "she has learnt [the part] quite perfect, of her own accord" (*Letters* 1.100). Rather than embodying innocence, most of these children played distinctly adult parts, and the more demanding role coveted by Annette was no exception. As Dodgson noted, "The part of Mrs. Mite (taken by a very clever child) involves a good deal of talking, including a violent 'scene' with her sour-tempered little husband" (*Letters* 1.100). Undisconcerted by the idea of a four-year-old engaging in such non-angelic activities, Dodgson instead seems fascinated by the ability of these children to transform themselves into people they are not, including their ability to transgress class lines. Winding up his letter to Edwin, he exclaims, "certainly I *never* saw such clever little things – the sharpest of the sharp race of London children. They had very nice manners, and talked extremely well. In fact you might introduce most of them into a drawing-room without anyone guessing their lowly birth" (*Letters* 1.101).

Dodgson was not alone in admiring the Living Miniatures. *The Era* described them as "accomplished in a triple sense [...] as actors and actresses, singers, and

---

6   I borrow the term "knowingness" from Peter Bailey, who argues that Victorian music hall performers often adopted a canny, self-consciously artful stance when relating to their rowdy audiences. He points out that performers such as Marie Lloyd often played the part of sexually aware youngsters in songs such as "I Asked Johnny Jones, So I Know Now!" – a fact that supports my contention that Victorian theatergoers were fascinated by precocity.

dancers" (Rev. of Living Miniatures, *Era* 10), while the *Times* dismissed their acting as sub-par, but characterized the songs and comic dances as "extremely well executed" (Rev. of Living Miniatures, *Times* 7). The *Times* also mentioned that, between the two pieces, "a brilliant fantasia on the pianoforte serves to display the precocious talent of the juvenile artist, Miss Sophia Flora Heilbronn" (7). As this coupling suggests, the goal of all-child productions and stand-alone performances by child prodigies was basically the same: to showcase children who were unusually talented for their age. Thus, a decade later, a reviewer describing the London debut of an American infant phenomenon noted that "in witnessing the performances this week of 'Baby Benson' at the Adelphi, we recall the doings of the 'living miniatures' who years ago found favour at the Haymarket" (Rev. of Baby Benson 12). Like Mr. Coe's troupers, Baby Benson

> possesses talent very far in advance of her years. She has had a remarkably good training, and has picked up all the ease of an *artiste* of long experience. Her every movement is graceful and easy, her enunciation is wonderfully distinct, her singing is praiseworthy, and her dancing is first class. (12)

This focus on the importance of training, experience and specific skills occurs frequently in Dodgson's descriptions of child actors as well. After seeing Vera Beringer in *Little Lord Fauntleroy*, for example, he called her "one of the cleverest children I have seen on the stage," but added, "No doubt much of the success of the acting is due to Mrs. Kendal's teaching" (*Diaries* 2.460). Dodgson particularly valued crisp articulation and the kind of "conscientious *thoroughness*" that enables an actor to "*forget* [herself] altogether, and *be* the character" ("'Alice'" 212; *Letters* 2.736). He frequently criticized child actresses who lacked these skills, as his dismissive account of Minnie Terry's turn in *Bootles's Baby* indicates: "she recites her speeches, not very clearly, without looking at the person addressed" (*Diaries* 2.460).

Dodgson was so impressed with the Living Miniatures that, when he began to contemplate putting *Alice* on the stage, he seriously considered making it an all-child production.[7] This is unsurprising, given how successful such shows were with the general public in the 1870s and 1880s. In December 1876, the Adelphi Theatre presented *Little Goody Two Shoes*, "a Children's Pantomime, performed entirely by Children [...] at Children's prices," which proved so popular with the women and children who crowded the morning matinees that evening performances were eventually added in order to cope with the extra demand (*Little Goody* 10). Encouraged by its success, producer F. B. Chatterton took the unusual step of offering another all-child pantomime, *Little Red Riding Hood* (1877), in the unseasonable

---

7   After registering his two children's books as dramas in December 1872, Dodgson records that he wrote to the stage historian Percy Fitzgerald "for advice about getting *Alice* dramatised: he advised against *my* idea, (the having it acted by children, etc.) but thinks it would suit the stage" (*Diaries* 2.315). A growing interest in such shows was clearly in the air, as revealed by the fact that Henry Savile Clarke, the librettist Dodgson eventually chose to dramatize *Alice*, had had the same idea; he "proposed that the play be acted entirely by children," a suggestion Dodgson successfully resisted, having been persuaded by Fitzgerald that this was a bad idea (Lovett 38).

month of August. It ran until November, just a month before the next all-child offering opened, *Robin Hood and His Merry Little Men*. All three of these shows were written by the famous pantomime impresario E. L. Blanchard. Reacting to complaints that his genre was growing unsuitable for children, Blanchard cut down on the political jokes and "vulgarity" that had begun to crowd out fairytale incidents, and proved himself "the faithful and constant friend of the good mothers who bless morning performances and are able to get the children safe in bed before the bell rings for supper" (Rev. of *Robin Hood*, *Era* 13).

Judging by the reviewers' often lengthy descriptions of audience reactions, children responded with great enthusiasm. "The shrieks of delight that came from all parts of the house told more plainly than any description we can give how thoroughly the children enjoyed themselves," wrote one reviewer of *Little Goody Two Shoes* (Rev. of *Little Goody*, *Era* [24 Dec. 1876] 12). Indeed, this critic was so certain that children formed the principal audience for the show that he addressed portions of his review directly to them: "And now, dear boys and girls, that we have told you all about Harlequin, Columbine, Pantaloon, and Clown, let us further inform you that there is the jolliest comic business in store for you that you can have imagined in your wildest dreams of Christmas revelry" (13). Similarly, a reviewer of *Robin Hood* announced, "It is eminently a children's pantomime, and on the first performance the theatre was taken by storm by children" (Rev. of *Robin Hood*, *Times* 8). Because children themselves did not write reviews, and rarely left records of their responses to drama, it is difficult to ascertain precisely what appealed to them about such performances. But the interactive aspect of such shows was evidently attractive. Describing some of the comic byplay that enlivened a performance of *Robin Hood*, the *Times* reported that

> the gallery was full of persons of tender age who were always ready to assist Master Coote, the Clown, when he paused for a word in the time-honoured song of "Hot Codlings." A boy who would address a grown-up Clown as "Sir," pays, apparently, no respect to a Merryman of his own age; but the interrupters were vanquished by the satire of Master Coote, who begged to be excused for observing that "one fool is quite enough at a time." (8)

It also seems reasonable to assume that children got a kick out of seeing their peers step into roles previously reserved for adults. Indeed, according to the same reviewer, the children watching Robin Hood cavort with his merry little men "were evidently gratified by the compliment to themselves implied in intrusting all the parts to young actors" (8).

Echoing the way these all-child productions were advertised, many reviewers described them as being performed "by children, for children."[8] At the same time,

---

8   The advertisement for *The House that Jack Built* (1894) provides an example of this sort of child-centered language; it describes the show as a "Fancy Play for Children (by Children)" (*House* 14). A review of another all-child production of *Little Goody Two Shoes* reveals that such shows were considered commonplace by the late 1880s: "Plays and comic operas have frequently before been acted by children for children" (Rev. of *Little Goody*, *Era* [29 Dec. 1888] 8).

however, they suggested that the appeal of such shows was far broader than that. Thus, *The Era* confidently predicted "*Little Goody Two Shoes* will be the talk of the town. Everybody will be asking 'Have you seen the children's Pantomime at the Adelphi?' just as they used to inquire three years ago 'Have you seen the Shah?'" (Rev. of *Little Goody*, *Era* [24 Dec. 1876] 12). As we have seen, this opinion was borne out by the commercial success of the show. Similar raves greeted *The Children's Pinafore*, an all-child version of W. S. Gilbert and Arthur Sullivan's popular operetta *H. M. S. Pinafore* (1878), which was produced at the Opera Comique in December 1879. "[I]f anyone asked me how best I could delight a private box full of children," the reviewer for *The Theatre* declared, "I should decidedly say by expending a little judicious capital at the Opera Comique, where some exceedingly clever youngsters act 'H. M. S. Pinafore' in admirable style" (Rev. of *Children's Pinafore*, *Theatre* 38). Notably, although this show was performed only in the mornings, while the "adult" *Pinafore* ran at night, critics again emphasized that it was "a thing for everybody to see, whether they are of tender years or are 'children of a larger growth'":

> Hoary-headed grandpapas will shake their sides with delight; cosy old dames will declare that it makes them feel young again; prim spinsters of uncertain age will relax their rigid muscles and forget there is such a subject as "Woman's Rights;" simpering maidens will give unwonted encouragement to bashful swains; and there will be one broad, universal grin of enjoyment on the faces of all who witness *The Children's Pinafore* at the Opera Comique. (Rev. of *Children's Pinafore*, *Era* 7)

Indeed, *The Children's Pinafore* garnered such large audiences that it was revived a year later, and was followed by an all-child production of *The Pirates of Penzance* in December 1884. Even the Prince and Princess of Wales went to see it. As for the children's *Pirates*, critics again raved about "the half hundred children whose singing at the Savoy has been the wonder and admiration of London during the past month" (Beatty-Kingston 80). According to Tony Joseph, its success inspired the Savoy management to consider producing all-child versions of *Patience* and *Princess Ida* as well (58).

Why were reviewers and other adults so strongly drawn to these shows? In her brief discussion of child actors who were not limited to functioning as mere stage props, Steedman surmises that children who played larger roles were valued for their adorable incompetence: "What is 'priceless' in the child's performance is its attempt to be part of the adult world, and the very uselessness of that attempt" (144). This explanation is in keeping with the widely accepted argument that Victorians involved in the cult of the child "placed an absolute line of division between childhood and adulthood," emphasizing the innocent "otherness" of children (Robson 8). Following this reasoning, we would expect all-child productions to capitalize on the comic incongruity of little people playing distinctly adult roles. But none of the existing accounts of any of these all-child shows suggests that the innocence of young performers rendered them unfit to understand or inhabit their parts fully. On the contrary, commentators either marveled that the children's acting was "full of intelligence and meaning" and guided by a deep "sense of character" (Rev. of *Children's Pinafore*, *Era* 7), or they complained when they felt that "docility rather than appreciation of character [...] lies at the basis" of an impersonation (Rev. of

Living Miniatures, *Times* 7). Either way, they appreciated the difficulty "of procuring little folks competent to undertake characters hitherto associated with 'grown-ups'" (Rev. of *Little Goody, Era* [24 Dec. 1876] 12), a remark that reveals their shared assumption that the appeal of child-performers depends on their proficiency.

Thus, reviews of *The Children's Pinafore* uniformly celebrate how successful the child performers were at stepping into extremely demanding adult roles. For example, *The Era*'s reviewer pronounced himself profoundly impressed by "the marvellous manner in which the children fitted their parts, and their characters fitted them [...]. All were competent, and more than competent indeed, for sometimes they displayed absolute genius" (Rev. of *Children's Pinafore, Era* 7). Many of the brilliantly executed songs, he reported, were "encored amidst thunders of applause," and despite the difficult dialogue, "these talented young *artistes* did not miss a word, and invariably gave the sentences with their true accent and suggestiveness. The sly drollery infused into such passages as 'What, never?' could not have been surpassed by the most experienced performers" (7). At the same time, commentators also marveled at the skill with which the children performed even the most difficult passages of music. Reviewing the all-child version of *The Pirates of Penzance*, for example, William Beatty-Kingston declared that the youngster who played the demanding role of Mabel was "already a mistress of the art of vocalization":

> She executes elaborate *fioriture* with the ease and *désinvolture* of a Frezzolini; her *attaccamento* exhibits the reckless intrepidity that is alone inspired by inward certitude of infallibility; her tone-production would gladden the heart of Lamperti himself; and the truth of her intonation is absolutely flawless. (81)

Stand-alone performances by child prodigies garnered the same sort of praise during this period, as when *The Theatre* described Josef Hofmann an "executant genius," whose musical intelligence placed him amongst the ranks of "many a professional critic old enough to be his grandfather" (Clavichord 91).

As such accounts suggest, fans of child performers dwelt not on their adorable incapacity and appealing "otherness" but, rather, on their uncanny ability to blur the boundary between adult and child, by exhibiting skill or knowledge far in advance of their age. Describing the efforts of Miss Effie Mason, who played Little Buttercup in *The Children's Pinafore*, one reviewer admiringly noted that she "has a woman's voice with a child's face" (Rev. of *Children's Pinafore, Theatre* 39). Similarly, in praising the flair for "comic business" exhibited by Master William Phillips, who played Dick Deadeye, *The Era* exclaimed, "Never has 'an old head upon young shoulders' turned to more whimsical account" (Rev. of *Children's Pinafore, Era* 7). Such comments recall the descriptions of working-class children seen in the writings of social reformers such as Mary Carpenter and Henry Mayhew, who also emphasized the preternaturally adult qualities of laboring youngsters. But whereas they characterized such precocity as a horrifying indictment of the values of Victorian society, admirers of child performers were delighted to see (mostly) lower-class children behaving like grown-ups.[9] For, although such shows were praised

---

9   For more on the class status of nineteenth-century child performers, see Tracy C. Davis ("Employment" 122-24) and Martin Danahay.

for containing less vulgarity, they nevertheless offered numerous opportunities for child actors to engage in representations of distinctly "adult" activities, including excessive drinking, rowdy violence, and passionate love affairs. The boy who played Frederick in the children's *Pirates*, for example, garnered praise for "the fervour of his love-making" (Beatty-Kingston 82), while Blanchard's *Robin Hood* included a scene in which the child impersonating Friar Tuck rolled about the stage "in a drunken and incapable state" (Rev. of *Robin Hood*, *Times* 8).

Even when child actors were called upon to impersonate purity, their mere presence onstage – flaunting their bodies in a public forum – undermined the image of the innocent child. Although the theater gradually became a more socially acceptable occupation over the course of the nineteenth century, "popular culture continued to ascribe immorality and sexual indiscretion" to performers, and particularly to actresses (Davis, "Actress" 104). Youthful entertainers were not considered exempt from the corrupting effects of stage life. Indeed, the intimation of sexual as well as professional precocity probably constituted a key part of their appeal for many audience members. Consider Gerald Dixon's description of an enticing child actress named Miss Minnie May, in a short story that appeared in *The Theatre* in 1878:

> There was a certain *abandon* in her movements which was at once attractive and strange. Her manner and utterance were easy, and her tone seemed to imply a thorough mastery of the situation, and a hint that, though she was young, she was experienced and was intimately acquainted "with her way about." (127-28)

The story's title, "Bashful Fifteen," is meant to be ironic. Having performed in public since the age of 12, Minnie has lost all modesty and shyness. After boldly accosting the male narrator in a public place, she describes her professional history: "'I have played Arthur in *King John*, Mamillius in the *Winter's Tale*, and Prince Bright Eyes in the pantomime. Quite a wide range of parts isn't it?'" (128). This brash girl then invites the narrator to see her perform "in the new burlesque at the Fortune" (128). The implication here is that Minnie's professional experience has accustomed her not only to public display but also to intimate interaction with the opposite sex. Her precocious knowingness fascinates the narrator, although he also recognizes that she is not the type of good girl he ought to marry.

Fans of child actors were not alone in emphasizing their uncanny maturity and prematurely developed capacities. Commentators who objected to the whole phenomenon of the stage child based their criticisms on this very point. In 1832, Gilbert à Beckett attacked a six-year-old child prodigy named Miss Waller Wybrow, by calling her "a little lump of precocious vulgarity" ("Theatricals" [22 Dec. 1832] 220), and objecting that she sang the music hall song "Oysters, Sir" with "very precocious accuracy" ("Theatricals" [24 Dec. 1831] 12). Similarly, the author of "Children on the Stage" expressed disdain for the public's fascination with children who exhibited capacities far in advance of their age, and who had therefore "grow[n] before their time into men and women" (186). Ellen Barlee, campaigning to rescue children from the stage and turn them into Christians, painted a picture of the stage child that is strongly reminiscent of Minnie May and the crafty children Dodgson described, only drained of any positive valency. Stage children, she complained, are "quick and sharp as needles, but as they approac[h] their teens, proportionately bold and irreverent" (14-15). The girls in particular exhibit "a precocious undercurrent, not of a too refined nature," that often leads them to lose "their characters before they [are] fifteen years of age" (22). The premature professionalism and ambition that so impressed Dodgson greatly perturbed Barlee:

> The children soon learn to measure their own abilities and worth, and trade with their talents with the cupidity of grown women; whilst to hear them discuss amongst themselves their engagements, gains, and successes, one would imagine that, far from being in the realm of childhood, one was in the company of scheming adults. (55-56)

Protests against the presence of youngsters on the stage peaked in the 1880s, when activists such as Millicent Garrett Fawcett campaigned to bar children under ten from any kind of theatrical employment. Committed to persuading the playgoing public that they were complicit in the wholesale destruction of childhood innocence, Fawcett and Barlee followed Dickens and Mrs. O. F. Walton in representing young performers as "miserable little victims" of adult exploitation (Barlee 99).[10] The title of Barlee's publication – *Pantomime Waifs: or, A Plea for Our City Children* (1884) – and her choice of topics reflects this tendency. *Pantomime Waifs* begins with chapters focused on stage children, but these are followed by others on "Gutter Children" and "Factory Children," inclusions that are in keeping with activists' efforts to characterize stage work as a form of child labor, and a sign of society's willingness to neglect and abuse its young. To drive home this point, Barlee paints a dark picture of stage life. Dismissing the number of children who played real roles as "comparatively [...] few," she proceeds to focus exclusively on the plight of youngsters placed in deeply exploitative positions: scantily dressed ballet girls who fall ill after spending long hours in bitterly cold theaters; circus performers forced to perform dangerous feats in the air or on horseback; freak show exhibits in which children are subjected to bolts of electricity and other indignities (28).

Needless to say, no mention is made of all-child performances, or of the many plays in which children had featured roles. Instead, as her title suggests, Barlee dwells on the "poor little pantomime 'Super,'" a faceless, voiceless being whose job is simply to swell the scene into a spectacle that the author finds morally repugnant (26). Although such shows are ostensibly aimed at children, she complains, "the number of gray-headed men and women who invariably form the larger proportion of the audience, prove that these entertainments [...] draw the world's *dilettanti*," who are thirsty for "the gratification of the senses" that occurs when they are allowed to view children in a state of "undress" (30). Because the appeal of child actors is wholly visual, she explains, they are "selected more for beauty and agility than intellectual powers, no great talent being necessary" to perform such minor roles (31).

In other words, Barlee anticipates in every aspect the characterization of the stage child recently advanced by Steedman and Rose. But to accept this dismal

---

10 Walton's immensely popular tract *A Peep Behind the Scenes* (1877) chronicles the unhappy adventures of a child actor named Rosalie, whose father exploits and abuses his family, forcing them to perform in his company of strolling players even when they are ill.

representation of child actors as the unvarnished truth about life on the Victorian stage is to ignore the fact that *Pantomime Waifs* was a partisan volley in an ongoing debate between child-savers such as Shaftesbury, Barlee, and Dickens, and their equally outraged opponents, who objected that "the philanthropic gush of [this] sentimental class" had drastically misrepresented the conditions of theatrical life (Jeune 6).[11] Among others, Dodgson, John Coleman, and Mrs. Jeune argued that critics grossly exaggerated the dangers faced by child performers, while downplaying any potential benefits to the children and their families. Scholars, however, have given no credence to their statements on the subject, despite the fact that, in certain ways, their accounts are more measured and accurate than their opponents'.

For example, whereas Barlee ignored the experience of stage children whose professional lives fail to illustrate her argument, Mrs. Jeune identified "two classes" of performing children: untrained youngsters who merely "walk on the stage and make one of a crowd" and another, more privileged, group of actors who, thanks to their unusual talent and careful training, make a good living by acting, singing and dancing, either on their own or in plays such as *The Silver King* and *Pickwick* (8). And while Barlee and company refused to see anything positive in the fad for child actors, Mrs. Jeune and Dodgson were willing to acknowledge its negative side. Mrs. Jeune admitted that theatrical training "does interfere seriously with the continuous education of the children engaged in it" (11), while Dodgson was upset to discover that Lizzie Coote, whose performance he had so admired in *Hop-o'-my-Thumb*, was being mistreated by her managers: "They are killing the poor child with overwork, and she is suffering some malady in the throat from so much singing" (*Diaries* 2.325).

Perhaps as a result of hearing such stories, Dodgson took a nuanced stance on the issue of whether children under ten should be allowed to perform onstage. In a lengthy letter to the *Times* that was reprinted in *The Theatre* in 1889, he freely admitted that "this practice needs certain safeguards not yet provided by the law," supporting a licensing system that would regulate and protect child performers, rather than the absolute ban called for by Fawcett and others ("Stage Children" 224). Such a system was adopted, and a version of it remains in place to this day.[12] Yet my point is not that we should change sides and accept as gospel the testimony of Dodgson, Jeune and other fans of child performers. Both camps undoubtedly twisted the facts to support their position. For their part, child-lovers such as Dodgson and Dowson justified their desire to see children onstage by a variety of means, including (as Steedman notes) a refusal to recognize stage employment as labor. For instance, Dodgson insisted that child actors enjoyed their job so much that they viewed it not as work, but as the best "game ever invented" ("Stage Children" 224) – surely a glorification of a demanding, often exhausting career. Meanwhile, as I have noted,

---

11   Barlee's involvement in the child-saving movement is unmistakable. *Pantomime Waifs* featured an introduction by Shaftesbury. On the page following the title page, there is a line saying that the book was published under the aegis of "Charles Dickens and Evans, Crystal Palace Press" (iv).

12   At the end of her article on Victorian child actors, Davis describes the evolution of the licensing system, noting that it has become less prohibitive over the ensuing decades.

critics of the fad drastically downplayed the importance of talent and versatility, and insisted that the appeal of child actors was almost wholly visual, a move that led them to ignore the wide array of performance opportunities open to child actors, and to represent them as voiceless victims.

Indeed, Dickens warped his source material in precisely this way when he created his infamous "infant phenomenon." As Malcolm Morley and Robert Simpson McLean have noted, Ninetta Crummles was most likely based on Jean Davenport, who also toured the provinces performing under her father's direction. However, in reshaping this real-life phenomenon for his fiction, Dickens strips her of her extensive speaking and singing parts, thereby rendering her speechless. But Davenport and her fellow child prodigies had been anything but mute. Besides singing and reciting in a variety of different dialects, they were also called upon to memorize and inhabit multiple large roles in the same evening. Although many reviewers celebrated the "versatile and extraordinary nature" of Davenport's talent (qtd. in McLean 148), Dickens erased any signs of it in her fictional counterpart, leaving readers with the impression that no one in their right mind would enjoy her performances.

At the same time, Dickens suggested that the appeal of the infant phenomenon lay in her innocence *per se* rather than in the contrast between her youth and the (pre)mature talent she displayed on the stage. This does not seem to have been the case with Davenport. Like Mr. Crummles, Mr. Davenport certainly exaggerated his daughter's childishness, but he did so *offstage* in order to heighten the scale of her dramatic achievements onstage. As William Davidge, another actor in his company, recalled,

> Davenport would pick out a lodging which all the churchgoers would have to pass on Sunday morning. He would dress up the infant phenomenon and make her sit dancing a big doll where she could be seen in the window, and the people would stand in groups open-mouthed in wonder at the baby who played with her doll in the morning, and trod the boards at night as Macbeth. (qtd. in McLean 134)

Davidge adds that Miss Davenport "was a very good actress in certain heavy lines – indeed quite remarkable in some heavy characters." This early promise was triumphantly fulfilled, for Davenport went on to have a stage career so successful that, in 1889, one critic declared that she "ranks among the most accomplished of the tragic actresses of the day" (qtd. in Mullin 155).

None of this, however, proves that Davenport was *not* exploited by her adult handlers. But it does suggest that she was valued for her metamorphic mutability rather than for functioning as a mute icon of innocence. Thus, the advertisements created for her performances trumpet her ability to play radically different roles, such as Little Pickle in *The Spoiled Child*, and Richard III.[13] Similarly, the lure of all-child productions included seeing children slip effortlessly into a variety of roles, many of which had previously been reserved for adults. For instance, Mr. Warwick Gray's juvenile comic opera company toured London and the provinces throughout the 1880s, performing familiar pieces such as *Les Cloches de Corneville* and *La Fille*

---

13 An example of one such advertisement appears on page 145 of McLean's article about Davenport.

de Madame Angot to great acclaim. All-child shows remained popular enough that producers in the 1890s continued to assume that "there is always room in London at Christmas for one performance by children for children" (Rev. of *The House That Jack Built* 7).[14] No doubt their appeal was partly visual; however, to focus only on adults' desire to consume "the child as spectacle" (Rose 97) requires us to ignore the extraordinary demands such shows placed on child performers, not to mention the mixed audiences that invariably attended them. Precocious competence was the lure that drew in such enthusiastic crowds, a fact that should prompt us to reconsider whether the cult of the child was really about freezing the child in place as the embodiment of artless innocence. The Victorians are routinely blamed for representing children as a separate species, whose remoteness renders them "exotic and heartbreakingly attractive" (Kincaid 30). At least on the stage, however, children inspired excitement not when they demonstrated their difference, but when they exhibited theatrical expertise "such as the 'oldest stager' might have envied" (Rev. of *Children's Pinafore*, *Era* 7), successfully blurring the line between innocence and experience.

I could not have written this essay without the assistance of Paula Kepich at the main branch of the Carnegie Library of Pittsburgh, and the helpful staff of the Interlibrary Loan and Microform departments at the University of Pittsburgh's Hillman Library. Thanks also to Catherine Booth, Dennis Denisoff, Ann Donahue, Richard Foulkes, Don Gray, Edward Gubar, Susan Gubar, Claudia Nelson, Jessica Richard, Kieran Setiya, Phil and Susan Harris Smith, and Ashgate's anonymous readers.

Works Cited

à Beckett, Gilbert. "Theatricals." *Figaro in London* (24 Dec. 1831): 11-12.

-----. "Theatricals." *Figaro in London* (25 Aug. 1832): 152.

-----. "Theatricals." *Figaro in London* (22 Dec. 1832): 219-220.

Auerbach, Nina. *Ellen Terry: Player in Her Time*. New York: Norton, 1987.

Bailey, Peter. *Popular Culture and Performance in the Victorian City*. Cambridge: Cambridge UP, 1998.

Barlee, Ellen. *Pantomime Waifs: or A Plea for Our City Children*. London: S. W. Partridge, 1884.

Beatty-Kingston, William. Rev. of *The Pirates of Penzance*. *The Theatre* (2 Feb. 1885). Rpt. in *The Theatre* V (Jan.-June 1885): 80-82.

"Children on the Stage." *The Theatre* 1 Oct. 1878. Rpt. in *The Theatre* 1 (Aug. 1878 - Jan. 1879): 185-88.

Clavichord. "Our Musical-Box." *The Theatre* 1 Aug 1887. Rpt. in *The Theatre* X (July-Dec. 1887): 91.

---

14   Other all-child productions toward the end of the century included *Dick Whittington and his Cat* (1882) at the Avenue Theatre, another version of *Little Goody Two Shoes* (1888) at the Court Theatre, *The Belles of the Village* (1889) at the Avenue Theatre, *Cinderella* (1889) at Covent Garden, and *The House That Jack Built* (1894) at the Opera Comique.

Cook, Dutton. "Ellen Terry." *The Theatre* 1 June 1880. Rpt. *The Theatre* VI (Jan.-June 1880): 340-41.

Crozier, Brian. "Notions of Childhood in London Theatre, 1880-1905." Diss. U of Cambridge, 1981.

Danahay, Martin. "Sexuality and the Working-Class Child's Body in Music Hall." *Victorian Institute Journal* 29 (2001): 102-31.

Davis, Tracy C. "The Actress in Victorian Pornography." *Victorian Scandals: Representations of Gender and Class*. Ed. Kristine Ottesen Garrigan. Athens: Ohio UP, 1992. 99-133.

---. "The Employment of Children in the Victorian Theatre." *New Theatre Quarterly* 11.6 (1986): 116-35.

Dick Whittington and His Cat. Advertisement. *The Era* (9 Dec. 1882): 12.

Dickens, Charles. *Nicholas Nickleby*. Ed. Michael Slater. New York: Penguin, 1978.

Dixon, Gerald. "Bashful Fifteen." *The Theatre* Sept. 1878. Rpt. in *The Theatre* 1 (Aug. 1878 – Jan. 1879): 126-33.

Dodgson, Charles. "'Alice' on the Stage." *The Theatre* (1 Apr. 1887): 179-84. Rpt. in Lovett 208-13.

---. *The Diaries of Lewis Carroll*. 2 vols. Ed. Roger Lancelyn Green. New York: Oxford UP, 1954.

---. *The Letters of Lewis Carroll*. 2 vols. Ed. Morton N. Cohen. New York: Oxford UP, 1979.

---. "Stage Children." *The Theatre* (2 Sept. 1889): 113-17. Rpt. in Lovett 223-28.

Foulkes, Richard. *Lewis Carroll and the Victorian Stage: Theatricals in a Quiet Life*. Burlington, VT: Ashgate, 2005.

"Haymarket." *Times* [London] (27 Dec. 1866): 7.

The House that Jack Built. Advertisement. *The Era* (22 Dec. 1894): 14.

Jeune, Mrs. "Children in Theatres." *The English Illustrated Magazine* 7 (1889-90): 6-14.

Joseph, Tony. *The D'Oyly Carte Opera Company 1875-1982*. Bristol: Bunthorne, 1994.

Kincaid, James R. "Dickens and the Construction of the Child." *Dickens and the Children of Empire*. Ed. Wendy S. Jacobson. New York: Palgrave, 2000, 29-42.

Knoepflmacher, U. C. *Ventures into Childland: Victorians, Fairy Tales, and Femininity*. Chicago: U of Chicago P, 1998.

Lebailly, Hugues. "C. L. Dodgson and the Victorian Cult of the Child." *The Carrollian* 4 (1999): 3-31.

Little Goody Two Shoes. Advertisement. *The Era* (17 Dec. 1876): 10.

Little Teddy Barber. Advertisement. *The Era* (13 Feb. 1870): 15.

Lovett, Charles C. *Alice on Stage: A History of the Early Theatrical Productions of Alice in Wonderland*. Westport, CT: Meckler, 1990.

Master John Manley. Advertisement. *The Era* (5 March 1871): 14.

McLean, Robert Simpson. "How 'the Infant Phenomenon' Began the World: the Managing of Jean Margaret Davenport (182?-1903)." *The Dickensian* 88.3 (1992): 133-53.

Morley, Malcolm. "Dickens Goes to the Theatre." Dickensian 59 (1963): 165-71.

---. "More About Crummles." Dickensian 59 (1963): 51-6.

---. "Where Crummles Played." Dickensian 58 (1962): 23-9.

Mullin, Donald, ed. *Victorian Actors and Actresses in Review*. Westport, CT: Greenwood, 1983.

Nickel, Douglas R. *Dreaming in Pictures: The Photography of Lewis Carroll*. New Haven: Yale UP, 2002.

Nicoll, Allardyce. *A History of English Drama 1660-1900*. Vol. 4. Cambridge: Cambridge UP, 1955.

Odell, George C. D. *Annals of the New York Stage*. Vol. 3. New York: Columbia UP, 1928.

Rev. of Baby Benson. *The Era* (24 Dec. 1876): 12.

Rev. of *The Children's Pinafore*. *The Era* (14 Dec. 1879): 7.

Rev. of *The Children's Pinafore*. *The Theatre* 1 Jan. 1880. Rpt. in *The Theatre* 4 (Jan.-June 1880): 38-39.

Rev. of *The House That Jack Built*. *The Era* (29 Dec. 1894): 7.

Rev. of *Little Goody Two Shoes*. *The Era* (24 Dec. 1876): 12-13.

Rev. of *Little Goody Two Shoes*. *The Era* (29 Dec. 1888): 8.

Rev. of Living Miniatures. *The Era* (30 Dec. 1866): 10-11.

Rev. of Living Miniatures. *Times* [London] (15 Jan.1867): 7.

Rev. of *Robin Hood and His Merry Little Men*. *The Era* (30 Dec. 1877): 13.

Rev. of *Robin Hood and His Merry Little Men*. *Times* [London] (27 Dec. 1877): 8

Robson, Catherine. *Men in Wonderland: The Lost Girlhood of the Victorian Gentleman*. Princeton: Princeton UP, 2001.

Rose, Jacqueline. *The Case of Peter Pan: or, The Impossibility of Children's Fiction*. Philadelphia: U of Pennsylvania P, 1992.

Steedman, Carolyn. *Strange Dislocations: Childhood and the Idea of Human Interiority 1780-1930*. Cambridge: Harvard UP, 1994.

The Theatre: A Monthly Review of The Drama, Music, and the Fine Arts. Ed. Clement Scott. 39 vols. London: Charles Dickens & Evans, 1878-1897.

Walton, O. F. *A Peep Behind the Scenes*. London: Religious Tract Society, 1877.

Waters, Hazel. "'That Astonishing Clever Child': Performers and Prodigies in the Early and Mid-Victorian Theatre." *Theatre Notebook* 50.2 (1996): 78-94.

Wullschläger, Jackie. *Inventing Wonderland*. New York: The Free Press, 1995.

PART 2
Consuming Desires

Chapter 4

"I'm not a bit expensive": Henry James and the Sexualization of the Victorian Girl

Michèle Mendelssohn

Actualities [...] kept the girl before her at times as asacrificed, truly an even prostituted creature.

Henry James, The Ivory Tower (1917)

I'm not a bit expensive – ask mother, or even ask father.

Henry James, The Awkward Age (1899)

Henry James's first novel, *Watch and Ward* (1871), begins with the hero's affections being rejected by yet another woman. Later the same night, the hero hears a man to whom he had refused a loan shoot himself in a hotel room. Out of remorse for his financial reservations, he adopts the stranger's 12-year-old daughter, Nora, and invests in raising her to become his wife. The *New York Times* commended James for his admirable depiction of "the perilous experiment of a man taking a child and bringing her up to be his wife," as well as his deft handling of an admittedly "troublesome topic" (Untitled). James subsequently disowned *Watch and Ward*, but the bonds between children and their guardians remained a pregnant theme for him. In *The Portrait of a Lady* (1881), Pansy Osmond embodies her father's morbid aesthetic preoccupations. In "The Author of Beltraffio" (1884), an innocent child is left to die, whereas, in "The Pupil" (1891), a willing child is given up to his tutor by debt-plagued parents. In *The Other House* (1896), a little girl is drowned by her father's admirer, and in *What Maisie Knew* (1897), bitterly divorced parents use their daughter as a cipher whose value increases or decreases in proportion to her capacity to be used by each to provoke the other.[1] "The Turn of the Screw" (1898) presents a young boy and girl protected and corrupted by their distraught governess.[2] And in

---

1   As John Carlos Rowe suggests, this novel also raises the specter of the incest taboo, when Sir Claude realizes that his relationship with Maisie would hopelessly entangle romantic and parent-child loves (133).

2   "The Turn of the Screw" is also receptive to a different reading to the one I suggest above. The children might be understood as the tale's agents of corruption, an interpretation that is given further legitimacy because of their erotic ambiguity. For interpretations in this

The Awkward Age, nubile little Nanda Brookenham competes with her mother for a man's affections, and comes to an agreement with an elderly man, who takes her from her home.

James's treatment of children is thickly enmeshed with adult power dynamics and systems of exchange. He uses the stories' sexual subtext to explore the taboo combination of childhood and adult desire. Rather than being removed from the games adults play, children are at the center of them. Intricately drawn into a web of relations that threatens to become overpowering, the child is an object of desire, distaste, disruption and, often, destruction. Thus, children inaugurate an awkward age for all concerned. As the subject of an adult's will to power, the child is often divested of agency, becoming a pawn whose value resides in its inherent potentiality; the child is, in Michael Trask's words, "the most valuable chip in an economic game" (125).

In James's fiction, the female child in particular is perceived as purely innocent, and therefore ready to be filled with meaning by the adult who controls her. The child is presented as a *tabula rasa* blackened by the sins of her father, mother, or guardian. For the adult observer, the girl's appeal resides in her unconscious ability to suggest both innocence and illicit knowledge. In *Watch and Ward*, Nora's guardian-to-be detects "in her appearance, in spite of her childish innocence and grief, [...] something undeniably vulgar" (*Novels, 1871-1880* 12). Both Nora and Nanda encapsulate the happy blank of idealized girlhood and the possibilities of womanhood. In the eyes of the adult who beholds her, however, the child is, as the guardian-to-be says of Nora, a "little forlorn, precocious, potential woman" who arouses "an irresistible sense of her childish sweetness, of her tender feminine promise" (13).

The Jamesian child is subject to an adult will-to-power that is simultaneously economic and sexual. The novels and tales do not try to dispense with serious and delicate moral problems; rather, they play with them, forcing readers to question their moral allegiances. If made to laugh, smile, sympathize, or feel a knowing kinship with a decadent narrator, do the readers *de facto* agree to his moral scheme? Do James's novels ask readers to join "in this playful erotics of children" and adults, as Ellis Hanson has suggested (372)? Or rather, don't the novels compel readers to question the adults' responsibility? This seems a more productive way of considering the destabilizations prompted by James's fictions and the way they induce readers to experience their own awkward moral stages in relation to the texts. But more on this later.

The tension inherent in the taboo – the conflict between innocence and forbidden knowledge – is precisely the anxious power that drives these fictions. In the preface to *What Maisie Knew*, James explains that:

> No themes are so human as those that reflect for us, out of the confusion of life, the close connexion of bliss and bale, of the things that help with the things that hurt, so dangling before us for ever that bright hard metal, of so strange an alloy, one face of which is somebody's right and ease and the other somebody's pain and wrong. (25)

---

vein, see Ellis Hanson, Michael Trask, and my *Henry James, Oscar Wilde, and Aesthetic Culture*, in which I devote a chapter to parsing the implications of the story's aesthetic and moral involutions.

Must an adult's right and ease come at the expense of a child's wrong and pain? Not always, it seems; in *Watch and Ward* and *The Awkward Age*, the happiness shared by child and guardian stems from their mutual investment in a nebulous moral dilemma – nebulous because the wrong refuses convenient categories such as "pedophilia" or "incest," but comes, as James acknowledges, "at the cost of many conventions and proprieties, even decencies" (*What Maisie Knew* 25-26). By "bringing people together who would be at least more correctly separate" (25), James appeals to his readers as moral actors, who must play the part of arbiter in the drama presented.

The unseemly and unmentionable business of child prostitution lurks just below the surface of *Watch and Ward* and *The Awkward Age*. James's fictional girls dramatize the very real threat of exposure – sexual, commercial, and public – to which children were increasingly subject in the last quarter of the nineteenth century.[3] By contextualizing James's treatment within the era's heightened regulation of child prostitution, we can read both novels as realistic representations of current problems, rather than prurient explorations of the perverse.

The appalling images of exploited girl-labor brought to the public's attention by nineteenth-century reports on child abuse proved that innocent girlhood was not an immutable fact but, as Catherine Robson has compellingly demonstrated, "an economically contingent construction" (13). In *The Awkward Age*, the treatment of girls' development, marriage and commodification reflected contemporary views on child prostitution and on labor markets. James explained the origin of his theme by offering, in the preface to the novel, that "half the attraction [of the theme] was in the current actuality of the thing [...] One had seen such a drama constituted, and always to the effect of proposing to the interested view one of those questions that are of the essence of the drama: what will happen, who suffer, who not suffer"? (5-6). Nanda's plight dramatizes the problems of the later Victorian marriage market, and echoes the public outcry regarding juvenile prostitution and child labor. During the 1880s and 1890s, adults' sexual preoccupations with children were brought to the fore as ancillary considerations of New Woman reformers, who saw that "modern respectability" came at the price of what Mona Caird considered to be "the degradation of womanhood in marriage and in prostitution" (197). Likewise, in her discussion of the modern girl, Sarah Grand objected to daughters being brought up "exclusively for the marriage market, and [...] exhibited like fatted fowls whose value depends upon the color and condition of their flesh" (712).

The dual threats of publicity and exposure to indecency swirl around James's children, menacing to carry them away into a vortex of degeneration. Nora "looks as if she belonged to a circus troupe" (*Novels, 1871-1880* 12), and Nanda "has stepped on the stage" (*Awkward Age* 106), where she "has her little place with the circus" (119). A self-described "circus-woman, in pink tights and no particular skirts" (118),

---

3   The names of *The Awkward Age*'s characters neatly divide them into erotic buyers and sellers. The prospective buyers evoke their pecuniary power with names such as Cashmore (more money), Vanderbank (of the bank), Longdon (long on money), and Mitchy (suggesting the verb "to mitch," meaning "to pilfer" ["Mitch"]). Sellers announce their need with names such as Brookenham (broken home), which is often abbreviated to Brook (suggesting the verb "to brook," meaning "to enjoy the use of, make use of, profit by" ["Brook"]).

Nanda's mother justifies her daughter's exposure by claiming "it's the way we earn our living" (119); Nora, whose mother was a public singer, has equally theatrical parentage.[4] Mrs. Brookenham's explanation evokes the plight of poor Victorian families forced to send their children to work, but her unmistakably sexual idiom turns what might have been a mother's repentance into a bawd's rationalization for her child's sexual commodification. Nanda's brother is also part of the family trade, and he plays his part by "keeping it up with Lady Fanny" (241) – note the male-female genital double-entendre – so that he can get more cash from her husband. With the finesse of a true procuress, Mrs. Brookenham praises her son's cunni-linguistic ability with Lady Fanny, notes with pleasure her fellatory response to him, and suggests the Duchess sample her son's oral erotics:

> "He's amazing," Mrs. Brook pursued. "I watch – I hold my breath. […] Those great calm women – they like slighter creatures."
> "The great calm whales," the Duchess laughed, "swallow the little fishes."
> "Oh my dear," Mrs. Brook returned, "Harold can be tasted, if you like – "
> "If *I* like?" the Duchess parenthetically jeered. "Thank you, love!"
> "But he can't, I think, be eaten. It all works out," Mrs. Brook expounded, "to the highest end. If Lady Fanny's amused she'll be quiet."
> "Bless me," cried the Duchess, "of all the immoral speeches –!" (241)

Mrs. Brookenham's coolness about these sexual and financial matters explains her lack of indignation when Cashmore shamelessly admits to her his attraction to Nanda. As Judith Walkowitz notes, "the brothel operated as a family business, run by women who needed to support their dependents" (28).[5]

While nineteenth-century reports on child abuse and prostitution took pains to veil in euphemism the unseemly trade they exposed, Mrs. Brookenham's stark revelations advertise her daughter just like "some fine tourist region shows the placards in the fields and the posters on the rocks" (107). Beyond the realm of prostitution, in polite society, girls' commodification and publicity were also yoked by the process of coming out. Yet a girl's entrance into society could, if improperly effected, just as easily put her out of society. A girl's passage from the schoolroom to the more public drawing rooms and ballrooms ensured an increased visibility that could easily

---

4   In Henry Robinson's account of nineteenth-century child prostitution in Scotland, he argues that girls growing up with the language, manners and morals of the brothel were at risk of falling into that line of work (9).

5   In an article on gender and juvenile criminality in Victorian England and in *Oliver Twist*, Larry Wolff argues that child prostitution was gendered. In Dickens's words, "the boys are pickpockets, and the girl is a prostitute" (qtd. in Wolff 227). Contemporary social reports by Henry Mayhew and William Acton confirm Wolff's and Dickens's views. As Mayhew points out in *London Labour and the London Poor* (1861-62), boys on the street had a variety of earning activities open to them, while girls could "do little but sell (when a livelihood is to be gained without a recourse to immorality)" (qtd. in Wolff 234). Note that, later in *The Awkward Age*, Harold takes on the role of procurer for his sister, by demanding that Longdon pay for the flower of her youth.

degenerate into publicity.[6] Located at either end of a continuum of female public behavior, exhibition is the dark sister that threatens a girl's coming out. Exposure lurks as a danger that puts the entire social enterprise at risk: a girl's reputation, fate and family hang in the balance. If coming out is theatrical and transformative – because it involves changes in a girl's dress, hair, and perhaps even make-up – it is also conditioned by "antitheatrical prejudice" (Bilston 96-97).[7] False-hearted and artificial, the actress embodies the hazard of the all too public woman. To the public, "the similarities between the actress's life and the prostitute's or demimondaine's were unforgettable and overruled all other evidence about respectability" (Davis 69).

I want to propose that the Victorians saw marriage and prostitution as part of a commercial continuum, indicating either end of a socio-sexual economy. Marriage was deemed moral and productive, because its telos was the production of offspring (and thus of potential new producers and consumers). Prostitution was deemed immoral and unproductive because its telos ended with the sexual act itself. James traces a continuum between varieties of male-to-female bonding and prostitution as a strategy for making generalizations about the moral climate of the late-nineteenth century and for fictionalizing the real social dilemmas of the day. Focusing on young females, James suggests that, at this point in time, it was becoming increasingly difficult to differentiate the precincts of procurers from those in which the mainstream marriage market plied its trade. As Vanderbank explains to Longdon in the opening pages of *The Awkward Age*, the problem with Nanda's plainness is that

"beauty, in London[, …] staring, glaring, obvious, knock-down beauty, as plain as a poster on a wall, an advertisement of soap or whiskey, something that speaks to the crowd and crosses the foot-lights, fetches such a price in the market that the absence of it […] inspires endless terrors and constitutes […] a sort of social bankruptcy. London doesn't love the latent or the lurking, has neither time, nor taste, nor sense for anything less discernible than the red flag in front of the steam-roller. It wants cash over the counter and letters ten feet high. Therefore, you see, it's all as yet rather a dark question for poor Nanda […] She's at the age when the whole thing – speaking of her appearance, her possible share of good looks – is still, in a manner, in a fog. But everything depends on it."

Mr. Longdon, by this time, had come back to [Vanderbank]. "Excuse my asking it again – for you take such jumps: what, once more, do you mean by everything?" "Why, naturally, her marrying." (31-32)

Vanderbank's equation of marriage potential and beauty is predictable enough, but his extension of this scale to include publicity, exposure, boldness and commercialism is less so. A girl's beauty is "the red flag" that will provoke a bull to put his "cash over the counter" in order to claim her for his own. This is not the language of marriage

---

6   For a discussion of this transitional stage and the theatrical, see Sarah Bilston (96-125).

7   The menace of immorality associated with the theater and the actress is well documented. See, among others, Angelique Richardson, Joseph Litvak, Jonas A. Barish, Nina Auerbach, Tracy C. Davis and Juliet Blair.

but of libidinal economics and commodified desire. Until Nanda's "attractions" become glaringly obvious and able to speak to the crowd, her future is dark and gloomy, and might include "social bankruptcy." She needs to attract business: she needs to be a bit of a vamp in order not to become a tramp.

The Victorians had a more inclusive and elastic conception of the state termed "childhood" than we do today. For much of the period from the 1870s through the 1890s, the average age of first marriage for women was 26 (Young 361), a figure that suggests just how socially awkward the subject of age might become for the Victorians. Nanda and Aggie, 18 and 17 respectively, are consistently referred to as children, an appellation that attests to the idea that childhood, especially in middle-class females, was thought usually to end with marriage, so that a girl might effectively remain a child into her twenties and beyond. Conduct manuals encouraged middle-class girls to prolong girlhood (Robson 171). As Sarah Grand notes, grown-up daughters were expected to "be ignorant of everything objectionable upon earth" (708) until they married. Aggie's experience confirms that these young women would, however, be swiftly and thoroughly informed about the ways of the world as soon as they were engaged.

Age is a running gag in *The Awkward Age*, but this frivolity belies serious late-nineteenth-century debates about juvenile prostitution and the age of consent. Mrs. Brookenham can hardly be bothered to remember Nanda's age: she variously gives it as only 16 (28), 30 (45), and nearer 20 (118). The Duchess circumvents a discussion of the age of consent by telling Longdon that Nanda, in whom the Duchess knows he is interested, is "supposedly young, but she's really any age you like" (151). Vanderbank acknowledges the problematic nature of the subject when he admits, "I never know how old – or at least how young – girls are" (26). Nineteenth-century reports on child prostitution take a line similar to the Duchess's. In *Prostitution, Considered in Its Moral, Social, and Sanitary Aspects in London and Other Large Cities and Garrison Towns* (1870), William Acton reported that "the extreme youth" of London's street-walkers was one of the scene's remarkable aspects (185-86). In William Logan's 1871 report on *The Great Social Evil: Its Causes, Extent, Results, and Remedies*, the age of prostitutes is rarely a concern; eight- and nine-year-old prostitutes are not uncommon, and statistics on those under 15 or 16 vary between 0.27 percent to over 12 percent (Kincaid 76). James Kincaid concludes that "some Victorians seem concerned that children may have their moral sense blunted by contact with prostitutes, but there is not a great deal of evidence, until very late in reformers like [William T.] Stead, that the *child*-as-prostitute is much of an issue" (77). The age of consent, which had been set at 12 since the thirteenth century, was reaffirmed in the Offences against the Person Act of 1861. The Criminal Law Amendment Act of 1885 increased the age of consent for girls to 16, and allowed for the police regulation of brothels (Ledger 26). By ruling on all sexual activity, the amendment affected girls from every social stratum and effectively made all children, regardless of class, equal in the eyes of the law (Robson 179). By the same token, social reformers believed that prostitutes, if rehabilitated, would be "absorbed into the so-called respectable classes" (Acton xi).

In his preface to *The Awkward Age*, James takes for granted that "the female young read the newspapers" (7), and it is significant that Nanda, who has fallen before she has even come out, is a newspaper reader. In 1885, Stead's infamous articles in the *Pall Mall Gazette* on "The Maiden Tribute of Modern Babylon" brought the problem of child prostitution to the fore. He documented the ease with which a man could procure a virgin, as well as his knowledge of "the sale and purchase and violation of children" (2). He published a letter from a London brothel-keeper, that included a promise to deliver two daughters whom their parents were "willing to sell", or "a pretty girl of eleven, for £5 […] *virgo intacta*" (4). The procurer promised "to deliver half-a-dozen girls, ages varying from 10 to 13, within a week or ten days," and the purchase price would be refunded "if the girls were found to have been tampered with." Stead revealed how children were made available to sexual consumers. Equally startling was the return policy on such children: the procurer essentially promised that, if his goods were not satisfactory, the consumer's money would be refunded. Of course, the marriage market admits no such return policy. Despite the Duchess's assurances that "my niece is a person *I* call fresh. It's warranted, as they say in the shops" (151), Mitchett is disappointed to learn that Aggie is not the stainless virgin he thought her to be when he married her.

The Awkward Age's moral fulcrum rests in the turn of the screw induced by Longdon's desire to rescue Nanda from her family. "I do want it *done*," he tells Vanderbank, "that […] is why I myself put on the screw. […] I want her got out" (164). Longdon's intentions are not as altruistic as they seem, and some critics have overlooked his moral ambiguity in favor of the general view that he is "Nanda's good angel, who rescues her" (Wagenknecht 144). This notion collapses, however, upon closer examination of his motives. Longdon's philanthropy is activated by his undying affection for Nanda's deceased grandmother, Lady Julia, whom Nanda resembles in the extreme. Nanda is thus a cipher, allowing him to carry out his unfulfilled fantasy of an alliance with Lady Julia, who rejected him long ago. Roger Lawrence, the child-loving hero of *Watch and Ward*, anticipates Longdon's logic by using a little girl as a cipher in order to fulfill his physical desire for her older relation: the little girl is "sent to bed having been kissed by her aunt and rekissed, or unkissed shall I say? by her aunt's lover" (*Novels, 1871-1880* 9). In both cases, the child becomes a surrogate for desires not adequately expressed elsewhere. The Duchess deduces Longdon's secret and tells him in no uncertain terms: "your sentiment for the living is the charming fruit of your sentiment for the dead" (153). Nanda offers Longdon the possibility of revising his personal history, so that it might end with romantic victory rather than defeat. Nanda is of little importance or worth to Longdon in and of herself; were it not for her resemblance to Lady Julia, she would hold out little attraction for him.

Respect for others as ends-in-themselves, to use Kant's formulation of moral duty, is not what activates Longdon. He fails to live up to the categorical imperative according to which an act is moral insofar as it treats humanity (both the actor and the person affected by the act) not simply as a means but, at the same time, as an end in itself (Kant 96). Examined in these terms, Longdon's actions clearly fail to live up to their altruistic claim. To be moral, an action must depend on good will; however, an action's moral worth does not depend on realizing a set purpose, but on an actor's reasons for doing it (Kant 67-68). If we examine the motives for Longdon's actions, we cannot infer with certainty that "it is not some secret impulse of self-love which has actually, under the mere show of the Idea of duty, been the cause of genuinely determining" his will (74-75). The Duchess calls Longdon's bluff: "I make you out[. ... You are] one of those horrible benevolent busybodies who are the worst of the class" (152). Her questions and declarations guide him through the moral maze, forcing him to confront the Minotaur of his unacknowledged desire, and so "with so many fine mysteries playing about him there was relief, [...] rather than alarm, in the thought of knowing the worst" (149).

The arrangement to which Longdon and Nanda come, mutually agreeable though it might be, does involve an overt correlation between financial investment and possession. Longdon feels that Lady Julia is his property (100), and his golden bond with Nanda reasserts the sentiment. Longdon's home contains "portraits of women dead" (197) and Nanda, whose portrait he appraises long before he meets her in the flesh, is the latest addition to his collection. Like her grandmother, Nanda has the face of a Gainsborough. While Vanderbank and Longdon's discussion of what they do and "oughtn't" do (27) with young ladies' pictures is droll enough, it nevertheless partakes in the same ironic humor, used by James elsewhere in the novel (as well as in *Watch and Ward*), to connote erotic mastery and adults' sexual preoccupations with children.

In *Watch and Ward*, Nora accepts her guardian's "hard business-like charity" (*Novels, 1871-1880* 11), and Nanda does the same, although for very different reasons. Nanda differs markedly from James's early figurations of girlhood insofar as she is intensely aware of the machinations and motives of those who surround her. She also knows that her reputation has been damaged by her mother's salacious talk, and that men "are not on the lookout for little brides whose usual associates are so up to snuff" (48). Nanda is "a beggar-maid" (139), someone who in today's terms would be called "damaged goods." She is grateful that Longdon accepts her for her damaged, slangy self; "I *am* like that," she tells him gravely (310), "that's what I mean by your taking me as I am. It *is*, you know, for a girl – extraordinary."

In his preface to the novel, James describes the circle surrounding Mrs. Brookenham as one in which people behave "very often quite rudely and violently and insolently" (8). The insistent idiom of violence applied to Nanda underscores her mistreatment at her mother's hands. That this hurt goes undetected owes much to the "childlike innocence with which [Mrs. Brookenham ...] could invest the hardest teachings of life" (173). Nanda not only appears before company "well slapped," she has been battered, bruised (151) and "dreadfully damaged" (63). She has already "been pitchforked – by talk and contacts and visits and newspapers" (48). Mrs. Brookenham's nature does violence both to the memory of her mother and to the future of her daughter; it is for these reasons that Longdon's offer appeals to Nanda. Nanda's position is summed up in her name, which evokes both the miserable but erotic "Nana", popularized by Zola in his 1880 novel of the same name,[8] as well as the grandmotherly "nana" she represents to Longdon.

---

8   Nanda's resemblance to Nana is bolstered by Longdon's remark to Nanda that she is "like a heroine" out of Zola: "You're perched in your tower or what do you call it? – your bower. You quite hang over the place, you know – the great wicked city, the wonderful London sky and the monuments looming through: or am I again only muddling up my Zola?" (283).

Though the Brookenham social circle is far removed from the harsh realities of the poor and working classes, economic concerns constantly threaten the children. Left by their parents to "play in the street" and be run over (150), Nanda and Harold are expelled from their parents' home, and are constantly in need of money. Nanda's bills are unpaid, although her mother does not rule out the possibility that they might be paid by someone, thereby making her daughter a kept woman (107). James's method of bringing Nanda into relation with the working girl allows him to cast a gloomy shadow of possibility over her future. What little security Nanda has depends on her socio-economic underpinnings (which distinguish her from the working girl), but her irremediable sexualization underscores some of their similarities. Nanda is aware of the problems of the working poor, and she visits the workhouse every Friday to read to old women (121). Her sympathies for the working classes stem from her character, as well as from her position in her mother's household, where she works hard to make herself useful. She brings a studied seriousness to the task of making tea, in common with another of James's neglected children – Pansy Osmond in *The Portrait of a Lady*. Pansy exists to preside over the tea ceremony, even approximating "a consummate piece" of Dresden-china (*Novels, 1881-1880* 560). The novels' clashes between the ornamental and the human are played out in the treatment of these girls.

Hoping to profit from Nanda's alliance with Longdon, the Brookenhams live off Nanda's position. Harold sees to the heart of the matter, explaining the situation in terms more evocative of prostitution than marriage: "she's working Mr. Longdon, like a good true girl" (228). If Longdon wants Nanda, then he should pay for the pleasure:

> I think we ought to *get* something. "Oh yes, dear man, but what do you *give* us for her?" – that's what *I* should say to him. I mean, don't you know, that I don't think she's making quite the bargain she might. If he were to want *me* I don't say he mightn't have me, but I should have it on my conscience to make it in one way or another a good thing for my parents. "You *are* nice, old woman" – he turned to his sister – "and one can still feel for the flower of your youth [...] For God's sake therefore – all the more – don't really close with him till you've had another word or two with me. I'll be hanged [...] if he shall have her for nothing!" (229)

Harold's correlation – an older man paying for the flower of a girl's youth – resonates with the most startling incident in W. T. Stead's 1885 article "The Maiden Tribute of Modern Babylon." In a subsection of the piece titled "A Child of Thirteen Bought for £5," Stead gives a journalistic account of how "Lily" was sold by her parents, her virginity verified, and how she was then deflowered by her purchaser. While Lily and Nanda are obviously from different social strata, they are subject to the same familial and economic pressures. Whether Longdon marries or adopts Nanda makes no difference to the Brookenhams, so long as he pays. "We must all help in our way to pull the coach" (193-94), Mrs. Brookenham reminds Nanda. Although Nanda is willing to give herself to Longdon so that she is no longer a burden to her family, Nanda's mother insists on receiving payment for her daughter's "surrender" (195). After all, the selfish mother reminds her self-sacrificing daughter, "[c]harity, love, begins at home."

Intelligent and capable of weighing up alternatives, Nanda decides that it makes financial sense for her to go with Longdon and to become a kept woman. Her situation links her to nineteenth-century prostitutes, whom Acton and others recorded as having "chosen" their position, not because they were seduced, but because of economic need and cultural demand (Kincaid 28, 108). *Watch and Ward* articulates both these demands in terms of Lawrence's feelings towards his ward: "Nora, Nora, these are not vulgar alms; I expect a return. One of these days you must pay your debt. [...] I love you less than you think, – and more!" (*Novels, 1871-1880* 35). The agreement to which Nanda and Longdon have come satisfies both of them:

> "I shall be one of the people who don't [get married]. I shall be at the end," said Nanda, "one of those who haven't."
> "No, my child," he returned gravely – "you shall never be anything so sad."
> "Why not – if *you've* been?"
> He looked at her a little, quietly; then, putting out his hand, passed her own into his arm. "Exactly because I have." (142)

Nanda is Longdon's alter ego and his altar ego: he offers her the possibility of an enduring alliance with an intimate and trusted friend. This is the basis for their mutual adoption. Longdon performs a double role as potential seducer (having lured Nanda from her home) and ultimate savior.[9] Lawrence and Nora share a comparable conversation that culminates in the girl's grave "promise never, never, never to marry, but to be yours alone – yours alone!" (42).

In my introduction, I noted the way in which James's authorial detachment proves morally destabilizing to readers. I want to return to this idea in order to clarify the contradictory dynamic at work in these novels, as well as in James's claims about them. The novels simultaneously acknowledge (and even moralize) their impropriety, while coolly advising readers that pleasure and pain are the stuff of life, *ma chérie*. James's ironic distance makes possible the exploration of these taboo themes. His detachment enables readers to take a subjective view of the issue. By removing himself from this ethical equation, James squarely places the moral onus on his readers. For example, "The Turn of the Screw" induces readers to take on the governess's role, by making them distrustful and paranoid of the children's secrets (Felman 239). The story's model of authorship is a "lure" for readers, "a scene in which audiences found it irresistible to 'read into' the story their own emotions and fears" (Flatley 105).

The more the author retreats under silence, euphemism and equivocation, the more readers are *de facto* obliged to invest in the task of evaluating the moral scene set before them. In *Watch and Ward*, for instance, Nora is shocked to learn from her cousin, Fenton, that her guardian wishes to marry her:

---

9   My thinking here is indebted to Catherine Robson (173).

"He has known me as a child," she continued, heedless of his sarcasm. "I shall always be a child, for him."

"He'll like that," said Fenton, with heat. "He'll like a child of twenty." (*Novels, 1871-1880* 52)

This scene reveals Fenton's vulgarity, and confirms James's dissociation from the relationship between Nora and her guardian, by demolishing the myth of intimate asexuality between them (Traub 374). In *The Awkward Age*, James disentangles himself from the novel's sexual intrigues through a similar series of authorial gestures: he disengages himself through ironic detachment but elicits the readers' investment, and then again evades the readers' demands for interpretative closure. This one-two punch also functions on a generic level. First, James privileges the Realist's sober matter-of-factness and scientific detachment – *The Awkward Age* is "the picture of contemporary manners, in 2 features of current English life" (*Notebooks* 177).[10] Second, he effects a neat refusal of Realism's implicit moral stance, adopting instead the aesthete's pose of *l'art pour l'art* and, therefore, literature's insubordination to moral, didactic, or political purposes. James's notes for *The Awkward Age* make clear his conscious positioning of "the question of the non-marrying of girls, the desperation of mothers, the whole alteration of manners – in the sense of the *osé* – and tone, while our theory of the participation, the *presence* of the young, remains unaffected by it" (118). The non-participant author is, in fact, an absence that is a presence.

Careful positioning also accounts for James's detachment concerning the subject of *Watch and Ward*, a novel with strong allusions to incest and pedophilia. To Grace Norton, he described the novel as "charmingly graphic" (*Life in Letters* 42). To her brother, Charles Eliot Norton, he winked, "the subject is something slight; but I have tried to make a work of art, and if you are good enough to read it, I trust you will detect my intention" (41). The playful description of "the subject" (both little Nora and the book's matter) as "slight," the intent to aestheticize moral ugliness ("I have tried to make a work of art"), the knowing pressure put on readers to "detect my intention": these positions conspire to remove James further from the novel's moral center, while bringing readers closer to it. James effectively hands the reins over to his readers, whose task is to assess the moral and aesthetic value of the stories before them.

In *The Awkward Age*, both Nanda and Aggie are unstintingly accompanied by the adjectives "little" and "small," by floral and rural echoes, and by daughterliness. These attributes combine to lay claim to the girl's ideal status, while consistently undermining it via the "accommodating irony" that James "invoked, for [his] protection" (*Awkward Age* 3). The sexualization of these girls is not *sub rosa*, however, and James fully exploits the playful erotics of his seduction scenes. *Pace* the lingering legends of James's sexual squeamishness, his flirtatious prose and suggestive imagery are not the elements that surprise readers. The need for protection – a recurrent image in his sexually aware letters of the 1890s – is what strikes a

---

10   Note how the definite article in "the picture of contemporary manners" intensifies the Realist claim and detachment, whereas an indefinite article would have had the opposite effect.

discordant note.[11] Why did he need such protection? What I have been suggesting is that James was always "finely aware and richly responsible" (*Art* 52) of the juvenile nature of his subjects, and the jarring effect this would have on his readers. In *Watch and Ward*, James attempted ironic detachment, but with less success than he achieved in *The Awkward Age*. One of the marks of his achievement in that later novel is the fact that, despite his characters' willful affectation of nonchalance, James anticipated readers' troubled response. The sexualization to which his children are subjected is, to borrow James's own response to an acquaintance's sordid sexual exposure, "beyond any utterance of irony" (*Life in Letters* 279).

Works Cited

Acton, William. *Prostitution, Considered in Its Moral, Social, and Sanitary Aspects in London and Other Large Cities and Garrison Towns*. 1870. London: Frank Cass, 1972.

Auerbach, Nina. *Private Theatricals: The Lives of the Victorians*. Cambridge: Harvard UP, 1990.

Barish, Jonas A. *The Antitheatrical Prejudice*. Berkeley: U of California P, 1981.

Bilston, Sarah. *The Awkward Age in Women's Popular Fiction, 1850-1900: Girls and the Transition to Womanhood*. Oxford: Clarendon, 2004.

Blair, Juliet. "Private Parts in Public Places: The Case of Actresses." *Women and Space: Ground Rules and Social Maps*. Ed. Shirley Ardener. New York: St. Martin's, 1981. 205-28.

"Brook." *The Oxford English Dictionary*. 2nd ed. 1989.

Caird, Mona. "Marriage." *Westminster Review* (August 1888): 186-229.

Davis, Tracy C. *Actresses as Working Women: Their Social Identity in Victorian Culture*. London: Routledge, 1991.

Felman, Shoshana. *Writing and Madness: (Literature/Philosophy/Psychoanalysis)*. Ithaca, NY: Cornell UP, 1985.

Flatley, Jonathan. "Reading into Henry James." *Criticism: A Quarterly for Literature and the Arts* 46.1 (2004): 103-23.

Grand, Sarah. "The Modern Girl." *North American Review* (June 1894): 706-14.

Hanson, Ellis. "Screwing with Children in Henry James." *GLQ: A Journal of Lesbian and Gay Studies* 9.3 (2003): 367-91.

James, Henry. *The Art of the Novel*. Ed. R. P. Blackmur. New York: Charles Scribner's Sons, 1950.

---. *The Awkward Age*. Ed. Ronald Blythe. London: Penguin, 1987.

---. *The Complete Notebooks of Henry James*. Ed. Leon Edel and Lyall H. Powers. Oxford: Oxford UP, 1987.

---. *Henry James: A Life in Letters*. Ed. Philip Horne. London: Allen Lane, 1999.

---. *Novels, 1871-1880*. New York: Library of America, 1983.

---. *Novels, 1881-1886*. New York: Library of America, 1985.

---

11   See, in particular, James's letters to Edmund Gosse regarding the arrest and trial of Oscar Wilde (*Selected Letters* 291).

---. *Selected Letters of Henry James to Edmund Gosse, 1882-1915: A Literary Friendship.* Ed. Rayburn S. Moore. Baton Rouge: Louisiana State UP, 1988.

---. *What Maisie Knew.* Ed. Paul Theroux. New York: Penguin, 1985.

Kant, Immanuel. *Groundwork of the Metaphysics of Morals.* Trans. H. J. Paton. New York: Harper & Row, 1964.

Kincaid, James R. *Child-Loving: The Erotic Child and Victorian Culture.* New York: Routledge, 1992.

Ledger, Sally, and Roger Luckhurst, eds. *The Fin-De-Siècle: A Reader in Cultural History, C. 1880-1900.* Oxford: Oxford UP, 2000.

Litvak, Joseph. *Caught in the Act: Theatricality in the Nineteenth-Century English Novel.* Berkeley: U of California P, 1992.

Mendelssohn, Michèle. *Henry James, Oscar Wilde, and Aesthetic Culture.* Edinburgh: Edinburgh UP, 2007.

"Mitch." *The Oxford English Dictionary.* 2nd ed. 1989.

Richardson, Angelique, and Chris Willis, eds. *The New Woman in Fiction and in Fact: Fin-de-Siècle Feminisms.* Basingstoke: Palgrave, 2001.

Robinson, Henry. *The Whole Truth and Nothing but the Truth About the Social Evil: Being Deeper Glimpses of the Business of Prostitution in Edinburgh.* Edinburgh: Henry Robinson, 1866.

Robson, Catherine. *Men in Wonderland: The Lost Girlhood of the Victorian Gentleman.* Princeton: Princeton UP, 2001.

Rowe, John Carlos. *The Other Henry James.* Durham: Duke UP, 1998.

Stead, W.T. "The Maiden Tribute of Modern Babylon." *Pall Mall Gazette* (6 July 1885): 1-6.

Trask, Michael. "Getting into It with James: Substitution and Erotic Reversal in *The Awkward Age.*" *American Literature* 69 (1997): 105-38.

Traub, Lindsey. "'I Trust You Will Detect My Intention': The Strange Case of *Watch and Ward.*" *Journal of American Studies* 29.3 (1995): 365-78.

Untitled. *New York Times* (12 July 1878): 3.

Wagenknecht, Edward. *Eve and Henry James: Portraits of Women and Girls in His Fiction.* Norman: U of Oklahoma P, 1978.

Walkowitz, Judith R. *Prostitution and Victorian Society: Women, Class, and the State.* Cambridge: Cambridge UP, 1980.

Wolff, Larry. "'The Boys Are Pickpockets, and the Girl Is a Prostitute': Gender and Juvenile Criminality in Early Victorian England from *Oliver Twist* to *London Labour.*" *New Literary History* 27.2 (1996): 227-49.

Young, Michael, and Peter Willmott. *The Symmetrical Family: A Study of Work and Leisure in the London Region.* London: Routledge and Kegan Paul, 1973.

Chapter 5

For-getting to Eat: Alice's Mouthing Metonymy

Carol Mavor

At meals he was very abstemious always, while he took nothing in the middle of the day except a glass of wine and a biscuit. Under these circumstances it is not very surprising that the healthy appetites of his little friends filled him with wonder, and even with alarm. When he took a certain one of them out with him to a friend's house to dinner, he used to give the host or hostess a gentle warning, to the mixed amazement and indignation of the child, "Please be careful, because she eats a good deal too much."

Stuart Dodgson Collingwood, writing about his uncle Charles Dodgson (aka Lewis Carroll) (300)

My dear Agnes,

At last I've succeeded in forgetting you! It's been a very hard job, but I took 6 "lessons-in-forgetting," at half-a-crown a lesson. After three lessons, I forgot my own name, and I forgot to go for the next lesson. So the Professor said I was getting on very well: "but I hope," he added, "you won't forget to pay for the lessons!" I said *that* would depend on whether the other lessons were good or not: and do you know? the last of the 6 lessons was so good that I forgot *everything*! I forgot who I was: I forgot to eat my dinner [...]

Lewis Carroll, letter to Agnes Hull, December 10, 1877 (*Selected Letters* 80)

For-getting: To Eat

The Alice stories are lessons in forgetting – "'And now who am I? I *will* remember if I can! I'm determined to do it! [...] L, I *know* it begins with L!'" (Carroll, *Annotated Alice* 177) – and eating – "it had, in fact, a sort of mixed flavour of cherry-tart, custard, pine-apple, roast turkey, toffy, and hot buttered toast" (17).[1] In both *Alice's Adventures in Wonderland* (1865) and *Through the Looking Glass* (1871), but especially in *Wonderland*, nearly every action turns hedonistically on eating/consumption. Like Marcel Proust's *In Search of Lost Time* (1913), the emphasis on food in *Wonderland* and *Through the Looking Glass* is in the absence of nourishment. But in contrast to

---

1   All further citations to *Alice's Adventures in Wonderland* and *Through the Looking Glass* are from *The Annotated Alice*.

Proust's bit of madeleine cake dipped in tea, which is now a cultural trope – even a cliché – for profound memory, Alice's eating is all about forgetting.

My text swallows Alice's reading-as-displaced-eating, as mouthing metonymy, not gorging on metaphor. Feeding forgetting rather than fulfilling memory, Alice's eating-as-withholding keeps desire in check. This anorectic labor, reflective of Carroll's own fear of indulgence, manifests itself in the Alice stories, in Carroll's letters to girl-children, in the 1890 *Wonderland Postage-Stamp Case*, in the 1892 *"Through the Looking-Glass" Biscuit Tin*, and even in Carroll's photographs of never-to-grow-old girls, nurtured solely by paper and wet collodion.

In *Wonderland* and *Through the Looking Glass*, Alice remembers very little about home, save for her always-hungry cat Dinah:

> Dinah'll miss me very much to-night, I should think! […] I hope they'll remember her saucer of milk at tea-time. Dinah, my dear! I wish you were down here with me! There are no mice in the air, I am afraid, but you might catch a bat, and that's very like a mouse, you know. But do cats eat bats, I wonder? (14)

Save for her reminiscing about Dinah, it seems that there is hardly a nostalgic (homesick, remembering) bone in Alice's fantastic, metamorphosing, textual, writ(h)ing,[2] always-hungry body.[3] As we know from *Through the Looking Glass*, Alice had once "really frightened her old nurse by shouting suddenly in her ear, 'Nurse! Do let's pretend that I'm a hungry hyæna, and you're a bone!'" (141). For Alice, bones hold no sacred memories or pasts; they're just food, and barely that. For a bone is for chewing and gnawing and tasting and picking and licking. It's really not much to eat. A bone feeds a hunger of a different order.

If Alice's eating is about anything, it is about morsels, nibbles and bits. Just try to imagine how teeny-tiny her bit of mushroom would have had to be when Alice was but three inches tall (53). Like Proust's *In Search of Lost Time*, the Alice stories insist on eating that is really not eating. When tasting the famed madeleine cake (given to him by Mamma on a winter's day during a return home), Marcel takes only a "morsel of the cake" in a mere "spoonful of the tea" (I.60, I.44).[4] From that crumb blossomed all of the volumes of *In Search of Lost Time*. The intellectual metamorphoses in Proust's work made possible by a nibble are strangely parallel to the magnificent, physical, but never meaningful (at least to Alice) metamorphoses caused by drinking a bottle not marked poison, or eating a bit of mushroom, or swallowing a pebble-turned-cake.

Throughout Proust's *In Search of Lost Time*, things meant for eating and even things not meant for eating are described deliciously, with tasty words at the tip

---

2   Recall in the Mock Turtle's tale that, in his schooling, that character could take only the "regular course" – no French music or washing, just "Reeling and Writhing" (97-98).

3   Alice does, however, seem to miss home (if only a little bit) when she says, after so much growing and shrinking, "It was much pleasanter at home" (39). Nevertheless, as quickly as she makes that remark, Alice says that it is as if she is in a fairy tale and that "there ought to be a book written about me, that there ought!"

4   Hereafter, parenthetical references to *In Search of Lost Time* will include the pages of the English version followed by those of the French version.

of the narrator's tongue. Rarely, however, does Marcel describe himself physically devouring food. In his boyhood home of Combray, the Sunday luncheon table typically included eggs, cutlets, potatoes, preserves, biscuits, a brill, a turkey, "cardoons with marrow," "a roast leg of mutton," spinach, gooseberries, raspberries, cherries, a cream cheese, an almond cake, a brioche and "a chocolate cream" (I.96-97; I.70). As I argue in *Reading Boyishly*, and as Proust makes especially apparent in his essay "On Reading Ruskin,"[5] despite such bounty, Marcel rarely takes a swallow; he would rather be reading than eating. He is an anorectic hedonist.

Carroll, in his thoroughly non-French, British way, has his own dressed tables with their own anorectic/hedonistic tendencies. These are displayed, for instance, in *Wonderland*'s "mad tea-party," where Alice is told that there is no room for her at the big table, when in fact there is plenty; where Alice is offered nonexistent wine; and where she learns of three girls named "Elsie, Lacie, and Tillie", who live at the bottom of the well, eating nothing but treacle (75). By the time we get to the end of *Through the Looking Glass*, "Queen Alice" arrives to find an even larger table, one set for "about fifty guests" (261). Having already "missed the soup and the fish," Alice is confronted by an animistic leg of mutton crowned with his own paper-frill coronet. With a little bow on the mutton's part and one returned by Alice, they meet: "Alice – Mutton: Mutton – Alice" (261). But how could Alice ever slice someone she has just met? "It isn't etiquette to cut any one you've been introduced to," the Red Queen scolds (262).[6] There's nothing to do but remove the joint and bring out the pudding. In an attempt to avoid more shameful embarrassment when faced with cutting food that talks, Alice hastily says, "I won't be introduced to the pudding, please [...] or we shall get no dinner at all" (262). No sooner has Alice said this than the pudding is removed. In a wink, things turn annihilative, with bottles turning into birds (with plates for wings and forks for legs), and the Red Queen's broad, good-natured face disappearing into the soup.

The effect of the Alice stories, like that of *In Search of Lost Time*, is to emphasize consumption based on withholding. Consider those tarts, stolen but not eaten. Or recall when the little bits of comfits are handed round at the Caucus-race: "the large birds complained that they could not taste theirs, and the small ones choked and had to be patted on the back" (33). And don't forget the Hatter, who complains that "the bread-and-butter" slices are "getting so thin" (114). As the White Queen makes as clear as pudding, "jam to-morrow and jam yesterday – but never jam *to-day*" (196), because "it will never be exactly time for Alice to eat the jam" (Cixous 247). The same is true of the plum-cake. "Hand it round first and cut it afterwards" (231), the Unicorn orders the baffled Alice. It's all about cutting up, whether it be the roast, the pudding, or the fish; but it involves eating of a different order.

Alice, we learn in *Wonderland*, "always took a great interest in questions of eating and drinking" (75). She is surprisingly willing to eat a bit of anything, as she moves

---

5   In French, Proust's essay is entitled "Sur la lecture."

6   The Reverend Robert Kirk's late seventeenth-century treatise on the secrets of fairies tells us that a joint-eater is a kind of fairy who sits invisibly by a victim and partakes of the latter's food, allowing the victim to continue to be lean despite a devouring appetite (Warner 201).

through those two dreamy landscapes that, undisputedly, evoke the unconscious. Alice is fearless in her bit-eating: the only thing that seems to be at stake is etiquette. When Alice says, "Nurse! Do let's pretend that I'm a hungry hyæna, and you're a bone!" (141), I smack my lips with dangerous thoughts of naughty, risky food (James Kincaid has schooled us well in the close ties between a kissing smack and a spanking smack.). With Alice's nurse-desiring, hyæna hunger on my mind, in rushes Merit Oppenheim's own 1936 feast on a nurse, her dangerously delectable *My Nurse* (fig. 5.1).

Served up, like yummy foods, on an eye-catching platter is a pair of Freudian slippers – white ladies' pumps, to be exact – bound together with sadistic, sexy string like a gift waiting to be untied (by one's teeth, of course).[7] And best of all, the most delectable parts, the devious heels, have slipped on their own little paper frills (like the mutton leg to which Alice is introduced) as if they were a pair of lamb chops. But there is nothing to nourish here in any kind of nutritional way; it is about a mouth that does not nurture its body and the pleasures and dangers of surface-oriented eating. As Freud has shown us, there is no "no" in the unconscious. This kind of eating is closer to kissing and licking; it is an eating that is about risk

To eat in Alice's world is to turn mouths into eyes, and eyes into mouths, in a substitutive practice that cooks up nonsense. In the words of Carroll's Mad Hatter, "Why you might just as well say that 'I see what I eat' is the same thing as 'I eat what I see'" (71). In Alice's world, as the Hatter knows, "it's always tea-time" (74). And if it's always tea-time, then we are always hungry, always wild with desire; we are endlessly chasing the White Rabbit, whom Hélène Cixous rudely and hilariously describes as a "penis on paws" (240). The Rabbit is a Lacanian, metonymic carrot on a string, *always* before us. The rabbit as our carrot is, as Lacan would surely claim, "eternally stretching forth towards the *desire for something else* – of metonymy" (Lacan 167). It is an endless series of displacements.

In this endless chain of Carrollinian *word-to-word* connections[8] – a chain of isolated signifiers, a place of nonsense where we find ourselves stripped of what lies on the other side of metonymy (metaphor, memory and meaning) – we just might find ourselves sipping from Oppenheim's 1936 *Breakfast in Fur* (fig. 5.2). Itself a portmanteau object of White Rabbit and Mad Hatter teacup, I savor it as a revolting glug of the dormouse stuffed into the teapot. Oppenheim's teacup is a horrific, fully sensate, image of tea drinking. Think of the smell of the fur – wet, warm, and soaking with tea. Open your mouth to the cup and dream up the feeling of rabbit pelt in your mouth. Suppose the queerness of the soft touch of the cup on the

---

7   In his essay on the fetish, Freud supplies objects such as a tube of lipstick and a pair of shoes as objects to fetishize. For him, such stand-ins for the penis represent both an acknowledgement of, and protection against, castration. In Freud's hands, the fetish object is always sexual and shielding, as are Oppenheim's high-heeled yet clean, pure white pumps. Through the tying up of the shoes, *My Nurse* plays into the double-edged quality of the Freudian fetish: the pumps represent the threat of sexual sadism, yet they are tied to protect against loss. Furthermore, Freud sees the child's governess, or nurse, as the one who most often teaches us about sexuality. See Jane Gallop on "Nurse Freud" in "Keys to Dora."

8   Lacan writes that "the connexion between ship and sail is nowhere but in the signifier, and that it is in the *word-to-word* connexion that metonymy is based" (156).

saucer. Hardly Proustian, this cup of tea is not likely to remind anyone nostalgically of his or her old aunt, at least in any kind of nurturing sense. Furthermore, *Breakfast in Fur* is padded against the possibility of even an aural memory prompt; no chance here of a memory evoked from a Proustian chance knock of "a spoon against a plate" (VI.257; IV.446). Stirring tea in a fur cup and placing a fur spoon on a fur saucer would be nearly soundless. *Breakfast in Fur*, like the Alice stories, is about forgetting the past, as well as about forgetting the future by experiencing the present in a most non-normative way.

Like Oppenheim's work, the Alice stories present us with plenty of feeding, but not much nurturing. Just as the Mad Hatter "bit a large piece out of his teacup instead of the bread-and-butter" (113), when you take a bite in Wonderland it is more about reading than eating. Wonderland reading entails metonymic surface-eating nonsense; there are no metaphors. No deep meaning here, despite the fall "down, down, down. Would the fall *never* come to an end?" (13). Through the use of punning and word-switching, Carroll's Alicious words become isolated signifiers that resist meaning, sense, and metaphor. According to Lacan, displacement is metonymy[9] and "desire is a metonymy" (175). Alice falls into a deep hole, but it is a special Carrollinian hole, where memory/meaning does not grow deeper but is evacuated. Metonymy, as Lacan tells us and Carroll shows us, is a "weapon [...] against nostalgia" (165).

Eating makes possible all the forgetting. Still today, perhaps with our own touch of Aliciousness, it is not uncommon to drown our sorrows in a large bag of potato chips, a carton of ice cream, a box of chocolate, a handful or more of cookies, for all of this immediate consumption is all too readily available. But Alice's forgetting comes out of eating almost nothing at all. She's a pecker, not a gorger; she pecks like a bird that Dinah might just eat. Perhaps that is why Carroll was so fond of picturing Alice Liddell and a host of other girl-child friends as little beggars. When we look at *Alice Liddell as "The Beggar Maid"* (fig. 5.3), her cupped hand is a hole not for small change, nor for food, but for Carroll as tiny White Rabbit to slip into – a hole in memory.

Although not named as such, nor even seen, Lethe, the meandering river of forgetfulness, is everywhere in the geography of *Wonderland* and *Through the Looking Glass*. ("'L, I *know* it begins with L'" [177].) Alice drowns in Lethe, swallowing its waters as she does her very own tears. Forgetting is the only thing that Alice is unlikely to forget.[10] She is in her own way – via the waterways of her alter-ego "L"ewis Carroll ("'L,' I *know* it begins with 'L'") – consumed by the art of forgetting.

Memory is a storehouse, a cellar, a well, perhaps even a rabbit hole or a treacle well. Gaston Bachelard has argued that, when one is in the attic, fears can be rationalized, even enlightened; but in the cellar, "darkness prevails both day and night" (19). "The cellar dreamer knows that the walls of the cellar are buried walls" (20), and the deeper Alice descends, the closer she comes to the dark place of forgetting.

---

9   Lacan writes, "In the case of *Verschiebung*, 'displacement,' the German term is closer to the idea of that veering off of signification that we see in metonymy" (160).

10   For an illuminating discussion of the impossibility of "the art of forgetting," see Umberto Eco's "An Ars *Oblivionalis?* Forget It."

As Harald Weinrich writes in *Lethe: The Art and Critique of Forgetting*, "Perhaps forgetting is also only, in trivial terms, *a hole in memory* into which something falls or *disappears*" (4).

Death is the ultimate form of forgetting. On the most basic level, forgetting makes it possible to live without death; but forgetting is also death itself. In Milan Kundera's view, forgetting "is the great private problem of man; death as the loss of self. But what of this self? It is the sum of everything we remember. Thus, what terrifies us about death is not the loss of future but the loss of past. Forgetting is a form of death ever present within life" (234-35). In the great multiplication table of the ever-expanding worlds of the Dodo, Do-do Dodgson's writings, and perhaps especially his photographs – themselves infinitely reproducible, never necessarily just one – are always already troubled by the mark of death.[11] Today, when we look at Carroll's 1875 photograph of Xie Kitchin beneath her umbrella, we know that she is dead; nevertheless she lounges before us as a child forever, protected against death by the wet collodion that holds her image. Yet this Xie, like her parasol, is nothing more than paper (fig. 5.4). Photography operates as a trace of a moment gone forever. Photography is a hole that is made physical in the aperture of the camera itself, the iris of the eye. The hole, then, might signify death, but it is also a place into which death might disappear and be forgotten. Photography is a trace of a moment forever held, forever young, without death. The *mise-en-scène* of "Alice" is a forgetting place, for-getting rid of death.

The hole, and the possibilities of leaving it open, are like an optimistic gap: a place not to fill, a stomach left hungry, a history promised but left untold: "'You promised to tell me your history, you know,' said Alice, 'and why it is you hate – C and D'" (33). And much to our frustration and our delight, the story is never really told. C and D remain empty signifiers with which we readers can form (perform) our own "long and sad tale" or even a "long tail" (33). But the point is that both *Alice* tales (whether you fall for her or go through her) are less narratives than romps; there's no Oedipal climax, no character development, no sentimentality, hardly a memory of what has happened just pages before. But that's just it: it's a staging of desire, a play left open – whether C and D are for Charles and Dodgson, Carroll and the Dodo, Cixous and Derrida. After all, Derrida, like Alice, loved cats, and understood Dinah's purring as the ultimate deconstructionist utterance. To this effect, he cites the following passage from *Through the Looking Glass*:

> It is a very inconvenient habit of kittens (Alice had once made the remark) that whatever you say to them, they *always* purr. "If they would only purr for 'yes,' and mew for 'no,' or any rule of that sort, she had said, so that one could keep up a conversation! But how *can* you talk with a person if they *always* say the same thing?"

---

11   "Lewis Carroll" is, of course, Charles Dodgson's pen name. He had a problem with stuttering, sometimes resulting in the pronouncing of his name as "Do-do Dodgson," hence the presence of the Dodo as yet another alter ego in Wonderland. It is said that Carroll lost his stutter in the presence of little girls; this would make Alice Liddell part of the cure.

On this occasion the kitten only purred: and it was impossible to guess whether it meant "yes" or "no." (377)

The kitten in question here is the offspring of Dinah, who starts both *Wonderland* and *Through the Looking Glass*. Dinah is one of the very few objects (whether they be people, places, pets, or things) toward which Alice shows any conscious nostalgia. Alice, the bourgeois snob, has no longings for someone like Mabel, whom she remembers as stupid and poor, in her "poky little house [… with] next to no toys to play with" (23). Furthermore, Alice sheds no tears for the lost mother or father. It is the cat – perhaps only the cat, whether it takes the form of Dinah, or the metamorphosed form of the Cheshire Cat, or the form of a black kitten or a white kitten as birthed by Mother Dinah – that Alice misses at least a little in this surprisingly nostalgia-bereft children's story. Alice, however, does tell us with atypical sentimentality that Dinah is "a dear quiet thing [that] sits purring so nicely by the fire, licking her paws and washing her face – and she is such a nice soft thing to nurse" (26). In *Wonderland* and *Through the Looking Glass*, cats can be understood as a metonymy for memory.

In *Wonderland*, Dinah is displaced by the Cheshire Cat, whom the ever-polite Alice addresses as "Cheshire-Puss," in the hope that this feline with "*very* long claws and a great many teeth" might feel respected (64). And of course, both Dinah and the Cheshire Cat are all mouth. While Dinah is associated with saucers of milk and hunting mice, her displaced image, as the Cheshire Cat, is literally all mouth: "'Well! I've often seen a cat without a grin,' thought Alice; 'but a grin without a cat! It's the most curious thing I ever saw in my life!'" (67). Like the rabbit hole, this Cheshire Cat hole is yet another spatiality of memory into which to fall. Anorectically metonymic, it feeds nothing. It stresses the void: rather than a recuperation of memory, it is its evacuation.

Eating Grammar

Falling headfirst right down that rabbit hole "filled with cupboards," Alice initiates the eating down under by grabbing a jar labeled "ORANGE MARMALADE," although "to her great disappointment it was empty" (13). Likewise, she drinks language through a bottle (not empty) tagged "DRINK ME" and chews language through a cake on which the words "EAT ME" are spelled out in currants. As with Proust, Alice's reading is eating, her eating is reading. In an echo of the Mad Hatter's paradox of whether the phrase "I eat what I see" is the same as "I see what I eat," Alice might say "I read what I eat" is the same as "I eat what I read." Getting biblical with *Alice*, I cannot help adding Jeremiah 15:16: "When your words came, I ate them." Carroll and his fictional Alice share the appetite of the withholding ascetic: their nutriment is textual; they eat words, not food.

When Alice eats the whole "very small cake, on which the words 'EAT ME' were beautifully marked in currants," she decides to "set to *work*, and very soon finished off the cake" (18-19, emphasis mine). I have never found a small cake laborious to eat. Small words, on the other hand, can be a real bother, especially verbs – the category to which the word "eat" belongs. As Humpty Dumpty claims, "They've a temper, some of them – particularly verbs: they're the proudest – adjectives you can do anything with, but not verbs" (213). And let's not forget that Humpty Dumpty, who claims to be the Master of Language, is an egg, something to eat, and, like the Cheshire Cat, is all mouth – to the point that he verges on decapitation. "'If he smiled much more the ends of his mouth might meet behind,' she thought: 'and then I don't know *what* would happen to his head! I'm afraid it would come off!'" (210). It's all about displacement, about mouthing metonymy.

Eating as grammatical work is a form of anorexic labor (for the anorexic, eating is always work) in that it not only keeps metonymic desire in check (for one is never full/fulfilled), but also always embraces death. Death is the soulmate of the anorexic. Nevertheless, eating also keeps one close to death, in that a person must eat to grow older, grow toward death. The coupling of "to eat is to die" with "*not* to eat is to die" is a double theme also found in J. M. Barrie's Neverland: a faraway island where Peter, a child who never grows up, hardly ever eats, and is as fond of pretend food as real food. As Wendy notices:

> He could eat, really eat, if it was part of a game, but he could not stodge [that is, gorge in order to experience a delicious, rich, filling quality] just to feel stodgy, *which is what most children like better than anything else*; the next best thing being to talk about it. Make-believe was so real to him that during a meal of it you could see him getting rounder. (135, emphasis mine)

Likewise in Alice's tales, the excess of growing, of language itself, of babies turning into omnivorous pigs, is always matched by the impossibility of a full meal, a real meal.

Alice's orderly suppression of eating in *Wonderland* and *Through the Looking Glass* is ultimately a purification of appetite. In the words of Adam Phillips, the world of the anorexic is one "in which nothing can be eaten, nothing must be taken in" (*Promises* 134). What might this suggest about narrative itself? Carroll claims that a story gives us a framework, a menu to peruse, but then ultimately withholds the narrative, at least one conventionally told. Filled to the brim with rich words – which can never have only one meaning, but always already have layers of meaning, there is no food into which to sink our teeth. To go underground and through the mirror is to be at once anorectic and hedonistic. Carroll seemingly says, "I would prefer not to tell a story," just as the anorexic politely refuses to eat, claiming in a seemingly indifferent tone, with all the power of Herman Melville's Bartleby himself, "I would prefer not to."[12] Nevertheless, the anorexic knows how to present a meal and trim a table, just as Carroll gives us one of the most excessive, complex, oft-quoted pieces of English fiction. A world is created in which *almost* nothing is eaten, and *almost*

---

12   Connecting Mellville's story "Bartleby, the Scrivener: A Story of Wall Street" (1853) to the plight of the anorexic is at the heart of Phillips's essay "On Eating, and Preferring Not To." As he writes, "At first the boss takes it for granted, in a commonsensical way, that Bartleby will do the work demanded of him; just as, in a commonsensical way, one might assume that people will eat, simply in order to live, or to feel well; as though food has only a use-value, and not an exchange value as well" (*Promises*, 283).

nothing can be taken in. And this always-hungry world fills us with desire. We want to sit down and read/eat.

Even in his photographs, as in his *Alice* books, Carroll plays at an eating that is not actually eating. (This eating without eating is further enhanced by the fact that every photograph is connected to the Real, without being the real thing.[13]) For example, in Carroll's 1857 photograph of Agnes Grace Weld as *Little Red Riding Hood*, we see in the girl's menacing eyes the wolf's desire to eat Little Red, and wonder whether Agnes is going to consume us, as viewers. True, there is a biscuit openly displayed in Agnes's basket, but this treatmeant for grandma looks stale and unreal: it is stage prop, play, not food. In Carroll's 1864 photograph of Agnes Price, the model holds a doll face to face, mocking the proper, nurturing mother; she is a duplication of Alice holding the Duchess's baby-turned-pig. As Nina Auerbach writes, "the doll becomes less a thing to nourish than a thing to eat" (167). But what kind of food is a toy doll? Likewise, when, in 1873, Carroll pictures Alexandra ("Xie") Kitchin sitting on crates that are painted with Chinese floral patterns and bound tight with rope, wearing her cap in *Tea Merchant (On Duty)*, but not wearing it in *Tea Merchant (Off Duty)* (fig. 5.5), there are no biscuit boxes among her crates of tea. How fitting that the focus is on tea, a drink free of calories, but rich with energy-inducing caffeine. Tea, like coffee, is ascetic: it masks hunger; it feeds without food. When Carroll endorsed the manufacturing of an Alice biscuit tin, decorated with Tenniel's illustrations (fig. 5.6), he claimed unease at the idea of endorsing a brand of biscuits. But perhaps his actual unease was with the biscuits themselves. While Carroll gave many tins away to his little friends, he gave them as he received them from the manufacturer, without the biscuits (*Lewis Carroll's Alice* 49).

An eating disorder such as anorexia is the ultimate ordering of eating, order being a form of obsession often hailed as a positive quality in other aspects of daily life. Carroll himself was filled to the brim with his own (one might claim) obsessive orderliness. Each day, Carroll lunched only on a glass of sherry and a biscuit. In a more reflective but related way, his journals record dinner parties mapping where each guest sat and what each person ate. When packing for a trip, he wrapped each article of clothing in so much tissue paper that there was more paper than shirts, trousers, shoes, or anything else. Carroll's pamphlet "Eight or Nine Wise Words About Letter Writing," sold with the *Wonderland Postage-Stamp Case* (fig. 5.7), included such precise directions (e.g., for logging letters in and out) that one might never want to write one. Such order and etiquette, however, seemed only to fuel Carroll's own pen. It is estimated that he wrote over 100,000 letters in his last 37 years alone – and this is leaving off his first 29 years! What kind of eating is all of this licking of stamps and envelopes, under the auspices of perfect order?

It is worth noting that the front of the *Wonderland Postage-Stamp Case* features Alice nursing the Duchess's baby, while its back depicts the Cheshire Cat. When

---

13   Carroll's photographs are delicious confections made of little girls (and little boys): we can safely eat them with our eyes, without using our mouths. See my *Pleasures Taken: Performances of Sexuality and Loss in Victorian Photographs*. On the concept of photography's relationship to the real and to personal desire, see Roland Barthes's *Camera Lucida: Reflections on Photography*.

one pulls out the interior stamp case, the baby turns into an omnivorous pig, while on the back one is left with only the cat's grin. Similarly, Carroll's rule for writing a letter that might "irritate your friend" is all about taste and making it sweet. In his own words:

> Another Rule is, when you have written a letter that you feel may possibly irritate your friend, however necessary you may have felt it to so express yourself, put it aside till the next day. Then read it over again, and fancy it addressed to yourself. This will often lead to your writing it all over again, taking out a lot of the vinegar and pepper, and putting in honey instead, and thus making a much more palatable dish of it! ("Eight or Nine" 450)

This two-sided notion of anorectic/hedonistic eating (or letter writing) is at the heart of the definition of consumption itself: to consume is to eat and to eat is to live, but to be consumed is to be eaten and to be eaten is to die. Consuming and being consumed are at the heart of many of Alice's strange conversations about who eats what; in other words, which animals wear signs that say "EAT ME" and to whom such signs are directed. For example, Alice gets stuck on the question of whether cats eat bats, and sometimes on whether bats eat cats. She also toys with the Mouse, like a cat with a bird, by feeding him stories of Dinah. Likewise, Alice brags that Dinah is "a capital one for catching mice" (26), and that she also knows "a bright-eyed terrier" who "kills all the rats" (27). When she is Tiny Alice, she fears that the "enormous puppy" might be hungry enough to eat her.[14] Most perplexing of all for Alice, the Pigeon accuses her of being a cannibalistic serpent because she eats eggs (56-57). As Nancy Armstrong has noted, "all the problems with Alice's body begin and end with her mouth" (16). And yet, it consumes hardly anything at all. It is there just for getting, for forgetting.

Kissing: To Eat Without Eating

Kissing, in Adam Phillips's words, "involves some of the pleasures of eating in the absence of nourishment" (*On Kissing* 94). Carroll enjoyed kissing his girl-child friends, as long as they were not so old as to wear their hair on top of their heads, or so far along into "grown-updom" that he would be required to tip his hat when greeting them (basically, they had to be under 12 years of age). He also liked to close his letters to his posse of girl-child friends by sending them 10,000,000 kisses, or 4 ¾ kisses, or a two-millionth part of a kiss. In other words, he licked his letters closed with the same anorectic hedonism that fed his Alice stories. Carroll liked to call his beloved child-friend Alexandra Kitchin, "my dear Multiplication-Sign" – not just a diminutive "Xie," but all the way down to "X" (*Selected Letters* 96). Along with

---

14   This is how Carroll must have felt in the presence of little girls who had grown up. In a letter to Florence Balfour, he likens himself, with the shock of finding her, the once tiny "microcosm[,] suddenly expanded into a tall young person" to "the old lady who, after feeding her canary and going for a walk, finds the cage entirely filled, on her return, with a live turkey," or "the old gentleman who, after chaining up a small terrier overnight, finds a hippopotamus raging around the kennel in the morning" (*Selected Letters* 117).

Alice and a whole chocolate box of other pretty young girls, Xie was one of Carroll's favorite subjects. And, of course, an X is a kiss.

Xs first became associated with kisses in the Middle Ages when, because most individuals were illiterate and could not write their names, documents would be scrawled with an X that would be followed by a kiss on an animal skin so thin that it served as paper. A little smack next to an X affirmed sincerity. X is also a kiss because it looks like two stylized people kissing. And most of all, X is a multiplier like Xie herself, like the infinitely reproducible photograph. Both the X and the photograph are multipliers of delight and love, especially when developed on the body of Alexandra Kitchin.

However, as Mark Crinson has suggested to me in conversation, calling Alexandra "Xie" – and especially calling her "X" – might have referred not so much to kisses as to Dodgson's debilitating stutter. Naming this beautiful girl X might have been a simple, if rather sexy, solution to pronouncing her difficult name. If language is about eating words (reading words), then to eat/read Alexandra as X is not to eat/speak much at all. Likewise, when Alice, as an alter ego of Carroll, cannot remember her name and says "L, I *know* it begins with 'L'," she is choosing anorectic speech as a solution to stammering speech. As Lindsay Smith makes clear, photography can also be read as avoidance of full speech, enabling Carroll to "hold the child without the flaw of language" (99). If one cannot speak the name of the beloved, one can at least commemorate her with a photographic picture:

The connection of photography to stammering might be read as working in a way similar to that in which naming does. [...] The photograph can't "speak" the name of the absent loved one but it can otherwise commemorate that individual by triggering a temporal flight. By definition, the visual medium of photography can't figure forth a stammering subject but perhaps photography can come closer to so doing than any other visual medium. (Smith 104)

Carroll could imagine nothing lovelier than Xie before his lens. Amidst such delicious anorectic Aliciousness is the story of a chocolate box, emptied of its chocolates, but filled with delicious glass-plate negatives of Alice and her sisters.

In the late 1970s, historian Colin Gordon found his way into the attic of Alice Liddell's granddaughter's home in Gloucestershire, and there, within a chest of drawers, found an old wooden chocolate box, *"Allen's Marvellous Chocolates,"* whose confections had been eaten long ago (fig. 5.8). On the outside was the injunction "Protect the contents from heat and damp." On the inside, within a nest of synthetic straw, were glass-plate negatives of Alice and her sisters looking as delicious as ever, "lolling on chairs" and "masquerading" in costumes that Carroll kept for just such occasions (Gordon 84). When we see *Edith, Lorina, and Alice Liddell in "Open Your Mouth and Shut Your Eyes"* (fig. 5.9) in their white cupcake skirts, and with their mouths ready for kisses and cherries, we cannot help reading them as delicious confections more than good enough to eat. Alice, the only one represented with an open mouth, is the subject of both a book and a photograph, and serves as an evacuation of memory, a hole to fall into. Forever Liddell girls, Alice and her chocolate-box sisters are for forgetting; they are a kind of eating that makes forgetting possible.

A Photograph is a Kiss

"When we kiss," writes Phillips, "we devour the object by caressing it; we eat it, in a sense, but sustain its presence" (*On Kissing* 97). The kiss, then, is like a photograph. Capturing what is fleeting, the camera loves people and places not just as the conventional *devouring eye*, but also as a consuming mouth. Photographs, as shutter kisses, might be understood as an extension of kissing with the eye as if it were a mouth, as butterfly kisses. Both the kiss and the photograph are stories of taking and preserving an object, especially if the kiss is placed on the mouth, an action that "blurs the distinctions between giving and taking" (Phillips, *On Kissing* 97). In other words, just as kissing can be described as "aim-inhibited eating" (97), photographs can be described as aim-inhibited picture production: photography both takes and gives. In *Edith, Lorina, and Alice Liddell in "Open Your Mouth and Shut Your Eyes"* Alice parts her lips for the two cherries in her sister's hand. She is caught/consumed by the camera, closing her eyes and opening her mouth as if ready to kiss. The 1850s have been appropriately labeled "the culinary period of photography" because, during this period, photographers held their stolen images physically as kisses, not with traditional photographic chemicals, but in sugar, caramel, treacle, malt, raspberry syrup, ginger wine, sherry, beer, and skimmed milk (Gernsheim 258).[15]

Leaving the Alice stories aside, I want to close with a lesser-known story by Carroll, "Novelty and Romancement," a tale that is far too dark and strange ever to be of interest to most children today (but a story Lacan would have loved: a sort of witty "Purloined Letter"). This sad tale involves one Leopold Edgar Stubbs, who quite by chance happens upon Simon Lubkin's shop and its signboard "SIMON LUBKIN, DEALER IN ROMANCEMENT." Stubbs concludes from the sign that he can buy and readily consume something that will "connect the threads of human destiny" (404). Sadly, however, as if lacking the most elementary introduction to the field of semiotics, he has misread the advertisement:

> Standing before that base mechanic's door, with a throbbing and expectant heart, my eye chanced to fall once more upon that signboard, once more I perused its strange inscription. Oh! fatal change! Oh! horror! What do I see? Have I been deluded by a heated imagination?
>
> A hideous gap yawns between the N and the C, making it not one word but two! (404)

"Romancement" has turned into "Roman Cement." Force-feeding every space with yet another twist of the letter (whether in a book, a poem, a pun, or the post), Carroll plays at forgetting the "hideous gap" between the words "Roman" and "Cement," while hailing it at every turn. His letters are as anorectically light (empty) as they are hedonistically heavy: romancement and Roman Cement at once.

In "Eight or Nine Wise Words About Letter Writing," Carroll insists on logging every letter received and every letter sent, carving out a space for every letter with which a person comes in contact. Despite such vigilant record keeping, letters come

---

15   For an excellent analysis of the concept of the devouring eye and the culinary aspects of photography, see Olivier Richon (8-14).

and go, even after death. Letters are lost. Some sit forever undelivered at the Dead Letter Office (where the anorectic Bartleby is an employee). Many are sent to the wrong address. Some are just meant to be forgotten. Nevertheless, there are plenty of envelopes to lick closed, without fear of absorbing the nourishment (the meaning) that each letter holds. The envelope is a spatiality, a rabbit hole, a cat hole, a mouth. The stamp is for dessert.

Likewise, the hideous gap between the N and the C of "Roman Cement" is a spatiality to which one is drawn, a language hole to fall into, not unlike the Rabbit Hole or the Cheshire Cat's mouth. It is a place to reside in, like an empty biscuit tin or a stamp case without stamps, to be held long enough to forget: both to forget to eat *and* to eat to forget. Metonymy is not about eating and consuming. Rather, it is a nutriment of non-nurturing substitution: like the Cheshire Cat for Dinah, and Alice for Carroll, and reading (or kissing) for eating, and, most importantly, forgetting for memory.

For her discovery of various useful quotations on Alice and hunger, I am indebted to Kate Arpen, a student in my graduate seminar on "Forgetting" (Spring 2006).

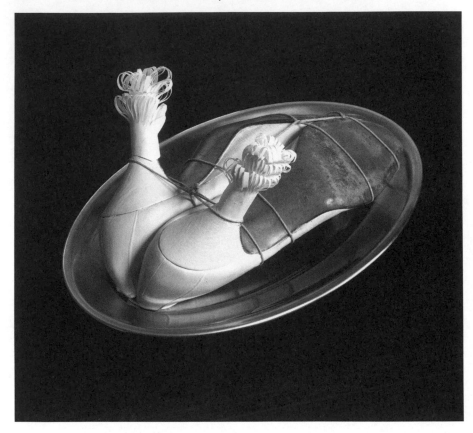

Fig. 5.1   Merit Oppenheim, *My Nurse.*

Fig. 5.2   Merit Oppenheim, *Breakfast in Fur.*

Fig. 5.3   Lewis Carroll, *Alice Liddell as "The Beggar Maid."*

Fig. 5.4   Lewis Carroll, *Xie Kitchin with Umbrella*

Fig. 5.5   Lewis Carroll, *Xie Kitchin as "Tea-Merchant (On Duty)"* and *Xie Kitchin as "Tea-Merchant (Off Duty)."*

Fig. 5.6   *"Through the Looking Glass" Biscuit Tin.*

The Wonderland

Postage-Stamp Case

PUBLISHED BY

EMBERLIN AND SON,

4, MAGDALEN STREET,

OXFORD.

(POST FREE, 13d.)

PRICE ONE SHILLING

Fig. 5.7   *Wonderland Postage-Stamp Case* (front and back).

Fig. 5.8   *"Allen's Marvellous Chocolates" Box.*

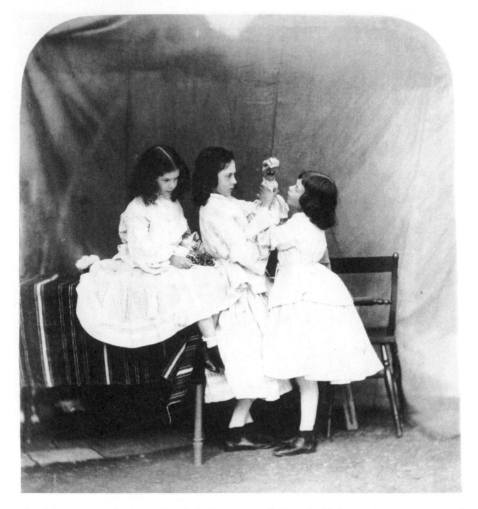

Fig. 5.9   Lewis Carroll, *Edith, Lorina, and Alice Liddell in "Open Your Mouth and Shut Your Eyes."*

Works Cited

"Allen's Marvellous Chocolates" Box. n.d.

Armstrong, Nancy. "The Occidental Alice." *differences: A Journal of Feminist Cultural Studies* 2.2 (1990), 3-40.

Auerbach, Nina. *Romantic Imprisonment: Women and Other Glorified Outcasts*. New York: Columbia UP, 1986.

Bachelard, Gaston. *The Poetics of Space*. 1958. Trans. Maria Jolas. Boston: Beacon, 1994.

Barrie, J. M. *Peter Pan in Kensington Gardens* and *Peter and Wendy*. Ed. Peter Hollindale. Oxford : Oxford UP, 1999.

Barthes, Roland. *Camera Lucida: Reflections on Photography*. 1980. Trans. Richard Howard. New York: Hill and Wang, 1981.

Bible. New International Version. Grand Rapids, MI: Zondervan Bible, 1984.

Carroll, Lewis. *The Annotated Alice: The Definitive Edition*. Ed. Martin Gardner. New York: Norton, 2000.

---. *Agnes Grace Weld as "Little Red Riding Hood."* 1857. Princeton University Library, Princeton, NJ.

---. *Agnes Price*. c. 1865. Harry Ransom Humanities Research Center, University of Texas, Austin.

---. *Alice Liddell as "The Beggar Maid."* c. 1858. Princeton University Library, Princeton, NJ.

---. *Edith, Lorina, and Alice Liddell in "Open Your Mouth and Shut Your Eyes."* 1860. Princeton University Library, Princeton, NJ.

---. *Xie Kitchin as "Tea Merchant (Off Duty)."* 1873. Princeton University Library. Princeton, NJ.

---. *Xie Kitchin as "Tea Merchant (On Duty)."* 1873. Princeton University Library. Princeton, NJ.

---. *Xie Kitchin with Umbrella*. Ca. 1875. George Eastman House. Rochester, NY.

---. "Eight or Nine Wise Words About Letter Writing." *Lewis Carroll: The Complete Works*. London: CRW, 2005. 450-54.

---. "Novelty and Romancement." *Lewis Carroll: The Complete Works*. London: CRW, 2005. 403-08.

---. *The Selected Letters of Lewis Carroll*. Ed. Morton N. Cohen. New York: Pantheon, 1982.

Cixous, Hélène. Introduction. Lewis Carroll's *Through the Looking-Glass* and *The Hunting of the Snark*. Trans. Marie Maclean. *New Literary History* 13.2 (1982): 231-51.

Collingwood, Stuart Dodgson. *The Life and Letters of Lewis Carroll*. London: T. Fisher Unwin, 1898.

Derrida, Jacques. "The Animal That Therefore I Am." *Critical Inquiry* 28.2 (2002): 369-418.

Eco, Umberto. "An Ars *Oblivionalis?* Forget It." *PMLA* 103 (1988): 254-61.

Freud, Sigmund. "Fetishism." *The Standard Edition of the Complete Psychological Works of Sigmund Freud, XXI*. Trans. James Strachey. London: Hogarth, 1961. 149–57.

Gallop, Jane. "Keys to Dora." *In Dora's Case*. Eds. Charles Bernheimer and Claire Kahane. Columbia UP, 1985. 200-20.

Gernsheim, Alison, and Helmet Gernsheim. *The History of Photography*. Oxford: Oxford UP, 1955.

Gordon, Colin. *Beyond the Looking Glass: Reflections of Alice and Her Family*. San Diego: Harcourt Brace Jovanovich, 1982.

Henrdrickson, Robert. *The Facts on File: Encyclopedia of Word and Phrase Origins*. Oxford: Facts on File, 1987.

Kincaid, James. *Child-Loving: The Erotic Child and Victorian Culture*. New York: Routledge, 1992.

Kundera, Milan. *The Book of Laughter and Forgetting*. Trans. Michael Henry Heim. New York: Viking, 1981.

Lacan, Jacques. "The Agency of the Letter in the Unconscious, or Reason Since Freud." *Écrits: A Selection*. Trans. Alan Sheridan. New York: Norton, 1977. 146-78.

Lewis Carroll's Alice: The Photographs, Books, Papers and Personal Effects of Alice Liddell and Her Family. London: Sotheby's Catalogue, 6 June 2001.

Mavor, Carol. *Pleasures Taken: Performances of Sexuality and Loss in Victorian Photographs*. Durham: Duke UP, 1995.

---. *Reading Boyishly: Roland Barthes, JM Barrie, Jacques Henri Lartigue, Marcel Proust and DW Winnicott*. Durham: Duke UP, 2007.

Oppenheim, Merit. *Breakfast in Fur*. 1936. 2006 Artists Rights Society, New York/ Pro Litteris, Zurich.

---. *My Nurse*. 1936. Moderna Museet, Stockholm.

Phillips, Adam. *On Kissing, Tickling and Being Bored: Psychoanalytic Essays on the Unexamined Life*. Cambridge: Harvard UP, 1993.

---. *Promises, Promises: Essays on Literature and Psychoanalysis*. New York: Basic, 2001.

Proust, Marcel. *À la recherche du temps perdu*. Ed. Jean-Yves Tadié. Paris: Éditions Gallimard, 1988.

---. *In Search of Lost Time*. Trans. C. K. Scott Moncrieff and Terence Kilmartin. New York: Random House, 1992.

---. "On Reading Ruskin." *On Reading Ruskin: Prefaces to* La Bible d'Amiens *and* Sésame et les Lys, *With Selections from the Notes to the Translated Texts*. Ed. and trans. Jean Autret et al. New Haven: Yale UP, 1987. 99-141.

---. "Sur la lecture." Préface du traducteur. *Sésame et les Lys*. By John Ruskin. Trans. Marcel Proust. Paris: Éditions Complexe, 1987. 36-97.

Richon, Olivier. *Allegories*. London: Salvo and the Royal College of Art, 2000.

Smith, Lindsay. "Lewis Carroll: Stammering, Photography and the Voice of Infancy." *Journal of Visual Culture* 3.1 (2004): 95-105.

"Through the Looking Glass" Biscuit Tin. 1892.

Warner, Marina. *Fantastic Metamorphoses, Other Worlds*. Oxford: Oxford UP, 2002.

Wienrich, Harald. *Lethe: The Art and Critique of Forgetting*. 1997. Trans. Steven Rendall. Ithaca: Cornell UP, 2004.

Wonderland Postage-Stamp Case. 1890. Author's private collection.

Chapter 6

Salome's Lost Childhood: Wilde's Daughter of Sodom, Jugendstil Culture, and the Queer Afterlife of a Decadent Myth

Richard A. Kaye

"Wilde's Salome – Jugendstil – for the first time, the cigarette. Lethe flows in the ornaments of Jugendstil."

Walter Benjamin, *The Arcades Project* (843)

Of all the myths of decadence that prospered at the European *fin de siècle*, that of Salome is perhaps the most enduring, rivaled, for the tenacious force of its procreative cultural success, only by Bram Stoker's Dracula. As with Stoker's bloodthirsty count, and his effect on subsequent incarnations of vampires, Wilde's Salome went far in effacing from popular consciousness all predecessors, emerging as the most potent of Salome texts. Just as we tend to think of Dracula as the most typical of Victorian vampires, we tend to see the Wildean Salome as the archetypal *femme fatale* of the era. With this Symbolist play, Wilde revisited the biblical legend and fashioned it into one of the most successful myths of the Decadent Movement. Its image, of a belligerent she-devil who consumes men, joins other craven creatures of debauched, imperious femaleness in animating *fin-de-siècle* culture: the eponymous ruler-vixen of Rider Haggard's *She* (1887), the dominatrix brothel-owner Señora Mendizabel of Robert Louis Stevenson's *The Dynamiter* (1885), and the numerous other fiendish females Bram Dijkstra has elucidated in his encyclopedic study *Idols of Perversity* (1986).

In *Salome*, Wilde often seemed to depict the princess as a sleekly commanding man-killer, a sense echoed in the 1894 drawings by Aubrey Beardsley, published with Wilde's play, and now irrevocably attached to it. Over the last several decades, nearly all commentators who have focused on Wilde's play have seen it as an especially successful transmutation to the stage of a pervasive *fin-de-siècle* fascination with the *femme fatale*, a castrating female who takes pleasure in destroying males. In *Dreamers of Decadence* (1971), Philippe Julian describes Salome as "the goddess of the Decadence," whose "terrified worshippers" included Beardsley, Gustav Klimt and Gustave Moreau, and whose spirit "dances again" in the figures of Lolita and the Marlene Dietrich of *The Blue Angel* (1930). Although Julian highlights a fierce, indeed Amazonian Salome – contrasting her in Western mythology with the "innocent

Ophelia" – he tacitly acknowledges Salome's girlish attributes by claiming her as a "*petite fille fatale*" (108-09). Dijkstra memorably refers to Wilde's play as a work that "did more than any other single image or piece of writing to make the head-huntress' name a household word for pernicious sexual perversity" (396). Dijkstra's conception of Salome as demonic man-eater has inspired Camille Paglia to insist that feminist critics have sought to downplay Salome's power. Paglia compares Salome to Elizabeth Taylor, Delilah and Helen of Troy, as women who had a "World disordering impact" and who wielded "the sexual power that feminism cannot explain and has tried to destroy" – a curious claim, given that feminist critics were among the first recent writers to herald Salome's key role as a sexual troublemaker in the late-Victorian and Edwardian era. Elaine Showalter, for example, in *Sexual Anarchy* (1990), not only explores Salome's erotically potent place in *fin-de-siècle* literature and culture, but also analyzes Beardsley's drawings for their pivotal role in lending Salome an aura of illicit androgyny, a coded late-Victorian means of conveying same-sex erotics.

There are reasons, however, for the persistent success of Wilde's play beyond its appeal as a tantalizing vehicle for actresses taking up the role of *femme fatale*. To be sure, Wilde's Salome is an avaricious, predatory woman who (in Dijkstra's schema) drew her power from the nineteenth-century fascination with *femmes fatales*, who depleted civilized males of their creative energies. Yet Wilde's anti-heroine is not quite the strident hellion that many interpreters have allowed. As Walter Benjamin notes, we can witness in Wilde's Salome the triumph of a Jugendstil aesthetic[1] – the youth culture on which Benjamin brooded at length in his *Arcades Project*, and that he ultimately rejected as an ornament-laden debasement, through the triumph of marketplace values, of a modernist tradition that reached a finer apotheosis in Symbolism. For Benjamin, Jugendstil was the failure of art to adjust to modernity's new, convulsive pressures; hence the seemingly strange leap in his comment quoted at the start of this chapter that Wilde's princess evokes a cigarette, a conjunction that suggested to Benjamin the glamorous but nihilistic aura of consumer culture.

A highly stylized, intensely consumerist youth ethos is thematized throughout Wilde's play, in which an errant daughter horrifies others through the imposition of her ghastly carnal tastes. This sense of Salome as a participant in a semi-repressed family romance – the quasi-incestuous drama, revolving around the figure of the nymphet that Vladimir Nabokov later explored so emphatically in *Lolita* – evokes a neglected, key element of the Salome myth: that the princess is a child. Her fundamental perversity is related not simply to her femininity, but also to her obdurate, spoilt girlishness. Wilde's text represents the most powerful nineteenth-century iteration of the notion of Salome as a child. The irreducible open-endedness of its generic status as a theatrical work, however, has obscured precisely this element, given that, historically, adult actresses have, necessarily, assumed the role of Salome in his play.

---

1   The term "Jugendstil" originated in 1896, when it was used in the German cultural weekly *Die Jugend*, founded by Georg Hirth, and based in Munich, to refer to a specific kind of graphic design then coming into vogue.

Given that childishness comes to be inextricably linked, in emerging psychoanalytic thought at the end of the Victorian era, with an inherent perversity, the image of Salome as a young girl has helped to fortify Wilde's play's reputation as a queer work that accommodates male same-sex desire. This link between, on the one hand, Salome's ambiguous status as at once youngster and woman and, on the other, an emerging homosexual identity, is further enhanced by Salome's connection to the mass, consumerist aesthetic of Art Nouveau (or Jugendstil) and kitsch. As Benjamin recognized, these often homosexually coded enterprises were linked to the hypnotizing powers of an emerging youth culture that demanded armies of consumers.

The portrayal of Salome as an unruly youngster has textual sources as far back as accounts in the Bible. René Girard points out that the Salome of the gospel is really a child (320), and that the Greek word for her is *koraison*, which means "little girl" (320). While Girard contrasts the Bible's girl-Salome with the "sultry temptress" (321), he sees as ubiquitous in the nineteenth and twentieth centuries a number of texts that did, in fact, stress a Salome who was decidedly a youth. A precocious "young girl" (321) of expressive movements but few words, Gustave Flaubert's Salome demands, with a childish lisp, the head of John the Baptist (whose name of Iokanaan she has difficulty recalling): "She went up, reappeared; and lisping slightly pronounced these words, with a childlike expression: I want you to give me on a dish the head [...]" (102-03). Coupling the princess's dual role as underage brat and social iconoclast, Jules Laforgue facetiously refers in his 1885 "moral tale" to "Salome, that dear child, who refused to hear of the joys of marriage" (91). In the German writer Oskar Panizza's play *The Council of Love* (1894), Salome is interrogated by the Devil, who addresses her as "pretty child" (111), but she, being but a youngster, can only nod mutely before his questions. In the final act, the Devil announces that Salome will give birth to his offspring, thereby becoming the "mother of a magnificent race which no aristocracy will ever equal" (115). The girl's degeneracy, however, will give birth to another's, for this offspring is syphilitic, meaning that the loveliest child in the world will poison all of humanity. In Stéphane Mallarmé's poem "Hérodiade" (1898), the drama involves a princess and a nurse who reiterates her distress that her impertinent charge is at once so lovely and so jaded: "So beautiful, my child, in your beauty so dreadful" (31).[2] The dialogue between nurse and girl encourages a sense of the princess as still a creature of an actual and metaphorical nursery. As Hérodiade herself movingly declares, she occupies "the armored halls of childhood's sad domain" (30).

Although nineteenth-century painters generally downplayed nymphet-Salomes in favor of predatory *femmes fatales*, there are several early twentieth-century images depicting the princess as a childlike *ingénue*. The French Symbolist Gustave Adolphe Mossa's *Salome: The Ballerina* (1904), a relatively small-sized work among the artist's numerous Salome images, evokes the princess's youthfulness in the tentative steps she appears to be making as she performs before Herod's court. As if to stress Salome's entrance into society, the king is flanked by a hall filled

---

2 Mallarmé began "Hérodiade" in 1864, and it appeared, in part, in 1871. The unfinished final sections were not published until 1959.

with onlookers. Mossa's Salome seems a timid debutante, her performance more a tremulous first step into adulthood than the lascivious act of a dominatrix. The French artist Edouard Toudouze's *Salome Triumphant* (ca. 1886), meanwhile, depicts the princess as a child curled up on an animal skin atop a throne. She gazes directly at the viewer, coquettishly licking her fingers as if she has just feasted on the lips of the prophet, whose severed head lies on a platter below her. Much of such *fin-de-siècle* arcana – excluding, of course, Mossa's 1904 work – may have cumulatively inspired Wilde in his depiction of Salome as a figure of destroyed childhood innocence, but there was at least one other significant precedent for the playwright's representation of familial disorder and hungry youth.

Keats's "Isabella" and Her Decadent Daughter: From Capitalist Critique to Decadent Consumerism

I have sketched the European tradition outside of Britain in which writers and artists sought to render explicit and problematic Salome's status as both an innocent girl and a too-knowing adult. Yet one important inspiration for Wilde's *Salome* lies within the British literary tradition – John Keats's "Isabella; or, The Pot of Basil" (1816). Wilde's poem "On the Grave of Keats" (1881) overtly discloses a fascination with Keats that is evident in much of the writer's early poetic writing. In later years Wilde remained indebted to his predecessor, if only in negation, no more so than in his drawing on Keats's "Isabella" in his most overtly poetic play, *Salome*.

"Isabella," the story of which Keats adapted from Boccaccio's *Decameron*, narrates a young woman's increasingly obsessive love for a working-class lover, Lorenzo, and his murder at the hands of Isabella's two brothers, who fear that their sister will not enhance her social status with a marriage to a low-born man. In a striking analog to Salome, Isabella digs up her lover's body, decapitates his head, kisses it, and then deposits it in a pot of basil. Isabella worships her dead lover's skull until her brothers destroy the morbid relic. Arguably one of Keats's most macabre poems, it is also one of his most socially aware works, a poem that features the perfidy of pure financial avarice, as that avarice vanquishes family bonds and romantic enchantment. Flamboyantly grotesque in imagery, sharp in its social critique, evoking a disturbed psychodynamic set within the context of a family romance, the poem is a likely inspiration for Wilde's *Salome*.

Viewing "Isabella" as a precursor highlights the way in which Wilde's play offers a Symbolist dissection of a girl's romantic yearning, as a frenzy of consumerist lust. Isabella and her brothers have been the beneficiaries of industrial progress, "Enriched from ancestral merchandize / And for them many a weary hand did swelt / In torched mines and noisy factories [...]" (179). The stress in the first stanzas of Keats's poem, however, is on its heroine's purity, depicting "poor simple" Isabella (177) who "lisped tenderly" (178) to her lover Lorenzo. He, meanwhile, is pure romantic ardor, an all-sentient being with a preternatural skill at anticipating and seeing his beloved: "He knew whose gentle hand was at the latch, / Before the door had given her to his eyes; / And from her chamber-window he would catch / Her beauty farther than the falcon spies" (177). Wilde inverts this scheme; his young woman is all-observing predator, while the object of her lust refuses even to gaze at her alluring physique. Most importantly, what in Keats is an allegorical meditation on materialist greed as a deadly impediment to romantic eros becomes, in Wilde's *Salome*, a troubled familial scenario in which another errant child, divided against two scheming parental figures in lieu of Keats's two conniving brothers, emerges as an obsessive erotic consumer who engenders murderous impulses in a relative (her stepfather, Herod).

Wilde's *Salome* rewrites Keats's poem so that a young female's desire is rendered perverse and wholly destructive, as a modern consumerist psychodrama replaces a Romantic drama of class ambition. Significantly, the events in both texts unfold within the context of a family whose members are capable of murder. But whereas Isabella's brothers kill her lover out of a rational (if murderous) entrepreneurial financial logic, in Wilde's play murder takes place to satisfy a berserk desire for possession. Significantly, Salome's lustful hunger is depicted as having been always perverse, whereas Keats's lovers first kiss (in a famously outlandish description) so that Lorenzo's lips "press with hers in dewy rhyme" (178) to create a moment of heightened romantic sublimity. Keats would seem to contrast these conjoined lips with an image of her brothers who, struggling to devise a plot to dispatch Lorenzo, "many times bit their lips alone" (181) – the line suggesting the failure of their erotic attachments as well as neurotic self-abuse.

Even in kissing, however, Isabella retains her purity, an innocence that is destroyed only in the necrophilic kiss that she repeatedly delivers to her dead lover: "Pale Isabella kiss'd it, and low moan'd," we are told, and this kiss is protracted into other kisses: "Sighing all day – and still she kiss'd, and wept" (187). Keats accentuates the ways in which Isabella's fugue-like devotion to her dead lover's head (and the pot of basil that comes to contain it) isolates her absolutely: "And she forgot the stars, the moon, and sun, / And she forgot the blue above the trees, / And she forgot the dells where waters run, / And she forgot the chilly autumn breeze" (188). The state of forgetful isolation from a cyclical natural realm becomes, in Wilde's play, an isolation through a familial and social stigmatization, that comes when Salome kisses John the Baptist's head, an act that provokes her execution.[3] Keats, however, depicts Isabella's blameless, sublime attachment as threatened by a financial avarice so venal that it degenerates into a mad fetishism. One might go so far as to say that the poem depicts a fall from romantic enchantment into erotic fixation. In Wilde's *Salome*, the image of the necrophilic woman gains an updated economic afterlife, where a female's insatiable lust negates both innocence and romantic desire. Indeed *Salome*, like its protagonist, can conceive of neither.

---

3   Martin Aske complicates a sense of "Isabella" as a simple parable of venal capitalist greed by arguing that the brothers react against the "narcissistic completeness" of their sister's attachment to Lorenzo, an attachment that mirrors their own greed.

Wilde's *Salome* as Paradigmatic Psychoanalytic Case of Polymorphous Erotics

Wilde's theatrical rendering helped to establish a sense of the Salome story concerning as childish erotomania, and not only because of his Salome's demand for the head of John the Baptist. Herod and his wife themselves act like greedy, obsessive youngsters who misuse their adult privileges. Such demands seem to reproduce themselves in Salome's arrogant insistence, in Wilde's text, that her stepfather stick to their agreement, and that she be allowed to kiss the lips of John the Baptist, a demand that resembles nothing so much as the lust-mad whining of a child.

Although disclosing classic hysterical symptoms (argumentativeness, moroseness, sexual aggression), Salome as conceived by Wilde is too psychologically controlled, too steely in her libidinal demands, to stand as a prototypical hysteric. In expressing a girl's erotic longing, the *fin-de-siècle* Salome myth articulated a crucial revelation of sexual theory and psychoanalysis at the time: children harbor "indecent" desires. In 1893, the Italian criminologists Cesare Lombroso and Gugliemo Ferrero wrote that children, especially female children, were more atavistic than adults, and close in temperament to the prostitute and the criminal (48). A decade later, Sigmund Freud located such "criminal" features in all children, in what became a contentious fundament of psychoanalytic thought. In 1905, the very year in which Wilde's play saw its initial performance in England at the Bijou Theatre, and Richard Strauss's opera *Salome* (based on Wilde's play) had its world premiere in Dresden, Freud published his first two extended arguments that sexual instincts have their earliest roots in childhood and adolescence – published, respectively, in *Three Essays on the Theory of Sexuality* (1905) and *Fragment of an Analysis of a Case of Hysteria* (1905), better known as the case history of Dora. The latter work, in coupling an adolescent female's sexuality with her unconscious lesbian inclinations, stressed specifically homosexual aspects of the polymorphous perversity that the *Three Essays* broadly understood as encompassing both heterosexual and homosexual desire (59). For Freud, libidinal desires in a little boy or girl encompass a fluid erotic life, while the common denominator of the perversions was their pursuit of pure pleasure rather than reproduction, echoing late-Victorian concerns about society's own move from a productionist ethos toward a consumerist one: "The abandonment of the reproductive function is the common feature of all perversions. We actually describe a sexual activity as perverse if it has given up the aim of procreation and pursues the attainment of orgasm as an aim independent of it" (*Three Essays*, 61). Elsewhere in the *Three Essays*, Freud makes explicit the connections between childhood, polymorphous sexuality, and sex as consumerist, declaring that:

> under the influence of seduction children can become polymorphously perverse, and can be led into all possible kinds of sexual irregularities. […] In this respect children behave in the same way as an average uncultivated woman in whom the same polymorphously perverse disposition persists. Under ordinary conditions she may remain normal sexually, but if she is led by a clever seducer she will find every sort of perversion to her taste, and will retain them as part of her own sexual activities. Prostitutes exploit the same polymorphous, that is, infantile disposition for the purposes of their profession; and, considering the immense number of women who are prostitutes or who must be disposed to have an aptitude for prostitution without becoming engaged in it, it becomes impossible

not to recognize that this same disposition to perversions of every kind is a general and fundamental human characteristic. (57)

Freud here offers a psychological foundation for a consumerist erotic economy, in which the girl infant, as much as the adult female, must barter for sexual attention and satisfaction, a set of needs that Freud describes in the terms of a business exchange (namely, prostitution). The pertinence of Freud's colorful analysis to a discussion of Salome lies in the way in which the extremities along a continuum of archetypal females – the seemingly innocent but in fact sexually knowing infant, the average "uncultivated" woman, the lecherous prostitute – collapse into the make-up of a single Everywoman.[4] Moreover, the endless stress on watching and being watched in Wilde's text constitutes the kind of "peeping mania" (62) that, in *Three Essays on Sexuality*, Freud maintains is a common form of perversion. Indeed, the voyeuristic and fetishistic impulses so apparent in *Salome* have their basis, as Jen Spitzer notes, in the relinquishment of the normal sexual aim for an unfit sexual substitute, predilections that Freud traced to a "perverse" erotic disposition, specific to childhood.

Wilde's *Salome*: The Afterlife of a *Fin- de-Siècle* Myth of an All-Devouring Child-Princess

A fusion of varying archetypal females is precisely what one finds in Wilde's *Salome*. The princess is, alternately, a peevish, erotically discerning girl, an unworldly adolescent (like Freud's Dora), and a woman who prostitutes herself by cannily bargaining for sexual favors. Throughout the play, Wilde emphasizes these diverse Salomes by sharply juxtaposing them, sometimes within the course of two or three sentences. Thus Salome declares of the tetrarch, her stepfather, in what are her first spoken words in the play, "It is strange that the husband of my mother looks at me like that. I know not what it means. In truth, yes I know it" (341). Thus, at the very outset, an important motif is established, in which the cloistered, repressed princess co-exists with the "Daughter of Sodom" who is too blackened by knowledge to be pure. Like Dorian Gray, whose depravity as a feminized dandy is established early in the novel, Salome – the too-aggressive female – is almost instantly a debauched creature, a synthesis of girl, adolescent, and woman. And like the other characters in Wilde's play, she does not deteriorate or de-evolve, so much as simultaneously embody different, overlapping moments in a female's lifespan. By the time Salome voices her lust for John the Baptist a few moments later, she certainly appears depraved, but she is also, in a sense, the "essential female."

The question of whether Salome is a young girl is transformed into a matter of competing subjective views. At the outset of the play, the Young Syrian (who invariably calls Salome "the Princess," as if to accentuate her youth) announces:

4　The preoccupation with childhood, with adolescence, and with what were thought to be characteristically adolescent concerns such as masturbation and homosexuality, was a hallmark of turn-of-the-century European literature, visual art, psychology and psychoanalytic theory.

"The Princess has hidden her face behind her fan! Her little white hands are fluttering like doves that fly to their dove-cots. They are like white butterflies" (340). This enraptured view of Salome insists on her status as a shy, nervous youth, her "little white hands" as fluttery as a butterfly's wings. This perspective, however, is contradicted by others in the play, either directly or indirectly. This is initially done by the Page of Herodias, who continually warns of Salome's dangerous powers, as he admonishes the Young Syrian to control his fetishistic impulses and avoid gazing at her. Later, with a similar accent on the girl's treacherous erotic hunger, Herod speaks of the moon (already associated with the princess) as being like a "mad woman who is seeking everywhere for lovers. She is naked, too. [...] She shows herself naked in the sky. She reels through the clouds like a drunken woman [...] I am sure she is looking for lovers" (349). In a sense, the power of Wilde's anti-heroine to disturb depends on her status as a girl who is motivated by voluptuous hunger. At the same time, a reliance on childish innocence becomes an instrument – perhaps the most potent instrument – for an adult female's destructive power over men.[5]

The childishness of Wilde's princess is matched by the immaturity of her warring parents, whose sexual impasse, barely disguised by their incessant bickering, temporally precedes, and therefore seems to engender, Salome's shrill demands for satisfaction. She vocalizes her degenerate needs, and, in breaking away from societal restrictions (in Wilde, as much Victorian as biblical), is destroyed by them. Salome's request for the prophet's head duplicates Herod's wish to see his stepdaughter dance. Wilde's young temptress, however, also strikingly resembles her mother, Herodias, whose erotic delinquency replicates, but also generates, that of her daughter. Yet it is Salome who most forcefully projects an image of the child as a consumer, for whom all earthly and non-earthly things are viewed as objects and even currency. "How good to see the moon!" she declares, "She is like a little piece of money" (341). Her fanatical adoration of John the Baptist also expresses itself in terms of a lavish materiality: "How wasted he is! He is like a thin ivory statue" (345). As the play gathers force, she focuses more intently on his mouth: "Thy mouth is like a band of scarlet on a tower of ivory. The pomegranate flowers that blossom in the garden of Tyre, and are redder than roses, are not so red. The red blasts of trumpets, that herald the approach of kings, and make afraid the enemy, are not so red" (347). Salome exults over John the Baptist with the epicurean fussiness of the connoisseur, but one whose allusions, emanating from the subjectivist isolation of Symbolist speech, insure that he remains a privately appreciated specimen. Her consumer fetishism, endlessly drawing out distinctions, refuses the vulgar generalities of mass production.

In presenting Salome as a more venal version of her mother, Wilde might have been leaning on earlier French texts. That the biblical Salome was a budding duplicate of her mother is an idea evident in Flaubert's "Herodias" (1877). "Up on the dais she took off her veil," notes the narrator; "It was Herodias, as she used to look in her youth" (101). Similarly, in Jules Massenet's opera *Herodias* (1881), Herod's wife, on discovering that Salome is her daughter, exclaims in shock, "She? My rival!" (qtd. in Annesley 298). Pablo Picasso's *Salome* (1905) depicts a nude princess

---

5   I owe this last insight to Jen Spitzer.

kicking up her legs in an athletic, flagrantly erotic dance. Her back is turned toward the viewer as she faces a plump, seated Herod and a stiff, standing Herodias, who stonily gazes away from the spectacle. Herodias's bared breasts provide a mirrored, decayed specter of those of her sexually self-confident daughter. Picasso focused on the fundamental point that, by the start of the twentieth century, the repressed eroticism of the adolescent Salome had become a touchstone for the stifled desires of other potent figures (in this case Herodias but, in the conceptions of other artists, the New Woman and the homosexual).

In Wilde's *Salome*, however, childishness is not confined to the title character. Through language, it becomes a quality shared by nearly all. Indeed, to many English-speaking readers and audiences, the repetitive rhythms of the play's dialogue, especially in its French incarnation as *Salome: Drame en Un Acte*, evoked children's speech that seems faltering on account of a weak mastery of language. One anonymous reviewer of Wilde's French text, writing in the London *Times* in 1893, noted that the play was an "arrangement in blood and ferocity," and compared its opening scene to a "page from one of Ollendorf's exercises" – Ollendorf being a popular nineteenth-century method of language instruction that stressed repetitive patterns. Similarly, just under 20 years later, Arthur Ransome (who offered the first serious study of Wilde's writings) suggested that the speeches in the play are "made of short sentences, direct assertions, and negations, that run like pages beside the progress of the play" (161). Ransome wryly concludes that "[Salome], Herod, and Herodias and all their entourage, speak like children who have had a French nurse."

At the level of textual ancestry, too, Wilde's Salome met condemnation for being a degenerate child. An 1893 review in the *Pall Mall Gazette*, reporting on the Lord Chamberlain Office's decision to ban Wilde's play because of its biblical subject matter, saw the text as overly indebted to French sources, especially Flaubert. In a pun on Salome's French literary influences and her status as a possible bastard child, the reviewer concludes that the youngster "is the daughter of too many fathers. She is the victim of heredity. Her bones want strength, her flesh wants vitality, her blood is polluted" (136). In such a way did the nineteenth-century medical comprehension of degeneration dovetail with British anxieties about decadent French aesthetic influences.

In terms of performance on the stage, striking a balance between *enfant terrible* and *femme fatale* has been crucial for actresses taking on the role of Salome, with too much of one persona spoiling the over-all effect. For her celebrated 1922 film, Alla Nazimova chose to play a 14-year-old Salome because, as she told an interviewer, otherwise the character "would have been married" (qtd. in Lambert 189). Wilde's remark that Sarah Bernhardt "was the only person in the world who could act Salome" has proven so convincing that *The Cambridge Guide to English Literature* (1993) reported that she actually did perform it (Oulsby 826). Vincent Sullivan, an acquaintance of Wilde's, maintained, however, that the playwright would never have chosen Bernhardt because she was too old: "It seems impossible that however infatuated he and those who advised him were with Sarah Bernhardt, however stunned by her tumult, he should ever have thought of her, at the age she had then reached, for the part of Salome" (183). "Salome was a child," insisted

Sullivan, "Even following the Gospel narrative without criticism, she was little more than a child. It is a hard strain on plausibility to see Wilde's 'Salome' played by even a young actress – young as actresses are when they are thought capable of tackling such a part" (183-84). In the 1918 libel trial against Maud Allan, one witness described Salome's desire to kiss the Baptist's head as akin to the "mutterings of a child suffering from an enlarged and diseased clitoris" (qtd. in Kettle 172).

The centrality of the notion of the child to images of sexual greed is apparent, moreover, from the numerous productions of both Wilde's and Strauss's *Salome* that have played up the princess's youthful qualities. Strauss saw her as "a sixteen-year-old virgin with an Isolde voice" (Wilhelm, 168), a notion he underscored when he offered to lessen the orchestral requirements of his opera for a 1930 performance by the silvery voiced singer Elizabeth Schumann, thereby allowing a light soprano to perform a role that previously had demanded singers of Wagnerian powers. Loïe Fuller began her Salome performances as a young woman picking flowers, and resembling a milkmaid. In her celebrated Covent Garden debut as Salome in 1949 (a production directed by Peter Brook with sets by Salvador Dalí), the heavy-set soprano Ljuba Welitsch sang uncannily like an adolescent girl. In his memoirs, the film director Michael Powell records that Hein Heckroth (celebrated for his designs for Powell's film *The Red Shoes*) suggested to the producer, Alexander Korda (then considering a Hollywood version of *Salome*), that the movie should feature "a very, very young girl – twelve years old perhaps," an idea that never came to fruition in a Hollywood film (qtd. in Powell 316). Luc Bondy's 1996 production of Strauss's *Salome* at the Lyric Opera of Chicago and Paris's Théâtre du Châtelet, starring Catherine Malfitano, offered a frenzied climax during the "Dance of the Seven Veils," in which Salome sheds a red-stained scarf. The performance thus exploited a latent implication of Wilde's text by suggesting that the princess is a virginal girl deflowered through her orgasmic encounter with John the Baptist.

The filmmaker Atom Egoyan's 1996 production of Strauss's *Salome*, for the Canadian Opera Company in Toronto, saw its protagonist as an abused daughter. Egoyan has demonstrated an obsessive fascination with the Salome legend as a myth of shattered childhood. In addition to directing the opera *Salome*, his 2000 film *Felicia's Journey* depicts its serial killer protagonist, a celebrated chef named Joey (Bob Hoskins), as traumatized when, as a boy, his mother takes him to the opera, and he witnesses the princess feasting on the Baptist's severed head. As an adult, Joey accidentally glimpses Rita Hayworth as Salome on a television screen, and Hayworth's screams at the sight of the Baptist's decapitated head echo with those of the young women Joey has murdered. As in the director Egoyan's 1995 film *Exotica* (which, in conversation with the author in 1996, he described in Salome-like terms as a movie "structured like a striptease"), his version of Strauss's opera is a feminist drama about the trauma of incest. Egoyan set his opera in a contemporary sanitarium, as he built up in flashback sequence a detailed past illustrating how Salome (Ljuba Kazarnovskaya) arrived at her uneasy state of mind, focusing on the middle-class family as the source of his heroine's psychosis. During the "Dance of the Seven Veils," Egoyan projected onto the stage huge film clips – "home movies" – revealing Salome's early years in a picket-fence home. Despite such references to bourgeois ideals, the sequence culminated in her being raped by her stepfather and his corrupt handlers.

What saved Egoyan's conception from the pop-psychological banalities of daytime television was his intensely lyrical visual imagination. With its absorption in burning contemporary issues such as child-abuse and incest, its dependence on a variety of experimental filmic techniques popular today in both avant-garde and mainstream theater (including a huge video close-up of the sensual lips of John the Baptist as he fulminates against the sins of Herod's household), and its repeated stress on Salome as destroyed innocent, Egoyan's revival is the truest postmodern Salome to date At the same time, his production was indebted to Wilde, in that all of its insights into its heroine's character were latent in the playwright's text. The villain of Egoyan's *Salome* was not only Herod, but also John the Baptist. "As much as she has been called obsessive and hysterical," Egoyan has stated, "I think there's something really hysterical about his own refusal to even address her, his own refusal to acknowledge her presence" (qtd. in Kim 35). A principal sequence in the Canadian Opera Company production depicted the princess arising out of mud into clear, luminous water; in Egoyan's hands, the opera speaks of Salome's liberation from the cesspool of an incest-racked household into the purifying sublimity of full consciousness.

Salome and the Codes of Homosexual Myth

A key characteristic of modern youth culture has been its obsession with consumerism, a non-productionist trait some have also seen as an aspect of homosexuality. Similarly, Wilde's depiction of childhood polymorphous perversity as a deadly, all-consuming process helped to generate Salome's own continuing association with same-sex male desire. Almost from the very first performance of the play in Paris, there stood an understanding of the biblical myth as same-sex in character.[6] The accusation that the Salome story was emphatically homosexual (because it supposedly appealed to individuals of same-sex preferences) first surfaced in a 1905 review of one of the earliest performances of Strauss's opera. "If sadists, masochists, lesbians, and homosexuals come and presume to tell us that their crazy world of spirit and feeling is to be interpreted as manifestations of art," wrote the critic Alan Roder, "then steps must be taken in the interests of health" (qtd. in Tydeman 127). Such views hit a feverish pitch in Britain in 1918 when the actress Maud Allan, along with the dramatic critic of the *Sunday Times*, J. T. Grein, brought a libel action against N. Pemberton Billing for alleging that Allan's Salome was part of a plot to undermine neutral countries during World War I through the dissemination of indecent texts, *Salome* chief among them.[7] The charges of homosexuality were pointed: Allan was accused of promoting lesbianism, and lost in court. The Maud Allan scandal had

---

6   As Alan Sinfield notes, the widespread awareness that Wilde was homosexual did not occur until late in his career, with his prosecution (2-11).

7   For accounts of the Allan case, see Huntley Carter, *The New Spirit in European Theater, 1914-1924* (44-45); Michael Kettle, *Salome's Last Veil*; and Philip Hoare, *Wilde Last Stand*.

an impact far beyond suppressing performances of *Salome* in England. Indeed, one historian has credited the case with helping to pave the way for the 1921 Criminal Law Amendment Act, which for the first time made lesbianism a punishable offense in Britain (Weeks 105-06).

The 1922 film featuring Nazimova has won an enduring reputation as a "gay" version because, in addition to the large number of actors wearing only loincloths, some of the ladies at Herod's court were played by men (Lambert 256-57). Probably the first production of either Wilde's or Strauss's *Salome* to play up a transvestite angle was the Italian film director Luchino Visconti's 1961 production of Strauss's opera at the Spoleto Festival, in which the "Dance of the Seven Veils" was performed not by the black soprano playing Salome (Margaret Tynes), who appeared nude throughout the performance (and who at one point rolled around on the stage in a masturbatory frenzy with a bloody head of John the Baptist), but by a group of sensual young men. At each performance, recalled the conductor Gian Carlo Menotti, "three or four people fainted" (qtd. in Visconti 276). Maurice Béjart's *Salome* (with recorded music by Riccardo Drigo, a turn-of-the-century composer) was first produced in Geneva in 1983, and depicted Patrick Dupond as a Salome in an imposing gown, unequivocally linking the character to transvestitism. Among other recent productions of Wilde's play, the 1977 version directed by Lindsay Kemp at London's Roundhouse Theatre, described by one critic as a "colossal homo-erotic spectacle [...] lifted from the absurd to the impressive by the manifest artistic integrity of Lindsay Kemp," was a theatrical landmark in same-sex erotics (qtd. in Raby xi). Kemp himself starred as Salome in drag, complete with sequined nipples, powdered rump, plumes, mirrors and silver paints. Ken Russell's film *Salome's Last Dance* (1987), set in an all-male brothel, in which a champagne-sipping Wilde attends a presentation of his own play, fortified a sense of Wilde's work as ineluctably tied to same-sex carnality. At the culmination of her "Dance of the Seven Veils," Salome (Imogen Millais-Scott) reveals that she has a penis, as the camera cuts away to Wilde kissing a young male ephebe.

Salome's illicit child's lust is matched by the illicit carnal needs of other figures in Wilde's play. As Richard Ellmann has noted, Wilde's *Salome* entertained a variety of unsanctioned desires, none of them defined within the play as normative. "In *Salome* the pageboy loves the Syrian soldier, but this is only one of the erotic relationships suggested," observes Ellmann. "For the Syrian, like Herod, loves Salome, Salome loves John the Baptist, John the Baptist loves Jesus. All love appears as deviation, and no deviation is superior to any other. All bring their tragic consequences" (7-8). Ellmann's notion of *Salome*, as a round robin of frustrated compulsions, explains why Wilde's play harbors such intense implications of erotic decadence beyond Salome's necrophilic lust for the Baptist. Her gruesome kiss becomes the enactment of *everyone*'s consuming perversity.[8] If Wilde contributes a specifically homoerotic dimension to the nineteenth-century myth of Salome, he depicts same-sex lust as

---

8   In *Sexual Politics*, Kate Millet suggests that, in *Salome*, Wilde revealed his own homosexual predilections. Gail Finney similarly contends that, in the play, "Wilde used a female character as a mask for a male homosexual" (66). For Finney, Salome's lust for a dead man's lips duplicates the logic of Wilde's overtly homosexual texts such as "The Ballad of

ineluctably tied to a death wish. That note is struck at the outset of the play when, well before Salome is killed by her outraged stepfather, the Young Syrian commits suicide. As with *Dorian Gray*, *Salome* reveals the architect of modern homosexual consciousness in the throes of a tale that, while intensely stylized, is cautionary nonetheless.

Beginning with Wilde's version of the Salome legend, the inspiring enchantments of the nineteenth-century *femme fatale* function in tensile rapport with the underground grandeur of the *homosexuel fatal*. Yet, as I have been arguing, the sources for the *femme fatale*'s power – a sometimes covert, sometimes overt girlish eroticism – are accompanied by a myth of homoerotic desire. The playwright's pairing of Salome and John the Baptist notionally signals a coded pair of would-be homosexual lovers, a couple bound together in a sadomasochistic death-grip. For if Salome is a kind of sexually voracious youngster in Wilde's story, John the Baptist, in his taunting of the child princess, and in his suicidal refusal to save himself by responding to her advances, suggests a man whose self-renunciation borders on the masochistic. As a prophet, he surely foresees that he guarantees his own death by denying Salome. Wilde's homosexual narrative of Salome and John the Baptist harks back to classical myths such as Zeus and Ganymede, as well as to classical Greek and Roman military allegories of imperious men and their youthful male lovers. Refusing to render his play in anything but the stark terms of a homosexual counter-myth, Wilde takes a gimlet-eyed view of such tales: same-sex desire is not merely frustrated in his play, it ends in suicide and death, implicitly challenging the ethic of redeeming homosexual *amours* advanced by contemporaries such as Walt Whitman and Edward Carpenter.[9]

Walter Benjamin's Salome and the Perilous Allure of Jugendstil

One principal aspect of the historic standing of Wilde's *Salome*, as ineluctably a homosexual myth, is suggested by the entry from Benjamin's monumental *Arcades Project* that appears in the quotation prefacing this essay. Fascinated with the unstated cultural codes that define the modern urban landscape, Benjamin links Wilde's Salome to a sequence of freely associated ideas and figures: "Wilde's Salome – Jugendstil – for the first time, the cigarette. Lethe flows in the ornaments of Jugendstil" (843). During the late nineteenth and early twentieth centuries, Jugendstil, or "youth style," signaled a mode of architecture or decorative art similar to Art Nouveau, popular in German-speaking and Nordic countries, where it became integrated with the National

---

Reading Gaol," where the philosophy of "each man kill[ing] the thing he loves" suggests that homosexuality can be satisfied only through the death of the beloved (66-67).

9   In *Vested Interests*, Marjorie Garber shifts the focus from Salome's homosexual dimension to other, illicit "performativities." For Garber, the postmodern Salome bespeaks the "specter of transvestitism" and the mysteries of the veil, while the "impossibility" of determining Salome's gender comprises the primary "scandal" of the Salome myth (345). This ambiguous poly-gender potential seems to be part of the charged erotic force of the child Salome, who, in Wilde's play, takes on agency by demanding payment for a desire that she is not allowed to possess, or even to desire to possess.

Romantic Style. In Munich especially, Jugendstil became a successful movement. The art of Jugendstil represented the successful dissemination, into a wide range of products, of aesthetics affiliated to Art Nouveau furniture and architecture, in which, as Gillian Naylor notes, there was "no demarcation between fine and applied art" (293).

For Benjamin, one might fruitfully speculate, Wilde's Salome entered into an era of all-pervasive kitsch, an inordinately ornamented style that lures its consumers into forgetfulness (that is, into Lethe – in Greek mythology, a river that flows through the realm of Hades, from which the shades of the dead had to drink in order to forget about their past lives on earth).[10] Salome's seductions have entered the epoch of mechanical reproduction, and are likened by Benjamin to the irresistible power of the cigarette. Benjamin's notation suggests that Wilde's "Daughter of Sodom" spawned a kitsch style linked to a new, consumer-oriented youth style and culture. In expressing his concern about the excesses of Jugendstil, as embodied in Wilde's *Salome*, Benjamin might have been thinking of an artist such as Franz von Stuck (1863-1928). A major player in the Munich cenacles of Jugendstil, Stuck painted one of the most arresting images of Salome. More generally, however, Benjamin seemed disturbed by Jugendstil's easy accommodation of consumer culture, epitomized by an artist such as Otto Eckmann. A major exhibitor at the first Secessionist exhibit, Eckmann sold all of his paintings in 1894 in order to focus entirely on design, contributing Japanese woodcut prints to the journal *Jugend*.

Jugendstil drew on three key strands in turn-of-the-century art – the Symbolist aesthetic of von Stuck, the pragmatic embrace of applied arts, and a highly stylized depiction of nature. Such characteristically Jugendstil traits frequently hinted at an illicit erotics. One critic, for example, described Hermann Obrist's 1892 wall hanging "Cyclamen" – decorated with a single flower in a pattern of sharply curving lines and loops – as the "sudden violent curves generated by the cracking of a whip" (qtd. in Duncan 27-28). Anxiety about Jugendstil is apparent elsewhere in *The Arcades Project* when Wilde is invoked, as when Benjamin discusses the "sterile" and "unnatural" mother as an iconic image of Jugendstil culture: "The depraved woman stays clear of fertility, as the priest stays clear of it" (556). Benjamin then identifies two distinct lines of Jugendstil. One is the strain of "perversion" that, he claims, "leads from Baudelaire to Wilde and Beardsley," and the other is the hieratic strain that leads "through Mallarmé to [Stefan] George." A kind of dialectical third strain emerges, however – what Benjamin terms the "line of emancipation"; it "takes its departure from *Les Fleurs du Mal*," and reaches the "heights of Zarathustra" (556). For Benjamin, Jugendstil culture is a sterile aesthetic project, but one that hints at possibilities for freedom.

If Wilde's *Salome* is, as so many of its modern interpreters have suggested, not only a narrative of an errant nymphet, but also one of homoerotic consumption that registers at a destructive pitch, it owes much of its force to the specter of the hyper-masculinized girl Salome's desire to consume the passive John the Baptist. Wilde, much like Freud after him, declines to sentimentalize homosexual eros in narratives of

---

10   In her chapter in this collection, Carol Mavor offers further discussion of Lethe and death in relation to consumption.

love. Instead, in *Salome*, he depicts it as a ruthless struggle for power and ownership. The playwright's homosexual myth of the Daughter of Sodom thus emerges as one of the harshest configurations of same-sex eros in the late-Victorian period, one that draws its power from the theoretical insights established by Freud on the subject of a female child's adult sexuality. Compared to the era's other taxonomies of same-sex practitioners, such as Carpenter's third-sexers, Marcel Proust's swank *invertis* and (in the 1920s) Magnus Hirschfield's *sexuelle Zwischenstufen*, Salome and John the Baptist have more in common with the pathological figures explored by Richard Krafft-Ebing, for whom sadomasochistic desire was inextricably linked to same-sex eroticism. As in Panizza's *The Council of Love*, in which a princess gives birth to the Devil's child, Wilde's debauched child Salome ultimately mass-produced a powerfully resonant myth of same-sex erotics, as an endlessly consuming familial and personal psychodrama.

Works Cited

Annesley, Charles. *The Home Book of the Opera*. New York: Dial, 1937.

Aske, Martin. "Keats, the Critics, and the Politics of Envy." *Keats and History*. Ed. Nicholas Roe. New York: Cambridge UP, 1995. 49-66.

Benjamin, Walter. *The Arcades Project*. Ed. Roy Tiedemann. Trans. Howard Eiland and Kevin McLaughlin. Cambridge: Harvard UP, 1999.

Carter, Huntley. *The New Spirit in European Theater, 1914-1924*. New York: George H. Doran, 1925.

Dijkstra, Bram. *Idols of Perversity: Fantasies of Female Evil in Fin de Siècle Culture*. New York: Oxford UP, 1986.

Duncan, Alastair. *Art Nouveau*. London: Thames and Hudson, 1994.

Ellmann, Richard. "The Uses of Decadence." *A Long the River Run*. New York: Knopf, 1989. 3-17.

Finney, Gail. *Women in Modern Drama: Freud, Feminism, and European Theater at the Turn of the Century*. Ithaca: Cornell UP, 1989.

Flaubert, Gustave. "Herodias." 1877. *Three Tales*. Trans. A. J. Krailsheimer. Oxford: Oxford UP, 1991. 71-106.

Freud, Sigmund. *Dora: Fragment of an Analysis of a Case of Hysteria*. 1905. Trans. James Strachey. New York: Touchstone, 1997.

Freud, Sigmund. *Three Essays on the Theory of Sexuality*. 1901-05. Trans. James Strachey. New York: Harper Collins, 1975.

Garber, Marjorie. *Vested Interests: Cross-Dressing and Cultural Anxiety*. New York: Routledge, 1992.

Girard, René. "Scandal and the Dance: Salome in the Gospel of Mark." *New Literary History* 40 (1984): 311-24.

Hoare, Philip. *Wilde's Last Stand: Decadence, Conspiracy and the First World War*. London: Duckworth, 1977.

Julian, Philippe. *Dreamers of Decadence: Symbolist Painters of the 1890s*. New York: Praeger, 1971.

Keats, John. "Isabella or the Pot of Basil." 1816. *The Poems*. Ed. Gerald Bullett. New York: Knopf, 1992. 177-90.

Kettle, Michael. *Salome's Last Veil: The Libel Case of the Century*. London: Hart Davis, MacGibbon, 1977.

Kim, Goby. "Atomic Opera." *Venue* (Fall 1996): 44-48.

Laforgue, Jules. "Salome." 1885. *Moral Tales*. Trans. William Jay Smith. New York: New Directions, 1985. 87-106.

Lambert, Gavin. *Nazimova*. New York: Knopf, 1997.

Lombroso, Cesare, and Gugliemo Ferrero. *The Female Offender*. 1893. London: T. Fisher Unwin, 1895.

Mallarmé, Stéphane. "Hérodiade." 1896. *Collected Poems*. Trans. Henry Weinfield. Berkeley: U of California P, 1994. 25-36.

Millett, Kate. *Sexual Politics*. New York: Doubleday, 1970.

Mossa, Gustave Adolphe. *Salome: The Ballerina*. 1904. Gustav-Adolph Mossa Museum, Nice, France.

Naylor, Gillian. "Munich: Secession and Jugendstil." *Art Nouveau, 1890-1914*. Ed. Paul Greenhalgh. New York: Abrams, 2000. 287-309.

Oulsby, Ian, ed. *The Cambridge Guide to English Literature*. Cambridge: Cambridge UP, 1993.

Paglia, Camille. "On Actors and Actresses." 12 April 1997. <http://privat.ub.uib. no/bubsy/pagliaom.htm>.

Panizza, Oskar. *The Council of Love: A Celestial Tragedy in Five Acts*. Trans. Oreste F. Pucciani. New York: Viking, 1973.

Picasso, Pablo. *Salome*. 1905. Musée Picasso, Paris, France.

Powell, Michael. *Million-Dollar Movie*. New York: Random House, 1992.

Raby, Peter. Introduction. *The Importance of Being Earnest and Other Plays*. Ed. Peter Raby. Oxford: Oxford UP, 1995. 3-26.

Ransome, Arthur. *Oscar Wilde: A Critical Study*. London: Methuen, 1912.

Rev. of *Salome*. 1893. *Oscar Wilde: The Critical Heritage*. Ed. Karl Beckson. New York: Barnes and Noble, 1970. 135-37.

Rev. of *Salome*. 1893. *Oscar Wilde: The Critical Heritage*. Ed. Karl Beckson. New York: Barnes and Noble, 1970. 133.

Showalter, Elaine. *Sexual Anarchy: Gender and Culture at the Fin de Siècle*. New York: Viking, 1990.

Sinfield, Alan. *The Wilde Century*. New York: Columbia UP, 1994.

Spitzer, Jen. "Salome's Polymorphous Perversity." Unpublished essay, 2006.

Sullivan, Vincent. *Aspects of Wilde*. London: Constable, 1936.

Tydeman, William, and Steven Price. *Salome*. New York: Cambridge UP, 1996.

Visconti, Luchino. *Il Mio Teatro*. Vol. 2. Bologna: Nuova Casa Editrice Cappelli, 1979.

Weeks, Jeffrey. *Coming Out: Homosexual Politics in Britain, from the Nineteenth Century to the Present*. London: Quartet Books, 1977.

Wilhelm, Kurt. *Richard Strauss: An Intimate Portrait*. Trans. Mary Whittall. London: Rizzoli, 1989.

Wilde, Oscar. "Salome." 1894. Trans. Lord Alfred Douglas. *The Importance of Being Earnest and Other Plays*. New York: Barnes and Noble Classics, 2003.

PART 3
Adulthood and Nationhood

Chapter 7

Adult Children's Literature in Victorian Britain

Claudia Nelson

Propelled by rising literacy rates and ever-cheaper print technology, children's literature boomed, both in quantity and in quality, across the nineteenth century. Adapting to fit evolving adult notions of what children's reading, and childhood itself, should be, such texts mixed an increasingly large proportion of delight into the inevitable instruction, so that children's literature became newly pleasurable for adult consumers. *Treasure Island*, for example, flopped in its first incarnation as a serial in the periodical *Young Folks*, some of whose youthful subscribers wrote to the editor to express their displeasure with the tale (Jackson 31), but garnered glowing reviews and popularity among adult readers when published as a single volume (Ymitri Mathison points out elsewhere in this collection that its admirers included W. E. Gladstone). Such responses were sufficiently common to cause worry among some Victorian critics that adult fans of children's books were regressing to childhood, perhaps a signal of widespread social degeneration. As Andrew Lang commented in the 1880s, "The flutter in the dovecots of culture caused by three or four boys' books is amazing. Culture is saddened at discovering that not only boys and illiterate people, but even critics not wholly illiterate, can be moved by a tale of adventure" (qtd. in Jackson 28).

The reverse side of the phenomenon of the children's book enjoyed by adults is the adult text that makes use of strategies more usually associated with children's fiction – what Lynne Rosenthal has dubbed the "children's book for adults." Arguably, such works do not constitute a genre, not because examples of the form are few, but because the phenomenon is so far reaching. It extends from sentimental fiction, romance and adventure to inspirational non-fiction, humor, poetry and stage plays (*Peter Pan*, which played to packed adult houses in 1904, is the ultimate example of the latter). The children's book for adults is often, but by no means always, about childhood. It embraces both the realistic and the fantastic. Its purpose wavers between offering readers a vacation from the burdens of the mundane world of adulthood and improving them, particularly by inculcating sympathy with childhood's more difficult aspects or by privileging a childlike mindset, conducive to the absorption of practical or moral instruction. For a crucial characteristic of such works is that they see their readers as imperfect or incomplete, acutely in need of resocializing. Because of that outlook, as this chapter will argue, such works can help to illuminate Victorian ideas about the relationships between adulthood and childhood, text and reader. And because of its ostensible separation from the adult marketplace, childhood becomes, in these texts, the ultimate commodity to (re)fit grown consumers for that forum. By temporarily separating readers from the demands of capitalist maturity, the children's book for adults seeks to enable its audience to meet those demands in new ways.

To date, few scholars have explored the possible influence of children's fiction on Victorian literature for adults, save for the occasional discussion of fairy-tale imagery in works by authors such as Charlotte Brontë, Charles Dickens and Elizabeth Gaskell. Even here, investigators sometimes perceive this imagery as differing in meaning and emotional weight from its counterpart in children's texts. For instance, Carole Silver argues in her informative *Strange and Secret Peoples* that nineteenth-century faëry art (including literature) was initially an adult mode, an expression of interest in folklore and the paranormal rendered jejune after the 1860s by a flood of children's titles that drove "the elfin peoples" out of the sophisticated texts they had once populated (187). In Silver's construct, Dickens's use of changeling figures, say, such as Paul Dombey and Quilp, derives less from his childhood reading than from a self-consciously adult Victorian tradition of medical and anthropological inquiry (Silver 73–80). Evidently, where Victorian literature is concerned, crabbed age and youth cannot live together.[1]

Even if we grant that assumption, however, a shared interest in the supernatural is not the only possible common ground between children's literature and adult literature. Yet scholarly investigation into overlaps in outlook and authorial strategy has not progressed substantially beyond Rosenthal's early article on one of the most popular novels of 1869, Florence Montgomery's *Misunderstood*. In an effort to extend and contextualize Rosenthal's valuable insights, I begin my chapter with a discussion of Montgomery's novel and then explore texts by Samuel Smiles and George MacDonald, each of which represents a different way of adapting children's literature to adult purposes.

The preface to *Misunderstood* opens with the line, "The following is not a child's story." Montgomery goes on to note that nonetheless, her work is intended to teach: "It has been thought that the lives of children, as known by themselves from their own little point of view, are not always sufficiently realised, that they are sometimes overlooked or misunderstood; and to throw some light, however faint, upon the subject, is one of the objects of this little story" (7). In other words, as Rosenthal observes, "Montgomery hoped to change the behavior of parents rather than of children" (94). Because *Misunderstood* posits a family consisting of two boys and their widowed father, and indicates that the lost mother's parenting skills needed no amendment, Montgomery plainly shares the perennial Victorian suspicion that social dominance and authority might be shutting out adult men, in particular, from something important.

---

1   To be sure, not all investigators draw a firm line between childhood experience and adult literary output. Studies such as Michael Kotzin's *Dickens and the Fairy Tale* (1972) and Harry Stone's *Dickens and the Invisible World* (1979) have traced the influence upon Dickens's fiction of a childhood spent with Aesop, the brothers Grimm, Charles Perrault and the *Arabian Nights*. Useful as investigations of this type are, however, they address a somewhat different phenomenon than the one that forms the subject of the present chapter.

The title *Misunderstood* thus refers ultimately to an apparently large number of real children, represented in the fiction by seven-year-old Humphrey Duncombe. Humphrey is what the mid-Victorians termed a "pickle," a good-hearted and attractive child who is constantly in trouble because of his inability to be guided by authority. His father, Sir Everard, prefers the delicate and biddable younger son, Miles, who looks like the boys' dead mother. He interprets Miles's submissiveness as affection and uses him as an emotional substitute for his wife. Lady Duncombe, however, was especially attached to Humphrey, and one of Montgomery's objectives is to demonstrate that inside the noisy, active and apparently hypermasculine "pickle" may lurk a sensitive, deeply emotional and feminized true self. Sir Everard, whose public duties as a member of parliament have often kept him away from home, comprehends that self only when Humphrey is paralyzed in a fall and is joyfully reunited with his mother in death. The adult male realm of politics, self-discipline and deference to authority is thus explicitly identified as incomplete, and readers are urged to expand their worldviews to embrace a different sensibility.

Rosenthal has observed that, in focusing on "the polarities of restraint and spontaneity," *Misunderstood* recalls a number of eighteenth- and nineteenth-century children's books that seek to influence children to make "the rational or virtuous choice" (96, 97). The novel, however, is not a cautionary tale about Humphrey's foolhardiness and disobedience, even though these traits lead to his fatal accident when a rotten branch, upon which he has been forbidden to climb, breaks under his weight. Rather, it is a cautionary tale about the dire consequences of Sir Everard's lack of perception, which ultimately leaves him not only contrite, but also deeply powerless. Much of the pathos of the deathbed scene depends upon this powerlessness, which mirrors Humphrey's sudden physical immobility:

> "Humphrey, my darling," [Sir Everard] exclaimed, in his longing to do something, be it ever so little, to soothe his boy's dying hour, "what is it? What can I do for you?"
>
> Nothing! With all his love and all his yearning, nothing! [...]
>
> Vain is the father's endeavour to reach a trouble of this kind [Humphrey's religious anxieties]; vainly, bending over him, does he seek to discover its cause, in his longing to remove or alleviate it. (284-85)

Unlike Sir Everard, we adult readers understand the cause of Humphrey's distress, since the narrator has spelled it out for us. Nevertheless, because we are an audience rather than actors in the drama, we share not only Sir Everard's "longing to remove or alleviate it," but also his impotence.

We might thus ask *why* Montgomery imposed this particular sensation on her audience. Rosenthal suggests that she "hoped to shock her adult readers into an awareness of the paralysis of their own lives; to make them conscious of the degree to which they had become alienated, not only from their children, but from the sources of their own inner vitality" (101-02). The obvious source of this alienation is Victorian society's emphasis on economic advancement, which required middle-class men to direct their attention to business in preference to their family relationships. I would, however, add two further purposes here. First, Montgomery dramatizes through an adult sensibility a point that she has elsewhere made via a focus on the child: adults and children sometimes fail to grasp each other's feelings and concerns, and this mutual misunderstanding can cause pain to parents as much as to their offspring. Second, the scene is plainly intended to be deeply pathetic; our enforced helplessness should result in tears. But these tears are not, like the tears shed in earlier didactic texts for children, a punitive stick designed to cause us to make a moral choice in future. Rather, they *are* a moral choice.

For earlier in the novel, the narrator has implied that Humphrey's boisterous behavior, which has caused his father to condemn him as unfeeling, is in part a mechanism for coping with his grief at the loss of his mother. The text notes that this response has its counterpart in adult consumerism:

> Children of a larger growth, but children in understanding still, do not many of us wrestle with this undefined feeling in the same way? This mysterious thing, which we, with our maturer experience, call sorrow, is not our first thought when it assails us, 'How shall we drive it away?' [...] Does it not drive the rich to society, travelling, or excitement, and the poor to the public-house? (166-67)

Montgomery continues, however, by suggesting that better than evading sorrow is moving through it toward God – a model for which is provided by Humphrey's fortunate fall, which leads him to Heaven. Adult readers, then, made conscious of their inadequacy by their pain at Humphrey's situation, are presented immediately with a religious resolution, whose joyfulness we can feel only if we have experienced the grief toward which Montgomery directs us. Significantly, however, while Sir Everard is a necessary player throughout, our attention is always primarily on the child, to whom the narrator repeatedly compares us. And significantly, too, our simulacrum is specifically a "*stricken* child," a "child, crushed and despairing" (170, my italics). If "one of the objects" of *Misunderstood*, as Montgomery notes in her preface, is to encourage adult empathy with children so that childish sorrow may be reduced, another would seem to be to transfer that sorrow to adults, on the grounds that woe will improve their chances of salvation.

The gender composition of *Misunderstood*'s audience is also relevant. The novel's dominant subject is the adult male's emotional inadequacy, which apparently matters only in the absence of his idealized wife. Men and women are thus likely to respond to this fiction differently – women taking it as a validation of their domestic irreplaceability and comparative emotional expertise, men asking themselves nervously about the extent to which Sir Everard's faults are also theirs. In effect, *Misunderstood* is not only a children's book for adults, but also a woman's domestic novel about men. It translates into an all-male world the plot that Nina Baym has identified as central to the woman's novel in mid-nineteenth-century America, in which a "poor and friendless [female] child" must cope with "mistreatment, unfairness, disadvantage, and powerlessness," ultimately triumphing over them by developing "a strong conviction of her own worth [... and changing] the world's attitude toward her" (35, 17, 19). Thus, while Montgomery's novel identifies mothers as superior to fathers in their insight and empathy, it simultaneously seeks to diminish "misunderst[anding]" between women and men, as well as between adults and children. Women are to see that men and boys, too, may feel undervalued and powerless, while male readers, by identifying with male characters of this type, are to project themselves into an emotional situation already familiar to many women. The favorable reviews and wide sales that *Misunderstood* enjoyed suggest that adult readers of the day got the point.

Misunderstood was participating in a commitment to moral uplift that was widespread in the nineteenth century. Influenced by modernism's aesthetic dictates, however, we tend to define the didactic urge as a hallmark of the marginalized or second-rate writer. Thus, when Dinah Mulock takes exception to *The Mill on the Floss* in an 1861 *Macmillan's* article, instructing the reader to ask, "What good will it do? [Will it] lighten any burdened heart, help any perplexed spirit, comfort the sorrowful, succour the tempted, or bring back the erring into the way of peace[?]" (444), we may see the question as itself somewhat juvenile, a sign that Mulock does not understand how George Eliot's masterpiece "should" be read. By the standards of the day, however, perhaps it was Eliot who was missing the point. As Sally Mitchell notes, Mulock's name "was frequently paired with Eliot's during these [mid-nineteenth-century] years in a context which implies 'good literature' as opposed to the other sort" (114). Advice manuals and novels designed to inculcate principles of upward mobility in both a moral and a practical sense proliferated; didacticism was not confined to works for children. Yet because literature for the young was considered to have a particular responsibility to be didactic, writers who wanted to preach to adult readers might take children's works as their models.

This observation brings us to the central text of Victorian "success literature," Samuel Smiles's *Self-Help*, which seeks to teach ambitious working-class men the character traits that will turn them into gentlemen – in effect, to accomplish the mass-marketing of a particular brand of masculinity. Published in November 1859, *Self-Help* had sold 20,000 copies by the end of the year (it required three reprints in November alone), and some 250,000 by its author's death in 1904.[2] The book's appeal has been traced to various sources, including Smiles's ability to express his era's optimism and energy while simultaneously addressing its anxiety about social class, his "muscular and succinct" prose style and his habit of drawing his illustrations from all levels of society (Joseph 7-8). But an additional reason for *Self-Help*'s perceived effectiveness, I suggest, is its shrewd adaptation of the techniques of the children's literature of Smiles's youth, which similarly focuses on the consumer's replication of characteristics that authors have identified as desirable commodities.

Like many Victorian texts for children and adults alike, *Self-Help* focuses on the honing of the male character, one trait at a time. In a characteristic chapter, "Men of Business," Smiles offers his audience – originally, young artisans belonging to a mutual improvement society in Leeds in 1845 – a taxonomy of masculine energy, which he subdivides into accuracy, method and dispatch, among other qualities. In order to illustrate the benefits of these virtues, he tells anecdotes about the lives of great men, advising the reader to rise by cultivating in himself, for example, Napoleon's mastery of detail and the Duke of Wellington's punctuality. In other words, Smiles sees character as flexible. Far from being fixed at one social level by heritage, upbringing or innate talent, Smiles's readers, though nominally adult, are

---

2   For publishing information, see Houghton (191), Richards (52) and Joseph (7).

presumed to be *tabulae rasae* who may effectively become their own preceptors, recognizing weaknesses and acquiring attributes that they may hitherto have lacked. Middle-class status becomes, in this formulation, equivalent to adulthood; moreover, like chronological adulthood, it is potentially available to all. All that is needed is a set of blueprints, which this text provides through a host of readily consumable mini-biographies.

Smiles's narrative style is not universally admired. As Christopher Clausen puts it, in his lack of organization, and in his tendency to pad his chapters, "Smiles resembled nothing so much as a vacuum cleaner that rolled from room to room of a large dusty house filling up its bag" (407-08). Yet as Clausen also indicates, the book's unsophisticated structure, a result of its emphasis on anecdote and its refusal to subordinate one anecdote to another, was a major source of its appeal for the working-class men who constituted its original audience (407). *Self-Help* makes few demands upon its consumers. As in the children's books it resembles, the sketches it contains are simple, clearly written and short, their points readily apparent even to inexperienced readers. It is a book made to be dipped into by those who have limited leisure for reading, and if the reader has forgotten where he left off last time, no harm is done, as each moral is repeated again and again.

Here, for example, is an extract from Smiles's account of surgeon and scientist John Hunter:

> He received little or no education until he was about twenty years of age, and it was with difficulty that he acquired the arts of reading and writing. He worked for some years as a common carpenter at Glasgow, after which he joined his brother William, who had settled in London as a lecturer and anatomical demonstrator. John entered his dissecting-room as an assistant, but soon shot ahead of his brother, partly by virtue of his great natural ability, but mainly by reason of his patient application and indefatigable industry. (97-98)

To readers familiar with the rational moralist writers who flourished around the beginning of the nineteenth century – and Smiles, who was born in 1812, would have grown up on their works – this sketch should have a familiar ring. In its emphasis on the cause-and-effect relationship of character trait and personal success, its assumption that personality may be described in terms of a concentrated quality consistently displayed, and especially its implication that the point of writing about admirable individuals is that readers may be inspired to emulation, the passage adopts strategies associated with children's authors such as Thomas Day, Maria Edgeworth and the anonymous producer of an 1804 work resoundingly titled "The Renowned History of Primrose Prettyface, Who by Her Sweetness of Temper and Love of Learning Was Raised from Being the Daughter of a Poor Cottager to Great Riches and to the Dignity of the Lady of the Manor, Set Forth for the Benefit and Imitation of Those Pretty Little Boys and Girls Who by Learning Their Books and Obliging Mankind, Would to Beauty of Body Add Beauty of Mind."

According to Patricia Demers and Gordon Moyles, rational moralism – essentially, the principle that good sense and virtue are equivalent – continued to animate children's literature as late as 1850 (121). Its heyday began in the 1780s, with the appearance (over a six-year span) of Thomas Day's *The History of Sandford and Merton*. A wealthy eccentric, Day resembles the early Henry James hero described in Michèle Mendelssohn's contribution to this volume. Day believed so fervently in the theories of Jean-Jacques Rousseau that he adopted two orphan girls in order to rear them according to his idol's precepts, planning to marry whichever of his charges turned out better. In other words, Day took seriously the idea that character is malleable. Thus, like the anecdotes contained in *Self-Help*, the various episodes of *Sandford and Merton* provide a laundry list of desirable character traits, from kindness to animals to diligence at learning to read, which are, of course, being recommended to the reader as well as acquired by little Tommy Merton. And although Day's upper-class status might seem to have won out in his own life, in that he ultimately married an heiress instead of either of his working-class wards, the ideology on display is essentially a leveling one – the novel decries its culture's tendency to emphasize class differences.

So too, of course, does Smiles, who assures his readers that social mobility is possible, that the gulf between them and dukes or emperors may be lessened by taking the latter as inspirations and models. Like Day, Smiles implies that members of different classes can interact as equals, in this case by juxtaposing anecdotes of the well-born with accounts of the plebeian and refusing to distinguish between the two. But my point here is not only that Smiles's message resembles those of certain rational-moralist children's authors popular in his youth, since similar messages may be found in many texts for adults that might equally well have shaped his outlook. There are striking similarities of strategy between Smiles and the rational moralists as well.

Take the techniques on display in Edgeworth's 1796 story "The Purple Jar," published in her *Early Lessons*. On one level, "The Purple Jar" is a cautionary tale about the foolishness of impulse buying, in which little Rosamond prefers what she takes to be an attractive *objet d'art* to a useful pair of shoes – and lives to regret it. Not only do Rosamond's increasingly shabby old shoes inhibit her activities and pleasure, but the jar also turns out, when she looks more closely at what she has purchased, to be a plain white container whose purple color derived from its former (and now discarded) contents. Rosamond cannot benefit from her mother's advice; she is the kind of child who can learn only by experience. Yet clearly the story is written from the assumption that other children need not settle for her laborious trial-and-error approach, but can profit vicariously from her mistakes.

What drives the point home for the reader is less Edgeworth's evident faith in the utility of the lessons than the way she embeds them in story and personality, which, as in Smiles's work, gives them emotional weight. Whereas many protagonists of pre-Victorian children's works tend to be generic, Edgeworth individualizes Rosamond enough to make her stand out from a somewhat featureless crowd. Rosamond not only shares the intended reader's age and class status, but also is described in enough detail to come to life; although the story is brief, Rosamond herself is unexpectedly complex. If some authors of cautionary tales focus on a single disastrous trait, Edgeworth suggests that character consists of chains of interlocking and sometimes contrasting qualities. Just as Tommy Merton's unfortunate upbringing led not only to laziness but also to timidity, discourtesy, smugness and incompetence, Rosamond's impulsiveness is linked to her love of beauty and her desire to assert herself, and is balanced against a willingness to acknowledge that she is in the wrong. Similarly,

Smiles's model men rarely embody only the virtue under immediate scrutiny; industry, for example, will be shown to coexist with a network of additional traits, such as (in the case of artist and blacksmith James Sharples) thoroughness, good sense, "genuine right-heartedness" and uxoriousness (135). Like Rosamond, Smiles's exemplary characters are distinct from the mob; paradoxically, however, this individuality is offered to consumers as something to imitate.[3]

Anne Baltz Rodrick observes the rhetorical importance to the ethic of self-improvement of what we might term the "unimproved Other": members of the working class who failed to embrace the culture of improvement, and were consequently viewed with hostility by their aspiring brothers. She identifies as Smiles's chief innovation "his articulation of the links between individual self-help and the overall improvement of a larger civic body," so that those who rejected personal ambition were also implicitly rejecting their duties as citizens (40). Yet in the context of rational moralism, Smiles was by no means the first to make this connection. Rational-moralist works focus in roughly equal numbers on good examples and on bad, often in the same text, readers being invited to follow the one and despise the other. For instance, Tommy Merton is contrasted to Harry Sandford, Rosamond's foolish behavior in "The Purple Jar" to her sensible behavior in "The Marble Pear," and the six children who make up the "Bad Family" in Mrs. Fenwick's *Lessons for Children* (1809) to the six who make up the "Good Family." The larger purpose of these works is clearly to use individual cases to construct a kind of corporate childhood identity among readers – to improve in bulk, as it were, as a means of shaping a particular model of future citizen. The composite recommendation of an individual who is sensible, industrious, kind, responsible, attentive to detail and obedient to authority is designed to further national stability; even while rational moralists may espouse democratic or class-blind attitudes, they eschew the hot-headed, romantic impulses that may be leading to revolution elsewhere. As in Smiles's work, what is being engineered here is essentially the improvement of an existing society, not its wholesale replacement.

Critics have noted that *Self-Help* influenced subsequent children's works; for example, Clausen cites the fiction of Horatio Alger (407), Richards the novels of G. A. Henty, and Elleke Boehmer *Scouting for Boys* by Robert Baden-Powell (xiv). But what are the implications of viewing *Self-Help*, or for that matter *Misunderstood*, in the context of earlier works for children? I would argue that what is at stake here is more than a simple mapping of sources. For one thing, the fact that Day, Edgeworth and their colleagues wrote for a primary audience of pre-pubescent middle-class children, while Smiles addressed young men who were by Victorian standards adult and by our standards at least adolescent, tells us something about nineteenth-century understandings of both children and the working classes. The latter, who made up some 85 percent of the Victorian population, were frequently represented

---

3   This strategy would remain popular in later texts for self-improvement. Anne Morey, for instance, notes of a Hollywood correspondence school for aspiring screenwriters in the 1910s and 1920s that "while standardization was the key to turning students into successful screenwriters, the apparent promotion of individuality was the key to recruitment of students in the first place" (72).

as undisciplined, dirty, poorly educated and unrestrained in their appetites – in short, as childish, in the most negative sense of the word.[4] Yet in Smiles's work the textual infantilizing of the working classes is intended as a precondition for their empowerment, just as in Montgomery's novel the adult male reader is forced into powerlessness as a means of inculcating broader sympathies and new forms of sensibility. By reading exemplary lives, with their simple diction, straightforward sentence structure and strategic similarities to rational-moralist writings for small children, Smiles's ambitious audience can learn how to become respected adult citizens; by reading a cautionary tale, Montgomery's can learn how to understand the limitations of privilege. Both *Misunderstood* and *Self-Help* thus suggest the extent to which performing the role of the child could bestow cultural authority in the world of Victorian Britain.

Smiles wrote originally for an audience composed primarily of young men, some perhaps still in their teens, most in their twenties, and all (or nearly all) self-supporting. Montgomery wrote for an audience of well-to-do adults, although her novel was readily accessible to children as well. In contrast, their near contemporary George MacDonald addressed a readership that he imagined as simultaneously insightful and uncontaminated, emotionally mature without being intellectually jaded. He describes his ideal reader as "childlike," explaining in his 1893 essay "The Fantastic Imagination" that such a person might be "five, or fifty, or seventy-five" (25). In adapting the conventions of children's literature to the sophistication of the adult world, then, MacDonald rejects the convention that an author writes for a particular age group rather than for a set of ageless character traits. Or, as Amy Sonheim puts it, "MacDonald refuses to polarize the world of adults from the world of children" (1).

Sonheim discusses MacDonald's fairy tale "The Light Princess," which today is classified as a children's story because of its genre and brevity, and also because of its twentieth-century illustrator, Caldecott winner Maurice Sendak. And indeed, Sonheim notes, the tale was originally created for MacDonald's own children. It was not, however, offered to the Victorian public as a juvenile fantasy. Perhaps influenced by John Ruskin's advice, MacDonald incorporated it into the episodic structure of his adult novel *Adela Cathcart* (1864), within which, Sonheim cogently argues, it offers an inverted commentary upon the events, setting and concerns of its frame. Thus, as Sonheim notes, Adela lives in a house known as "The Swanspond," the Light Princess in a lakeside castle. Adela suffers from excessive melancholy, the bewitched Light Princess from insufficient gravity, in both a literal and a metaphorical sense. Above all, the Light Princess is saved by a man's self-sacrifice when the hero demonstrates his willingness to immolate himself for her sake, while Adela is saved by a man's recognition that women must be granted spiritual and intellectual stimulation, notwithstanding conventional gender roles (Sonheim 5-6). In short, in "The Light Princess" MacDonald plays with questions of audience. Not only does

---

4   Samuel Garratt's "The Irish in London," in *Motives for Missions* (1852), can afford to be particularly forthright because its subject is a despised minority. "For the most part, the native Irish of London know nothing," he notes, adding, "You must speak to them as if they were children" (qtd. in Garwood 263).

he redirect toward adult readers a tale first told to children, he also constructs the adult-oriented frame tale in a way that illuminates the themes of the fairy tale, and is simultaneously illuminated by them. Together, Adela and the Light Princess provide both direct and indirect discussion of the fraught issue of women's social place and intellectual needs – a subject that might normally be considered "adult," but that in MacDonald's hands is represented as transcending age.

This approach is characteristic of MacDonald's authorial strategy, which frequently juxtaposes realism with fantasy, and stories that seem adult-oriented with those that seem child-oriented. Apparent opposites are ultimately revealed to be complements, the underlying similarity of their messages revealed by proximity. As "The Fantastic Imagination" makes clear, MacDonald saw the reader's interpretative task as the ultimate creative act in literature, trumping the author's attempt to inculcate a message:

> Everyone [...] who feels [a] story, will read its meaning after his own nature and development: one man will read one meaning in it, another will read another.
>   'If so, how am I to assure myself that I am not reading my own meaning into it, but yours out of it?'
>   Why should you be so assured? It may be better that you should read your meaning into it. That may be a higher operation of your intellect than the mere reading of mine out of it: your meaning may be superior to mine. (25)

The author, then, should endeavor to provide opportunities for independent thought on the part of the reader – and the unexpected chiming of apparently unlike genres and modes of address will enhance such opportunities.

Consider the seemingly disparate plot threads in MacDonald's "The Gifts of the Child Christ" (1882). The tale concerns a neglected five-year-old, Phosy Greatorex, who, haunted by the saying "Whom the Lord loveth, he chasteneth," has been praying that God may chasten her (32). On Christmas Day, she wakes to discover in the guest room what she at first takes to be "the most exquisite of dolls [...] the gift of the child Jesus," and subsequently identifies as "baby Jesus himself." Holding the infant (her newborn half-brother) tenderly, she becomes a Mary figure, "at once the mother and the slave of the Lord Jesus," but gradually realizes that the object of her worship is not an artificial child but a dead one (54-56). The household discovers the strange sight, and when Phosy sees her father, she wails out her anguish. For the first time, she becomes real to him; in a sense, she makes in his eyes the same transition from symbolic object to individual that the baby has just made in hers. The father's subsequent behavior suggests that MacDonald is urging his audience to reconfigure its own conception of childhood, although perhaps readers are simply to exchange one way of commodifying children for another. Picking up his daughter, Mr. Greatorex comforts her, laying the groundwork for a relationship in which he will learn to respect her spiritual gifts. Like Montgomery's Humphrey, Phosy will no longer be "misunderstood"; father and child, as well as husband and wife, will draw closer together, making the hitherto unhappy household a place of joy. Meanwhile, Phosy's nursemaid, Alice, is likewise "chastened" when she learns first that a newly deceased uncle has left a substantial sum to his legal next of kin, and later that she and her brother cannot inherit it because, it turns out, their parents were not married.

The revelation is intensely humiliating to a woman who has prided herself on her respectability and has begun to develop grandiose fantasies about spending her new wealth. Nevertheless, the loss of the money is fortunate, as it preserves Alice's future with the man of modest means who loves her.

"The Gifts of the Christ Child" may initially seem to lack unity. Both Alice and Greatorex are flawed; however, at first sight their situations do not appear parallel. Alice is a servant whose anticipated legacy has gone to her head, so that she speaks disrespectfully to her employers and breaks her engagement. Greatorex is a merchant who tends to value those around him only to the extent that their minds resemble his own, so that neither of his marriages has been emotionally successful. To a conventional middle-class Victorian reader, Alice's crime is her transgression against the behavioral standards required of female domestic servants: humility, deference and the responsible performance of her duties (for example, she is somewhat neglectful and fierce toward Phosy). Greatorex, in contrast, appears to be hewing only too closely to the stereotype of the successful businessman, as laid down in novels such as Dickens's *Dombey and Son* (1847-48). Like Dombey, if to a lesser extent, Greatorex is honest but also proud, insensitive and cold – and desperately in need of redemption at his daughter's hands.

Because these unlike strands are juxtaposed, however, the reader recognizes a need to discover their underlying commonalities. Both plot lines, of course, illustrate that divine "chastening" ultimately increases happiness. Both, as Rolland Hein observes, demonstrate "that true conversion is a change of heart that issues in reconciled or renewed personal relationships" (342) – a theme that runs throughout much of MacDonald's fiction, whether marketed primarily to adults or to children. And the parallel between Alice and Greatorex encourages us to see him, too, as an impertinent servant in God's household, a man who needs to learn obedience and to jettison his arrogance. Various terms used in the narrator's uncomplimentary early description of Greatorex, including "meanness," "presumptuous[ness]," "cramped [...] development" and "vainest hopes" (33-35), strengthen this parallel.

Works such as "The Gifts of the Child Christ" may be classified as children's stories for adults not merely because they are didactic, but also because of the mindset into which they urge adult readers: humble, self-questioning, eager to seek the author's meaning by profiting from the clues he drops. MacDonald held that "it is God's things, his embodied thoughts, which alone a man has to use, modified and adapted to his own purposes, for the expression of his thoughts" ("Imagination" 27). In this context, it is possible to see a connection between the story's focus on God's chastening of his beloved children and the way in which the narrator both challenges his readers intellectually and warns them of the dangers of presumption. Although MacDonald believed in empowering readers, he simultaneously established his own position as their teacher, and therefore as their superior in understanding. Like Montgomery and Smiles, that is, MacDonald considered that the childlike adult reader – especially when taking direction from the adult author – is most amenable to improvement.

In their different ways, all three authors illustrate the common nineteenth-century conviction, developed in the Romantic period but extending throughout Victoria's reign, that far from being a mere apprenticeship to adulthood, childhood might be the superior state. Over the course of the century, one can hear many voices implying that childhood is wasted on the young. For example, although it predates by a generation or more the texts examined in this chapter, a comment published in *Blackwood's* in 1822 aptly summarizes the mindset shared in particular by Montgomery and MacDonald:

> The frequent recurrence of [childlike] feelings is beneficial to the human heart, [in] that it helps to purify, to refine, and spiritualize its worldly and corrupt affections, restoring a sort of youthful elasticity to its nobler powers, and at the same time a meek and childlike sense of entire dependence no longer indeed on the tender earthly guardians of our helpless infancy, but on our Father which is in Heaven, *their* Father and ours, in whose sight we are all alike helpless, alike children. ("Childhood" 139)

Children's literature for adults seeks to induce such a "recurrence of [childlike] feelings." Authorial strategies for accomplishing this end varied, as did the uses (for example, sacred vs. secular) to which the state of adult childhood was put. Nevertheless, the extent of this phenomenon in Victorian literature illuminates the cultural position assigned to childhood – childhood as a construct, if not childhood as actually experienced.

Works Cited

Baym, Nina. *Woman's Fiction: A Guide to Novels by and about Women in America, 1820-1870*. 1978. Ithaca: Cornell UP, 1980.

Boehmer, Elleke. Introduction. *Scouting for Boys: A Handbook for Instruction in Good Citizenship*. By Robert Baden-Powell. Oxford: Oxford UP, 2004. xi-xxxix.

"Childhood." *Blackwood's Magazine* 12.67 (1822): 139-45.

Clausen, Christopher. "How to Join the Middle Classes: With the Help of Dr. Smiles and Mrs. Beeton." *American Scholar* 62.3 (1993): 403-18.

Demers, Patricia, and Gordon Moyles, eds. *From Instruction to Delight: An Anthology of Children's Literature to 1850*. Toronto: Oxford UP, 1982.

Edgeworth, Maria. *The Parent's Assistant, or Stories for Children*. 1796. London, Macmillan, 1903.

Garwood, John. *The Million-Peopled City; or, One-Half of the People of London Made Known to the Other Half*. London: Wertheim and Macintosh, 1853. 24 July 2004. <http://www.victorianlondon.org/publications4/peopled.htm>.

Hein, Rolland. *George MacDonald: Victorian Mythmaker*. Nashville: Star Song, 1993.

Houghton, Walter E. *The Victorian Frame of Mind, 1830-1870*. New Haven: Yale UP, 1957.

Jackson, David H. "*Treasure Island* as a Late-Victorian Adults' Novel." *Victorian Newsletter* 72 (1987): 28-32.

Joseph, Keith. Introduction. *Self-Help: With Illustrations of Conduct and Perseverance*. By Samuel Smiles. Abr. ed. Harmondsworth, UK: Penguin, 1986. 7-16.

MacDonald, George. "The Fantastic Imagination." 1893. *The Gifts of the Child Christ: Fairy Tales and Stories for the Childlike*. Ed. Glenn Edward Sadler. Vol. 1. Grand Rapids, MI: Eerdmans, 1973. 23-28.

---. "The Gifts of the Child Christ." 1882. *The Gifts of the Child Christ: Fairy Tales and Stories for the Childlike*. Ed. Glenn Edward Sadler. Vol. 1. Grand Rapids, MI: Eerdmans, 1973. 31-60.

Mitchell, Sally. *The Fallen Angel: Chastity, Class and Women's Reading, 1835-1880*. Bowling Green: Bowling Green U Popular P, 1981.

Montgomery, Florence. *Misunderstood*. 1869. Leipzig: Tauchnitz, n.d.

Morey, Anne. *Hollywood Outsiders: The Adaptation of the Film Industry, 1913-1934*. Minneapolis: U of Minnesota P, 2003.

Mulock, Dinah. "To Novelists – and a Novelist." *Macmillan's* 3 (1861): 441-48.

Richards, Jeffrey. "Spreading the Gospel of Self-Help: G. A. Henty and Samuel Smiles." *Journal of Popular Culture* 16.2 (1982): 52-65.

Rodrick, Anne Baltz. "The Importance of Being an Earnest Improver: Class, Caste, and *Self-Help* in Mid-Victorian England." *Victorian Literature and Culture* 29.1 (2001): 39-50.

Rosenthal, Lynne. "*Misunderstood*: A Victorian Children's Book for Adults." *Children's Literature* 1 (1974): 94-102.

Silver, Carole G. *Strange and Secret Peoples: Fairies and Victorian Consciousness*. New York: Oxford UP, 1999.

Smiles, Samuel. *Self-Help: With Illustrations of Conduct and Perseverance*. 1859. Abr. ed. Harmondsworth, UK: Penguin, 1986.

Sonheim, Amy L. "The Unbearable Lightness of Childhood: George MacDonald Takes Seriously *The Light Princess*." Nineteenth Century Studies Association Conference. Augusta, GA. 12 March 2005.

Chapter 8

Home Thoughts and Home Scenes: Packaging Middle-class Childhood for Christmas Consumption

Lorraine Janzen Kooistra

In 1876, the front cover of the *Illustrated London News*'s *Christmas Number* displayed a full-page wood engraving of a middle-class family group (with the maidservant a humble participant in the background) watching a pretty mother lift her young son to crown the decorated tree with its final glory: not an angel or star but the nation's flag (fig. 8.1). Entitled "Hoisting the Union Jack," the image was accompanied overleaf by John Latey's narrative poem celebrating Christmas as the festival that enshrined a patriotic nationalism rooted in the domestic virtues of the patriarchal family.[1] The poem and picture packaged child, home, and nation for Christmas consumption. In the age of mechanical reproduction and an emergent commodity culture, a middle-class childhood representative of national cultural values was disseminated each Christmas in the pages of the illustrated press, from newspapers and periodicals to gift books and greeting cards. Aimed at a family market, the *Illustrated London News* (1842-1900) circulated to a wide audience the notion that Christmas "was the festival of the home and that the home was a deep-rooted English cultural expression" (Connelly 11). As one cover story emphasized in 1860, "It would seem to be a special characteristic of the Teutonic race to watch with the deepest interest and tenderest solicitude over the sanctities of *home*, and Christmas has been consecrated by them, from time immemorial, to the performance of domestic rites" ("Christmas Day" 575).This association of British Christmas celebration with Teutonic tradition made it easy for the German Christmas tree to become a national custom when middle-class readers throughout the kingdom, opening the *Illustrated London News Christmas Supplement* in 1848, saw a wood engraving of the "Christmas Tree at Windsor Castle" (fig. 8.2). The picture's heraldic frame, ornamented with a cornucopia of fruit, and with the carcasses of game and fowl sacrificed to feasts of the season, is inset with vignettes depicting the Christmas traditions of sleigh rides, benevolence to the poor, and ice skating. The ornate frame opens into a central medallion that functions as a peep-hole into the domestic life of the Queen, whose Christmas is being celebrated with family gathered around a decorated tree. Victoria stands in profile to the left, with the heir apparent, Edward,

---

1   I am indebted to Mark Connelly, whose *Christmas: A Social History* directed me to the *Illustrated London News*'s Christmas Numbers, and provided an historical context for the development of Christmas customs and cultural values in the Victorian period.

at her side. To the right stand the Prince Consort with the young Victoria, Alice, Alfred, and Helena (baby Louise is presumably sleeping in her cradle offstage). A maidservant on the left stands respectfully in the background as a crucial element of this representation of the Royals as an ordinary middle-class family.[2] For the benefit of readers unfamiliar with the decorated fir, the accompanying paragraph explained: "The Christmas Tree represented in the above Engraving is that which is annually prepared by her Majesty's command for the Royal children."[3] Within two years, as Liz Farr's chapter in this collection shows, the decorated Christmas tree was being celebrated by Charles Dickens in *Household Words* as a symbol of the maturation of desire within commodity culture.

By the time "Hoisting the Union Jack" was published in the *Illustrated London News* almost 30 years later, Christmas trees were being prepared annually for children across the kingdom – a familiar domestic rite, rather than an unfamiliar foreign one. As if aware that this national Christmas custom was produced by the power of the image in the age of the illustrated press, "Hoisting the Union Jack" makes specific visual reference to the engraving that introduced the tradition (fig. 8.1). Indeed, the image repeats, with great precision, the setting of the Windsor Castle Christmas tree and the arrangement of Queen Victoria's family group: to the left and right of the tree a maidservant and a father figure stand as silent symbols of the material culture and hidden labor on which this scene of luxury and pleasure depends. Grouped close to the father are the children who demonstrate successful domestic production and guarantee brand continuity, royal or otherwise. Central to this scene, as to the earlier image, is the ideologically charged triangulation of mother, son and nation. Just as Queen Victoria and Prince Edward constitute a separate visual unit, representing Great Britain's past, present and future greatness, so too the middle-class mother and her small son become the dominant focus in the later picture. As the mother lifts Freddy (a verbal echo of the Prince's name) to affix the Union Jack, the Christmas tree is transformed into a flagpole declaring Teutonic supremacy and Britain's greatness. The implication is that it is the role of mothers to raise sons who will uphold the nation's cultural virtues and rule the world. The accompanying poem underscores this pictorial patriotism, in a narrative that balances militant images of national power with sanctified images of domesticity, childhood and "the glorious Christmas season" (Latey 2).

This packaging of picture and poetry in the periodical press was as central to late-nineteenth century Christmas celebrations as the decorated fir, but was to achieve a more permanent position in the heart of the middle-class home than either disposable tree or weekly paper ever could. Even in a culture given to the making of albums and scrapbooks, illustrated poetry in newspapers and magazines was ephemeral, the detritus of print culture. Books, on the other hand, were permanent cultural

---

2   For an expanded context for this image, see Margaret Homans's analysis of how Victorian visual culture constructed Queen Victoria as a middle-class wife and mother.

3   In 1848, the Christmas tree was so unfamiliar to most Victorians that the engraving and paragraph entitled "Christmas Tree at Windsor Castle" were followed by a story, "A German Christmas Tree," intended to "throw some light upon the festive purposes for which [Christmas trees] are employed in Germany" (410).

objects, material repositories of a nation's greatness. Although annuals illustrated with steel engravings accompanied by fiction and poetry were an important feature of the Christmas season from the 1820s onward, it was not until wood-engraving became the dominant means of mechanical production that the illustrated book of poetry emerged as the standard Christmas gift. From the start, this new form of gift book was associated with national values. When S. C. Hall published his two-volume *Book of British Ballads* (1842-1844), his patriotic aim was to bring "the general reader" a treasure trove of national poetry ornamented with the art "of the more accomplished artists of Great Britain—as exhibited in drawing upon wood." According to Hall, this illustrated gift book would not only confirm "the supremacy of our English engravers," but also demonstrate "that the embellished volumes of Germany and France are not of unapproachable excellence, in reference either to design or execution" (Introduction ii, iii).

Like the Christmas tree, the gift book that became so central to Christmas celebrations in Britain – and, almost immediately, the United States and Canada as well – was influenced by the German art of wood-engraving and book illustration. By the mid century, the Christmas book industry was in full operation, with the poetic gift book marketed as a peculiarly British custom, the Teutonic influence having been fully absorbed into the nation's moral character: "The most noticeable mark of Christmas is the universal exchange of books. Our Leipzig fair in London is the announcement of the Christmas books; and being – or thinking that we are – a very good people, the run is upon good books" ("Christmas Books and Christmas-Boxes" 557), wrote the *Saturday Review* critic in 1857. Since national identity is always a contested and patrolled construction, the nineteenth-century boundaries were established in the press by contrasting Teutonic high seriousness with Gallic frivolity:

> [L]et France celebrate its Christmas [...] by sumptuous outlay in bronzes and jewels and the familiar *articles de Paris,* even down to its bonbons and chocolate. Be it ours, as befits the solidity and strength of the manly English character, to spend our money in a way which shall do us credit. [...] So let us go decently to Paternoster-row. (557-58)

The appeal of the gift book to the Christmas shopper lay in the successful marketing of its cultural and ideological freight. As Terence Hoagwood and Kathryn Ledbetter explain, "The book as an object in the material world of use vanishes, under the sponsorship of its sales staff, into the artificial idea of its supposedly spiritual, intellectual, or emotional meaning – that is, into its idealist illusion" (6).

Recognizing a large market, publishers and booksellers reorganized the book trade. As Simon Eliot's research has demonstrated, the emergence of Christmas as the period of greatest production and consumption can be seen in the dramatic redistribution of new titles from spring to fall, beginning in the 1840s. By the second half of the century, the months of October to December represented the year's highest concentration of sales (Eliot 34). The emergence of the gift book, marketed for Christmas consumption, was immediately evident in Victorian visual and material culture, a fact duly noted by the periodical press in its review columns: "The approach of Christmas shows itself on our Library Table, in every fantasy of gold and colour – covering every sort of poetry and illustration with binding worthy of the literary and pictorial artist" ("Our Weekly Gossip"). The gift book's success was also immediate. Within a few years of its appearance on the scene, the *Saturday Review* could declare, "The Christmas Book is a British institution" ("Christmas Books No. 1" 738).

The illustrated press ensured the gift book's marketability as the ideal Christmas present, in articles and reviews that connected the object to the season and its associated cultural values. By 1857, as the *Saturday Review* columnist noted, a new kind of seasonal consumption – associated with commodities rather than food – had emerged: "our Christmas-boxes have become Christmas books, and our Christmas books must reflect what, when we talk fine, we call the characteristics of the age" ("Christmas Books and Christmas Boxes" 557-58). The poetic gift book's "linked evocation of childhood and domesticity" (Maxwell 391) had enormous appeal, because the child it made ideologically central to home, nation, and season was iconic and, hence, endlessly reproducible and consumable.

As contemporary reviewers generally agreed, "The publishers of Christmas books aim[ed] very reasonably at domestic circulation" (Maxwell 391). The primary recipients of these illustrated quartos were women, who generally received them from husbands and fathers; however, their prominent display in middle-class drawing-rooms ensured that the pages would be frequently turned by children and visitors. As one of the rooms of the middle-class house that permitted both inter-generational familial activity and the reception of guests, the drawing-room, with its central book table, was an important cultural site for the construction and reinforcement of values and identities. By offering a refined material object combining art and literature in one complete and tasteful package – as suitable for public display as for family consumption – the gift book had immense appeal for middle-class consumers. Its elegant architecture put a miniaturized home into the hands of its domestic audience, who had the pleasure of viewing ideal reflections of themselves in its beautiful pages.

As had happened with the British adaptation of the German Christmas tree, within a generation the illustrated quarto had become a central feature of Victorian Christmas celebrations. In her review of Christmas gift books for *Blackwood's* in 1861, Margaret Oliphant remarked that

> Books did not rain down out of all the clouds in the firmament of old, when *we* had our holidays; and as for the miracles of paste-board and gilt paper, the glories of Russia leather and *papier maché*, which allure every passer-by into the prevalent mania for Christmas gifts, such delights had certainly not appeared within our horizon. (107)

Notable here are the equation of Christmas gift with Christmas book, as well as the appeal of the material object. Oliphant, however, also celebrates the gift book's cultural content and ideological function: "It is pleasant […] to note what stores of home gratification, what tender mementoes, and treasures of youth, to be gratefully remembered in darker days, are lighting up into a common exhilaration the everyday craft of buying and selling" (107). Then as now, beautiful images of youth and home authorized Christmas excess. The gift book's connection to Christmas did not reside in any explicit reference to the season that produced it, but rather in its ability to package and sell the cultural associations central to it. As A. Alexander explains in *Everyman's Christmas* (1931), "In the course of our English civilization, Christmas has come to stand for and inspire many worthy sentiments and customs, such as the glorifying of childhood and the English love of home" (qtd. in Connelly 10).

Home, childhood and cultural values were all linked in the aptly titled Christmas gift book *Home Thoughts and Home Scenes in Original Poems and Pictures*. The Dalziel Brothers' engraving firm, whose series of fine-art gift books defined the genre and established the market, produced *Home Thoughts and Home Scenes* for Christmas 1864.[4] The book was immediately hailed as the great success of the season. According to the *Art Journal's* critic, "Neither pen nor pencil ever produced truer phases of child-life than are found here" ("Opinions" n. pag.).[5] As I hope to demonstrate, the perceived authenticity of these "Original Poems and Pictures" derived from the powerful combination of aesthetic images and sentimental verses that reinforced Victorian patriarchal ideologies of gender, class and nation.

I

From its inception, *Home Thoughts and Home Scenes* was conceived as an object of domestic consumption, with childhood as its all-consuming theme. The Dalziel Brothers initiated the book's production by commissioning the artist, Arthur Boyd Houghton, to draw 35 pictures on the subject of "Child Life." The Dalziels engraved the drawings and distributed them (in proof) to seven separately commissioned female poets, who were asked to produce a poetic page in response to each design they were given. The book was assembled by printing the pictures and poems on fine paper and encasing them in a splendid red and gilt binding designed by John Leighton. As was their practice, the Dalziels had Routledge distribute *Home Thoughts and Home Scenes* as a guinea book for the festive season, doing their part to ensure sales by advertising, both in the periodical press and in publishing-lists, and by sending copies out for review.

The reviews were almost uniformly positive, a testament to the attractiveness of the aestheticized child at Christmas. The *Saturday Review* predicted "popularity, and a deserved popularity," for this volume "all about childhood, childhood's ways, and childhood's joys and sorrows" ("Christmas Books – No. II" 758). That indefatigable promoter of Christmas as a national event, the *Illustrated London News*, enthusiastically endorsed the purchase of *Home Thoughts and Home Scenes*. "Blazing outside with scarlet and gold and sparkling inside with poetical gems and brilliant specimens of illustrative talent," its critic wrote, this gift book "will make a right royal present" ("Christmas Books"). The gift, as the *Daily News* noted, would be a royal present indeed in the castle otherwise known as the Englishman's

---

4   Throughout this chapter, I cite the 1868 issue of this book. In keeping with Victorian forward dating practice, the first edition was published in 1864 but dated 1865. The Dalziels used Routledge as their publisher/distributor for all their Christmas books.

5   This is an excerpt from the publisher's advertisements at the back of *A Round of Days*, the Dalziel fine-art gift book for 1866.

home; *Home Thoughts* was "A work which will be doated [*sic*] over by ladies and which will even be tenderly regarded by those of the male sex who have an amiable fondness for children" ("Opinions"). Meanwhile, *Notes and Queries* recognized the cross-generational audience the book would enjoy in the domestic drawing-room, and praised the Dalziel firm's achievement: "Oh! how many little critics will turn over with delight the thirty-five pictures which Mr. Houghton has designed for them! pictures which will, if possible, add to the reputation of the Brothers Dalziel, and it would be hard to give them higher praise" ("Opinions"). Given the enthusiastic response, the Dalziels initial "Advertisement," declaring they believed "the theme chosen was certain to excite wide and general interest," showed they knew their market (Preface, *Home Thoughts and Scenes*, n. pag.).

The life of the nineteenth-century middle-class child was so completely absorbed in the domestic that the phrase *Home Thoughts and Home Scenes* was sufficient to suggest the subject, while also indicating the book's format of poems (home thoughts) and pictures (home scenes). The unspoken child in the title bespeaks a coyness about its production, not unlike the silence attendant upon the arrival of infants in Victorian households. Indeed, the book's mode of production was ideologically in keeping with the conservative impulses common to Christmas traditions and patriarchal family arrangements. While the typical gift book of the period was a collection of recycled poems accompanied by illustrations by various hands, *Home Thoughts and Home Scenes* is a throwback to the annuals of the 1830s, when women poets such as L. E. L. were commissioned to write verses in response to steel engravings. In *Home Thoughts and Home Scenes,* the poets illustrated the pictures, rather than the other way around.

This mode of production creates the child as a commodity for domestic consumption by replicating what the Victorians understood to be the sexual role of each gender in the reproductive process – that is, by coupling a generative male with female reception and nurture. The Dalziels chose the artist Arthur Boyd Houghton to provide the book's *Home Scenes* because of some particularly charming illustrations of family life he had done for *Good Words*, using his own wife and children as models. The Dalziels valued Houghton as a bourgeois realist who gave middle-class readers pleasing images of themselves in scenes celebrating contemporary domesticity. Later commentators have recognized the element of fantasy in this idealized and sentimental representation of middle-class family life, suggesting that, in *Home Thoughts and Home Scenes*, Houghton "created an extraordinary universe of rosy-cheeked children, of long-haired beautiful women, of impulsive youth and venerable old age, in settings so various and idyllic as to make it all a never-never land, threatened by the reality of the outside world" (Hogarth 11).

Houghton's pictures for *Home Thoughts and Home Scenes* portray the domestic world as the domain of children, women and the elderly, a space rarely shared with the fathers who supported it. This representation reinforced middle-class ideals of domestic leisure and material comfort. As in John Ruskin's contemporary *Sesame and Lilies,* home is conceived as an idyllic sanctuary of Queen's Gardens completely cut off from the busy world of King's Treasures.[6] Children appear alone or in groups in almost half of Houghton's pictures; with a mother figure in a little under a third; with senior citizens in almost a quarter; and with fathers only twice, or about five percent of the time – and then only in pictures that feature multi-generational family groups.[7] Houghton's depiction of this self-enclosed, beautiful childhood carried considerable emotional weight for consumers purchasing gifts for Christmas. As Claudia Nelson comments, such aestheticized and sentimentalized images of "middle-class children, who operated outside the economy, suggested that life has other purposes than financial profit," providing a treasured icon of hope "in a culture distressed by the undesirable side effects of money-making" (80). In this idealist domestic economy, the children were *in* the King's Treasures but not *of* them. Reflecting and reinforcing this comforting fantasy, *Home Thoughts and Home Scenes*'s images made children particularly desirable objects for adult Christmas consumption.

In their attention to the details of clothes, toys, household furniture and domestic objects, Houghton's pictures emphasize the child's world as a place of great comfort, presumably upheld by the absent father's material acquisition (fig. 8.3). Outdoor scenes place children in bucolic settings, implying their organic connection to nature while emphasizing their absolute separation from the world of trade and business (fig. 8.4). The images are claustrophobic in their compression of figures in pictorial space, and the strong black lines of the wood engravings reinforce this sense of restriction. Rich in decorative details and constrained in spatial boundaries, Houghton's scenes suggest that the Victorian middle-class home needs strong protective barriers in order to maintain its sanctuary from the world of getting and spending.

The Dalziels chose female poets to provide the *Home Thoughts* for Houghton's *Home Scenes* because they believed children and the domestic to be a special feminine preserve – despite the fact that none of these women had, at the time, written children's verses; most were single, childless, independent wage-earners; and several had published on women's rights. For the Dalziels, however, the poets' gender guaranteed credibility for their domestic market. As shrewd businessmen, the Dalziels also recognized the authors' value as household names, whose appearance on the title page of a Christmas book would likely enhance its desirability. Jean Ingelow, Dora Greenwell, Dinah Mulock, the Hon. Mrs. Norton and Amelia Edwards were all well-known writers in 1864. Lesser known, or perhaps even unknown, were Jennett Humphreys and Mrs. Tom Taylor. The latter had, however, made a significant – though unacknowledged –contribution to the Dalziels' previous year's gift book, *Birket Foster's Pictures of English Landscape with Pictures in Words by Tom Taylor.* Although only Tom receives title-page credit, his wife, Laura, contributed two of the poems, modestly appending the initials "L.W.T." after her verses. A published poet

---

6   Ruskin delivered his "Of Queen's Gardens" lecture in 1864, the same year *Home Thoughts and Home Scenes* appeared. It was published the following year, together with "Of King's Treasures," in *Sesame and Lilies.*

7   The series of 35 pictures includes 16 that contain only children; 9 that combine a mother figure with children; 6 that combine a senior citizen with children; 3 that combine children, parents and grandparents (2 of these include fathers), and 1 with a physician, a mother and children.

before marriage, her poetic identity was now subsumed in her husband's (Dalziel 144). Like *Home Thoughts and Home Scenes*, this Christmas book was created by the Dalziels on a theme powerfully resonant with its middle-class readership. Its focus on the bucolic appealed to a nostalgia for rural simplicity in an age of urbanization and industrialization. Foster's pictures, however, did not include the innocent child figure that had been associated with the pastoral at least since Blake. Houghton's pictures for *Home Thoughts and Home Scenes* retained the idyllic and secluded imagery of the Birket Foster volume, but shifted the focus from the English landscape to the English home, adding the child so central to Christmas, and to the cultural values it represented.

Just as the image "Hoisting the Union Jack" required John Latey's poem to draw out its narrative and ideological meanings, Houghton's pictures of children for *Home Thoughts and Home Scenes* needed poetic accompaniment. The texts, however, were to be secondary; they were not to overwhelm the images, which the Dalziels saw as the chief selling feature of the book.[8] When they distributed Houghton's pictures to the seven poets, the Dalziels directed the women to write precisely one "page of verse, either descriptive of or in sympathy with each picture, so that [the gift book] might possess literary as well as pictorial interest" (Dalziel 142). The mode of production of *Home Thoughts and Home Scenes* thus replicated a middle-class domestic economy in which, as Ruskin extolled in *Sesame and Lilies,* a woman's role was to be sympathetically responsive and deferentially secondary to a creative male intelligence (135-36). In art as in life, however, it is no easy matter for intelligent women to restrict themselves to sympathetic vibration and passive reflection. Thus, the division of the theme of child life into pictures by a male artist and poems by female writers also had the perhaps unanticipated effect of dividing the book's miniature world into separate spheres whose orbits were not always aligned. Far from undermining each other, however, these two renditions reinforce the implicit theme of *Home Thoughts and Home Scenes*: that child life is a construct made for the gratification and edification of the adults who both produce and consume it.

II

If, for a Christmas book, as one contemporary critic commented, "the *videri* is part of the *esse*" ("Christmas Books" [1859] 744), the spectacle of aestheticized childhood in *Home Thoughts and Home Scenes* made the volume a particularly appealing cultural commodity. Its iconic pictures and emblematic poems deploy the domestic as the site where middle-class children rehearse their future roles on the adult stage, as bourgeois capitalists, national defenders and moral and spiritual exemplars. The theatrical appeal of Christmas gift books was not lost on reviewers; as one critic enthused: "Here were bindings as gorgeous as the proscenium of any theatre, and within were pictures and stories" (Christmas Books – I" 726). Like the

---

8   In fact, the pictures had significantly greater longevity than the poems. In 1875, Houghton's images were recycled in a book for children entitled *Happy-Day Stories for the Young,* where the pictures were re-captioned and attached to stories written by H. W. Dulcken.

toy theater described by Liz Farr in this collection, the illustrated gift book was a product of nineteenth-century commodity culture, deeply embedded in everyday middle-class domestic life, and involved in shaping the imaginations of children while confirming the fantasies of adults. A reader leafing through the poems and plates of *Home Thoughts and Home Scenes* would have been constantly reminded, as one title declares, that "The Sports of Childhood Show the Future Man" (8).

While the majority of pictures in *Home Thoughts and Home Scenes* feature groups of children alone, an implicit adult presence – in speaker, audience, symbol, or reference – makes children and their world meaningful to grown-ups, and, therefore, marketable. Houghton's picture for "Noah's Ark," for example, depicts three children on their own in a very comfortable middle-class nursery full of books and toys (fig. 8.3). The title is taken from that most ubiquitous of nineteenth-century children's toys, the wooden ark designed to hold an assortment of colorfully painted pairs of animals. In the context of this gift book packaged for Christmas consumption, the title might as well refer to the popular shop, Messrs. Hamley's Noah's Ark Toy Warehouse in High Holborn (Burton 85), as to the biblical story of global destruction followed by salvation of the few. Houghton's bourgeois realism seems more suggestive of Hamley's shop, while Dora Greenwell's poetic interpretation of the image attempts to redirect attention to a spiritual meaning underlying both scene and season.

In the picture, a little boy and girl play on the floor, absorbed in an activity we cannot see, but assume to be connected to the line of animals advancing toward the ark. A third child, apparently bored with the game, has his head on a plump chair cushion, while his feet kick the back of a rocking horse. Overseeing the scene from the window ledge is a jack-in-the-box, perhaps the pictorial surrogate for the absent adult. Tousle-haired and sturdy, these well dressed and evidently pampered children are neither angelic nor ethereal. Nevertheless, Dora Greenwell finds the material features of this familiar middle-class scene full of spiritual meaning. Claiming that the children love "with equal care" the Raven and the Dove, Greenwell sees their "childish play" as rehearsing the Peaceable Kingdom foretold by the Prophet Isaiah:

See the Cow and Bear
Together dwell and feed,
Ox and Lion there
In sweet peace agreed;
Wolf and Lamb one pasture share,
With a little Child to lead. (2)

Greenwell's emblematic method of reading material signs for their spiritual significance glorifies childhood as the type of past and future innocence, perhaps not inappropriate in a book given at Christmas. In the context of the season's orgy of spending, however, the poem, by interpolating these self-absorbed middle-class children into a transcendental and transhistorical schema, also has the comforting effect of removing them from the capitalist economy that supports and justifies their play.

Greenwell's poetic reading is in tune with the Christian festival that celebrates the birth of a child as the harbinger of peace on earth; in this sense, its production for Christmas domestic consumption seems particularly apt. However, its confident association of the "happy lives" of the "old world's old / Fathers with their wives" with the play of contemporary children is unsettled by a troubling visual detail that must be ignored by the poetic text in order to proclaim its message of hope and good will. Houghton's nursery contains a knife embedded in the meshes of the chair on which the disengaged child has laid his head – a suggestion of violence undermining the future paradise that Greenwell reads into this picture. Easy to miss, but impossible to forget once noticed, the blade sharply reminds us not only of the impossibility of perfect children in an eternally harmonious home, but also of the cut-throat capitalism on which the luxury, peace and security of this scene depend.

Home Thoughts and Home Scenes presents the middle-class child's world as a place of great comfort, presumably upheld by the material acquisitions of absent fathers. At the same time, the gift book celebrates the child as capitalist manqué, an implicit confirmation of the domestic and national system in which adult producers and consumers operate, and on which the season's commodity culture relies. This is particularly evident in two scenes that take consumption itself as their subject: "At the Sweets" (3) and "A Scramble for Sugarplums" (21).

Houghton's picture for "At the Sweets" shows a group of five children clandestinely engaged in emptying the pantry's jam pots (fig. 8.5). One child has her hand stuck in a jar, much to her chagrin, but the others remain self-absorbed in pursuing their own pleasures and do not come to her aid. The accompanying poem, written by Jennett Humphreys, conveys sympathetic identification with the pleasure of the many, completely ignoring the anguish of the one. Spoken in the voice of a "grey-hair'd dunce," the grandmotherly speaker addresses the children indulgently, saying "I can understand ye!" and urging them to eat "All the sweets at once!" and to "Fill your hands quite full!" (3). Her identification with the children's greed affirms a human condition in which "For sweets to surfeit we are all athirst!" In this paired picture and poem, there is not only a tacit acceptance, but also a positive encouragement of the individualistic quest for maximum personal pleasure and profit. The message must have made its bourgeois audience feel very comfortable in their stuffed chairs by the drawing-room hearth. Figured here as "father to the man," the child is an emerging capitalist, validated for taking what he can without regard for others.

"A Scramble for Sugarplums" (21) follows a similar theme, but its accompanying poem takes a less positive view of the process of maturation, reading the childhood desire for sweets as the innocent emblem of tainted adult desires to come. In Houghton's composition, the children are again pictured without an adult present, though one must imagine a mature hand distributing the largesse directly in front of the scene – precisely the position of the reader/viewer (fig. 8.6). Intent on getting as many treats as possible, the children are oblivious to the pain they inflict on their companions, as they tumble in a heap of flying limbs and grasping hands. Amelia Edwards's poetic response to this picture begins by celebrating the "innocent delight" of the "happy children," but then uses the occasion to moralize on how soon "childhood passes": "Life soon loses its completeness, / Sugarplums their pristine sweetness." The words "soon" and "lose" reverberate throughout the poem, and, in such a context, it is not surprising that the lyric speaker ends with "Dust and ashes, tears and sin!" wishing to be "a child again." Despite this apparent opposition of childhood innocence and adult experience, however, Edwards draws an analogy between the sugarplums for which children scramble and the "worldly prizes" for which adults jockey:

Rank and title, place and power,
Fame, the triumph of an hour,
Gold that fetters, Love that changes,
Friendship that a word estranges,
Fashion, pleasure, empty station,
Beauty, homage, admiration—
These profane and hollow joys
Are *our* sugarplums and toys. (21)

The emphasis on the plural personal pronoun "our" effects a solidarity between the lyric speaker and the adult reader, a rhetorical move that recognizes the continuum of sensuous and materialistic desires between childhood and maturity.

This continuum is also captured in images that repeat the triangulation of mother, son and nation popularized in the periodical press, and seen in the Christmas supplements of the *Illustrated London News*. "The Enemy on the Wall" (fig. 8.4), for example, presents an idyllic outdoor scene whose central feature is a beautiful young mother and her small son, who buries his face in her skirts. In the background two bigger children brandish garden implements at a rooster perched on the wall, while a little girl appears on the verge of running away. This picture is often identified as one of Houghton's best because of its combination of bourgeois realism and decorative pattern (Reid 196). The central female figure's beauty and grace dominate the composition, almost transforming the children who are grouped around her voluminous skirts to merely decorative effects of shade against her luminous presence. The garden setting, with its profusion of flowers, adds to the ornamental patterning, while the wall in the background forms a dark and seemingly impenetrable barrier between the private, static enclosure of this Queen's Garden and the teeming public life beyond its gates. The masculine symbol of that outside world, the cock (so named in the poem), is identified as the "Enemy on the Wall," a liminal threat to this feminized domestic space. Like the absent father, this male bird can enter and leave the confines of the Queen's Gardens with a freedom of movement apparently denied to its enclosed and protected inhabitants.

The ideological work of this visual image is confirmed by its verbal text. Spoken in the voice of the mother, the accompanying poem by Dinah Mulock urges the older children to attack the cock "with hoe and spade," confident that "the enemy's day is brief" because "Kate will drive him to the park, / Like a second Joan of Arc," while big brother "Robert comes to her relief" (14). There is no gender distinction here regarding each child's duty to protect their garden paradise from foreign invasion. However, the mother castigates only the frightened boy, not the fleeing girl, for failing to join the assault. When the mother chides "little Willie," hiding "behind his mother's gown," for his lack of bravery, she is correcting him for his failure to rehearse his future role as patriarch. Through the mother's gentle mockery – "Frightened! Such a man as you? /At a cock-a-doodle-doo!" – the child learns that to be a man he must not only overcome his emotions, but also take a vigorous part in the protection of the home and, ultimately, the nation. His destined role, like Freddy's in "Hoisting the Union Jack," is to join the ranks of middle-class men whose off-scene labor produces and protects such fantasies of domestic paradise. The mother's teaching is in keeping with Ruskin's in "Of Queen's Gardens": "What the man is at his own gate, defending it, if need be, against insult and spoil, that also [...] he is to be at the gate of his country, leaving his home, if need be, even to the spoiler, to do his more incumbent work there" (165).

In "Grandpapa" (fig. 8.7), the scene shifts to a middle-class drawing-room, containing a multi-generational family group, mirroring the domestic setting in which *Home Thoughts and Home Scenes* was displayed and read. As in the *Illustrated News*'s "Hoisting the Union Jack" and "Christmas Tree at Windsor Castle," this image plays on the central Christmas image of mother and child, but in the context of the contemporary middle-class family and the national values it represented. At the centre, a Madonna-like mother holds up her cherubic infant for the admiration of an elderly man, while her daughter clings to her skirts and her small son pulls on Grandpapa's trousers. A cat plays with a spool of thread on the floor, adding to the scene's domesticity. Contributing to the room's evocation of material comfort are pictures on the wall and a piano adorned with flowers. Almost unnoticeable in the shadows at the left, a father sits in a stuffed armchair with his back to the room, playing with his little daughter. He is a peripheral part of the central family group, yet his presence recalls his crucial importance to it. Compositionally, he is linked to the elderly man and the infant, for the three figures connect in a strong diagonal.

In the poem that accompanies this picture celebrating middle-class family life, Dinah Mulock focuses on the elderly patriarch, and on the respect the children owe him. Spoken in the voice of a child, the poem recites the lesson taught by the angel in the house: "'You children, all of you,' says mamma, / 'Have need to look up to dear grandpapa.'" Inculcating a biblical commandment to honor and respect one's parents and grandparents, the poem ends with the reminder that, in a patriarchal society, both wives and offspring function as representations of the men who provide their homes: "'Remember, my children,' says mamma, / 'You bear the name of your grandpapa'" (19).

III

A gift, of course, always reflects the giver as much as, if not more than, the recipient. As a Christmas gift, *Home Thoughts and Home Scenes* commodified children for domestic consumption in a way that flattered both the giver – the paterfamilias – and the receiver – the lady of the house – by aestheticizing and sentimentalizing a Ruskinian domestic economy of Queen's Gardens and King's Treasuries. The sanctified images were an ideological necessity, a reminder that the nation's future lay in the promise of its children, in the virtues of home, and in the power of the patriarchal system. As a complete Christmas package, the pictures and poetry of *Home Thoughts and Home Scenes* celebrated the season by reinforcing the cultural values of family and nation associated with it in the illustrated periodical press. A marketing tour de force, a Christmas favorite and a joy (almost) forever, the Dalziels' gift book successfully deployed middle-class child life for the pleasure and profit of adult consumers.

I gratefully acknowledge the support of the Social Science and Humanities Research Council of Canada, whose generous funding made the research for this chapter possible. I also wish to express my gratitude to my indefatigable research assistants, Jennifer Douwes, Kate Schweishelm and Abigail Godfrey.

Fig. 8.1   Alfred Hunt, "Hoisting the Union Jack."

CHRISTMAS TREE AT WINDSOR CASTLE.—DRAWN BY J. L. WILLIAMS.—(SEE NEXT PAGE.)

Fig. 8.2   J. L. Williams, "Christmas Tree at Windsor Castle."

Fig. 8.3   Arthur Boyd Houghton, "Noah's Ark."

Fig. 8.4   Arthur Boyd Houghton, "The Enemy on the Wall."

Fig. 8.5   Arthur Boyd Houghton, "At the Sweets."

Fig. 8.6   Arthur Boyd Houghton, "The Scramble for Sugarplums."

Fig. 8.7   Arthur Boyd Houghton, "Grandpapa."

Works Cited

Burton, Anthony. "Small Adults: Education and the Life of Children." *The Victorian Vision: Inventing New Britain.* Ed. John M. Mackenzie. London: V & A Publications, 2001. 75-95.

"Christmas Books." *Saturday Review* (17 Dec. 1859): 744-45.

"Christmas Books." *Illustrated London News* (21 Dec. 1864): 653.

"Christmas Books and Christmas Boxes." *Saturday Review* (19 Dec. 1857): 557-58.

"Christmas Books No. 1." *Saturday Review* (5 Dec.1863): 738-39.

"Christmas Books – I." *Saturday Review* (3 Dec.1870): 726-27.

"Christmas Books – II." *Saturday Review* (17 Dec. 1864): 758-59.

"Christmas Day." *Illustrated London News* (22 Dec. 1860): 575-76.

Connelly, Mark. *Christmas: A Social History.* London: I. B. Tauris, 1999.

Dalziel, George and Edward. *The Brothers Dalziel: A Record of Fifty Years' Work in Conjunction with Many of the Most Distinguished Artists of the Period 1840-1890.* 1901. Rpt. London: B. T. Batsford, 1978.

Dulcken, H.W. *Happy-Day Stories for the Young.* London: George Routledge and Sons, 1875.

Eliot, Simon. "Some Trends in British Book Production, 1800-1919." *Literature in the Marketplace: Nineteenth-Century British Publishing and Reading Practices.* Ed. John O. Jordan and Robert L. Patten. Cambridge: Cambridge UP, 1995. 19-43.

Hall, S. C., ed. *The Book of British Ballads.* Second Series. 2 vols. London: Jeremiah How, 1844.

Hoagwood, Terence Allan and Kathryn Ledbetter. *"Colour'd Shadows": Contexts in Publishing, Printing and Reading Nineteenth-Century British Women Writers.* New York: Palgrave-Macmillan, 2005.

Hogarth, Paul. *Arthur Boyd Houghton.* London: Gordon Fraser, 1981.

Homans, Margaret. "Victoria's Sovereign Obedience: Portraits of the Queen as Wife and Mother." *Victorian Literature and the Victorian Visual Imagination.* Berkeley: U of California P, 1995. 169-97.

Home Thoughts and Homes Scenes in Original Poems and Pictures. Engraved by the Brothers Dalziel. 1864. London: George Routledge, 1868.

Hunt, Alfred. "Hoisting the Union Jack." *Illustrated London News Christmas Number* (Dec. 1876): 1.

Latey, John. "Planting the Union Jack." *Illustrated London News Christmas Number* (Dec. 1876): 2.

Maxwell, Richard, ed. *The Victorian Illustrated Book.* Charlottesville: UP of Virginia, 2002.

Nelson, Claudia. "Growing Up: Childhood." *A Companion to Victorian Literature and Culture.* Ed. Herbert F. Tucker. Oxford: Blackwell, 1999. 69-81.

Oliphant, Margaret. "Merry Christmas!" *Blackwood's Edinburgh Magazine* (Jan. 1861): 107-08.

"Opinions of the Press." Publisher's advertisement and excerpted reviews for *Home Thoughts and Home Scenes,* published at the back of *A Round of Day Described in Original Poems by Some of Our Most Celebrated Poets, and in Pictures by Eminent Artists, Engraved by the Brothers Dalziel.* London: George Routledge and Sons, 1866.

"Our Weekly Gossip." *Athenaeum* 31 (Oct. 1857): 1359.

Reid, Forrest. *Illustrators of the Eighteen Sixties: An Illustrated Survey of the Work of 58 British Artists.* 1928. New York: Dover, 1975.

Ruskin, John. *Sesame and Lilies.* 1865. London: George Allen, 1886.

Williams, J. L. "Christmas Tree at Windsor Castle." *Illustrated London News Christmas Supplement for 1848* (Dec. 1848): 409.

Chapter 9

Maps, Pirates and Treasure: The Commodification of Imperialism in Nineteenth-Century Boys' Adventure Fiction

Ymitri Mathison

R. M. Ballantyne's novel *The Coral Island* (1857), a story about three young boys marooned on an island in the South Seas, spawned a major subgenre of literature. Known as the Robinsonade, this species of adventure fiction, intended primarily for boys, was inspired by Daniel Defoe's *Robinson Crusoe* (1719).[1] A quarter of a century after *The Coral Island* appeared, Robert Louis Stevenson's *Treasure Island* (1881) and H. Rider Haggard's *King Solomon's Mines* (1883) offered readers revisions of Ballantyne's story, now as a quest for hidden treasure.[2] All three texts portray both the transnational spread of imperialist ideology and the increasing commodification taking place within western individuals' lives.[3] In both *The Coral Island* and *Treasure Island*, boys' adventures are conflated with the mercantile speculation and "get rich quick" schemes implicit in the era's capitalist culture. *King Solomon's Mines*, however, is intended primarily for adults, and its hero is 55 years old. Haggard's novel reveals that the textual means of instilling imperialist values into young males may be found also in adult-centered fiction. This similarity illuminates the ideological continuity between fictional youthful adventure and actual adult commerce. It also underscores the commodification for adults of childhood as a site of wish-fulfillment, and the commodification of adulthood for children as a sanction to act upon such wishes later in life.

In this chapter, I focus on three major stock devices that frame the genre of boys' adventure fiction: maps, pirates and treasure. In doing so, I aim to expose spaces in which imperial authority reinforced the anxieties experienced by Victorians as a result of imperial trade, the flooding of the domestic market with new commodities, and an increase in the ranks of the nouveaux riches. Adventure fiction rehearsed the

---

1   For a discussion of British and other European retellings of *Robinson Crusoe*, see Martin Green.

2   *King Solomon's Mines* is an adult adventure novel, written in the vein of boys' adventure fiction. Haggard was directly influenced by *The Coral Island* and *Treasure Island*.

3   Patrick Brantlinger's discussion of nineteenth-century fiction, as "a commodity, exchangeable for money" (*Fictions* 144), explores the place of literature in the influence of commodity culture on individuals' lives and identities.

colonial experience and offered a conduit to capitalism's economic and individual desires. The genre codified and mapped – in other words, taxonomically classified – the empire's exotic objects, lands and peoples so that they could be more readily consumed by a wide spectrum of the public – in particular, the middle class.

During the nineteenth century, literature in Britain became increasingly affordable for those with lower incomes, such as the working class, the poor and the young. Moreover, fiction was more frequently marketed to children, through materials such as penny dreadfuls, and magazines aimed specifically at boys and girls. In addition, as Peter Hunt notes, a shift toward a more child-centered approach in children's literature occurred about 1850, "the point at which books began to move from the didactic to the recreational" (9).[4] During the second half of the century, one of the most popular genres of literature aimed at boys was adventure fiction, with its stock elements of pirates and the search for hidden treasure in exotic landscapes. Pirates, as Liz Farr notes in her contribution to this collection, were equally common in the toy theaters that had become a staple of many middle-class boys' childhood. Because, historically, pirates trafficked primarily in human capital and in concrete forms of wealth, such as precious stones, currency and goods, these works for children epitomized the traditional conceptualization of wealth as material "treasure," even as they contrasted it with the contemporary industrialist and imperialist emphasis on capital, involving national debt and public credit.

This ideology of adventure was one of the British empire's major means of indoctrinating the young, who grew up to adopt its principles as a means of making their own fortunes. For boys and young men in particular, selfhood and subjectivity were circumscribed by a culture that defined worth through money and consumerism. Money was the ultimate commodity, traditionally based on a metallic standard of gold and silver; capitalism then transubstantiated it into abstract numbers in ledgers, so that "symbols [took] the place of tokens, as tokens had taken the place of money, and as money had taken the place of commodities" (Tilden 19).[5] Reinforcing an ideology of white domination and capitalist hegemony, boys' adventure fiction propelled an economic fundamental of the marketplace: individual desire expressed through a public mode of production. Meanwhile, adults' consumption of juvenile fiction guaranteed its success among a broader and more influential readership.[6] As Patrick Brantlinger argues,

> an adolescent quality pervade[d] imperialist literature. [...] And because imperialism always entailed violence and exploitation and therefore could never bear much scrutiny, propagandists found it easier to leave it to boys to "play up, play up, and play the game" than to supposedly more mature audiences. Much imperialist discourse was thus directed

---

4   Hunt further contends that the "first golden age" of children's literature began with the works of Lewis Carroll, George MacDonald and Charles Kingsley (30). Although I believe it is incorrect to suggest that these authors created the "first golden age," they definitely popularized children's literature.

5   Tilden wrote this in 1936, with reference to the American Great Depression; however, in the nineteenth century, money was already transubstantiating into abstract credit and debit on both sides of the Atlantic.

6   Prime Minister Gladstone read *Treasure Island* in one sitting (Saposnik 106).

at a specifically adolescent audience, the future rulers of the world. [...] Britain turned youthful as it turned outward, following a regressive parallel to "going native." (*Rule of Darkness*, 199)

While young readers consumed these works and thereby helped to commodify the British Empire, they were also being indoctrinated into furthering its ambitions of mapping the remotest parts of the globe, conquering foreign lands and exploiting indigenous peoples. Discussing J. A. Hobson's *The Psychology of Jingoism* (1901), Thomas Richards argues that the "English [...] believed that overseas expansion was necessary for capitalism to survive in England. [...] In truth, they were inclined to celebrate the circular logic of politico-economic expansionism, according to which expansion meant export and export meant expansion" (*Commodity* 131). At the same time, deeply invested in the imperialist project, the middle class's daily existence became increasingly consumerist. For this group, individual subjectivity became defined by states of desire and conspicuous consumption that, in fact, encouraged mass conformity and anonymity.

During the nineteenth century, the novel was one of capitalism's most important tools for self-fashioning, helping to consolidate the cultural and economic value system that commodified individuals' lives. Meanwhile, the cultural production of childhood as a site of innocence, the "fantasy of the child – essentially different from but in continuity with the adult – [spoke] to the British readership at the moment of the entrenchment of industrial capitalism, [which included] the unprecedented expansion of the empire, and the production of literary realism" (Armstrong xi-xii). Imperialist novels and children's fiction, for example, promoted a middle-class value of "manliness" congruent with a public-school ethos that prepared boys to take up positions of authority (Green 120-21). Under the banner of religious and cultural superiority, these works assigned value to Britishness, while placing it squarely within a masculinist and homosocial colonial administration. They prepared young male readers for participation in the appropriation of overseas territories and the subjugation of their native inhabitants.

Most boys' adventure fiction begins with a map, signifying the symbolic importance of cartography to heroes' quests for the wealth and social status that the empire promised its servants. During the nineteenth century, the science of cartography, the textual charting of geographical boundaries, fixed divisions among competing European nations as they scrambled to carve up the world. Cartography helped to create not just the impetus for imperialism, but imperialism itself, by mapping a territory's boundaries and wealth. Previously an exotic object or prosaic navigational tool, the map now became a familiar, domesticated item, reinforcing an economic program that construed the world as a giant marketplace. Offering idealized images of international relations, overseas maps became part of Britain's museum culture, what Thomas Richards describes as the "imperial archive," in which knowledge was classified and codified, and in which the fantasy of the "symbolic unity" of the empire was created (*Imperial* 3).[7] As events such as the

---

7   Discussing this issue in terms of nationhood, Richards argues that the "symbolism of the British Empire was built on an extended foundation of national symbols," such as

Great Exhibition of 1851 introduced more foreign commodities to the public, maps became more desirable as fetishistic objects whose "blank spaces" and red-colored imperial territories promised possibilities of adventure and easy wealth.

Gilles Deleuze and Félix Guattari argue that maps' symbolic discursiveness – their openness to revision and manipulation – renders meaningless the concrete, geographical boundaries they represent. In their view, a map is

> detachable, reversible, susceptible to constant modification. It can be torn, reversed, adapted to any kind of mounting, reworked by an individual, group, or social formation. It can be drawn on a wall, conceived as a work of art, constructed as a political action or as a meditation. (12)

Adventure fiction foregrounded such malleable maps, putting them within easy reach of consumers' imaginations. Stevenson, for example, drew the map of "Treasure Island," and only later wrote the novel that goes with it, for the amusement of his twelve-year-old stepson, Lloyd Osborne (Letley vii).[8] For the book's main character, Stevenson produced a scared but courageous boy with whom young people could identify, thereby encouraging them to participate in the map's imaginative manipulation.

Maps' artificial suggestion of bounded order belied the chaotic process of world-making entailed by imperialism. The concept of piracy reflected this same inconsistency. Both legitimate, state-sanctioned trade (as in the case of the East India Trading Company) and illegitimate trade or piracy (frequently unofficially sanctioned by the state) often involved the exploitation, and even destruction of natives in the name of progress. Nina Gerassi-Navarro suggests that, to Spain during the Renaissance, then Britain's arch-enemy, Sir Francis Drake "would certainly have been considered a pirate, [but] Philip Gosse in *The Pirate's Who's Who*, calls Drake a 'most fervent patriot.' [...] Thus the categories of pirate and patriot undoubtedly depended on the point of view from which they were presented" (17). [9] Such ambiguities with regard to the terms "pirate" and "patriot" exhibit the instability of imperial identities in general. The situation applies equally well to the nineteenth century, when colonial Britishness, for example, reflected an economy in which value was ascribed to individual entrepreneurship, characterized by predatory domination. The intense competition for claiming treasure, the "get rich quick" mentality and the "finders keepers" logic of the era: these were only further reinforced by the actual

---

"proclaiming Victoria 'Empress of India' and the creation of domestic institutions like the British Museum" (*Imperial* 3).

    8   In her introduction to *Treasure Island*, Emma Letley quotes a letter, written by Stevenson to a friend, showing his pecuniary interest in his writings, and his awareness of his audience: "I am now on another lay for the moment, purely owing to Lloyd, this one; but I believe there's more coin in it than any amount of crawlers [three-decker novels]: now, see here, '*The Sea Cook, or Treasure Island*: A Story for Boys'" (vii).

    9   Philip Gosse (1879-1959), an important early-twentieth-century historian on piracy, published *The Pirates' Who's Who, Giving Particulars of the Lives & Deaths of the Pirates & Buccaneers* (1924).

discoveries of gold and diamond deposits in the colonies, especially in the South African Transvaal.

Piracy often functions in adventure fiction by displacing Britain's greed, criminality and exploitation of natives onto the working class, thereby allowing the middle classes to partake of the image of an idealized, imperialist and chivalric Englishness – an identity originally characteristic of the upper classes, especially the aristocracy. When piracy is romanticized, and claimed by readers to embody the essence of their national character, however, it is defined, through the language of patriotism and competition, against a rival state such as Spain. In Stevenson's *Treasure Island*, for example, Squire Trelawney praises the buccaneer Captain Flint for the fear he instituted in the Spanish: "He was the bloodthirstiest buccaneer that sailed. Blackbeard was a child to Flint. The Spaniards were so prodigiously afraid of him, that I tell you, sir, I was sometimes proud he was an Englishman" (32). Britishness conveniently incorporates greed, betrayal and murder by rationalizing them as evils necessary for furthering the expansion of the British Empire. However, it is significant that Squire Trelawney, a Cornishman, incorporates into himself the nationality of Englishness, not the overarching nationality of Britishness, a more inclusive identity.

James Kincaid argues that "innocence is a faculty needed not at all by the child but very badly by the adult who put it there in the first place" (73).[10] As nineteenth-century adventure fiction reoriented public-school culture toward a world of travel and violence, it incorporated elaborate childhood fantasies, and took pleasure in the young's facility for role play and games. The Victorians thereby transformed imperialism into a delimited system stimulated by children's fantasies about outwitting pirates, subduing natives and discovering hidden treasure.

Both *The Coral Island* and *Treasure Island* are first and foremost children's novels foregrounding a delight in playing games. Each text, for example, is quick to introduce an impetus for adventure: in *The Coral Island*, three boys find themselves marooned on a deserted island and, in *Treasure Island*, Jim Hawkins inherits Billy Bones's treasure map because he died in his parents' inn (23). Even *King Solomon's Mines*, although not a children's novel *per se*, uses the frame of colonial chivalry, and incorporates the game of the treasure hunt for its three adult companions.

Haggard's text reflects Simon Gikandi's claim that, "if industrial England had come to be defined by the realistic novel[,] the colony continued to be the space that generated romance and utopia" (101). As Gikandi notes, "we enter the space of the other not to discover its unique history (does it have a history?) but to restage our unique national identity – to witness the triumph of the English spirit unencumbered by the disease of industrialization" (101). Similarly, in the adventure novels by Ballantyne, Stevenson and Haggard, adults commodify and resituate boyish adventure in the framework of an imperial economy in such a way that it "exalts the warrior-explorer-engineer-administrator-imperial paladin [... while] energizing and validating the

---

10   In her study of children and the theater, also in this collection, Marah Gubar demonstrates that adults did not always admire the young for being, by their innocence, distinct from adults. Indeed, child actors were frequently appreciated for their abilities to mimic adult identities.

empire as a vehicle for excitement, adventure and wish-fulfillment through action"
(Richards, Introduction 2-3). Ralph Rover's preface to *The Coral Island*, for instance,
situates his adult re-telling of his youthful adventures at the moment of consumption
by other boy readers. The narrator says he hopes these readers "may derive valuable
information, much pleasure, great profit, and unbounded amusement from its pages"
(xxx). Ralph's conception of information as something to be consumed reflects the
reifying influence of imperialist commerce in general.

In *The Coral Island*, the unmapped South Sea isle on which the boys are marooned
is a pre-lapsarian realm into which the adult world eventually intrudes in the form
of natives, pirates and missionaries. As Diana Loxley argues, however, even the
youths themselves function as mature conquistadors whose "ultimate identity, their
significant identity, resides in their Englishness rather than adolescence" (115). The
boys quickly establish a hierarchy based on age, with 18-year-old Jack as their leader.
In the play mode of children, they also invoke the imperial ethos of claiming the
territory for England, the first step before it can be named, mapped and administered,
and the natives civilized – as they saw it – through Christianity:

> "We've got an island all to ourselves. We'll take possession in the name of the king; we'll
> go and enter the service of its black inhabitants. Of course we'll rise, naturally, to the top
> of affairs. White men always do in savage countries. You shall be king, Jack; Ralph, prime
> minister; and I shall be – ." (16)

In this *tabula rasa* realm, the boys perform the colonial process of world-making
through an implicit belief in their racial superiority, creating a state through which to
govern not only the natives, but also each other.

In Ballantyne's novel, the natives' eventual political subjugation and conversion
to Christianity (with the coming of the missionaries) represents colonialism's grand
narrative, its subtext involving the circulation of commodities through the colonists'
easy access to raw materials (in this case, sandalwood). Ralph, who had been
kidnapped by pirates, inherits their schooner after its captain and crew are murdered
by natives. With the permission of Bill, the last dying pirate, Ralph sails to the Coral
Island to rescue his companions, Jack and Peterkin, and the vessel becomes the three
boys' treasure: "Here we are, on the wide Pacific, in a well-appointed schooner,
which is our own – at least no one has a better claim to it than we have" (260).

The problematic logic of the "better claim" extends to the characters' attitudes
toward non-Europeans as aspects of the geography. Nineteenth-century cartography
incorporated spatial surveillance by the imperial state through the dual imperatives
of geographical mapping of a territory and policing of its native inhabitants. When
the three boys systematically map the Coral Island on foot, the map's spatial
coordinates are reified linguistically onto Britain, as its geographic boundaries
become increasingly elastic:

> We found this to be the highest point of the island, and from it we saw our kingdom
> lying, as it were, like a map around us. As I have always thought it impossible to get a
> thing properly into one's understanding without comprehending it, I shall beg the reader's
> patience for a little while I describe our island. (47)

Ralph's carefully detailed account of the island's topography, which continues for two-and-a-half pages, is interwoven with taxonomic descriptions of its flora and fauna. A natural historian's articulation of the order of things is thereby embedded into colonial authority, legitimizing its domination of the landscape and the use of its goods.

For Ballantyne's boys, food is always plentiful and in a constant state of ripeness. The island boasts breadfruit, yams, plums, coconuts, small game, pigs and ducks. This congeries of freely available products brings to mind British consumers' insatiable appetite for goods from the colonies. By erasing the mode of production from the commodities they desired, British consumers were able to sustain a façade of innocence regarding the exploitation inherent to their imperial economy's access to goods. With *The Coral Island*, Ballantyne offers a similarly idealized vision of an economy's mode of production in which, even before the arrival of Europeans, natives are either an absent presence, or on the periphery in non-productive areas. This placement of the natives gives the three boys free rein to consume the island's abundant raw materials and resources, whether they are eating produce, or building a boat on which to explore the surrounding islands. Mapping the terrain is crucial, not only to survey and discover the territory's natural resources, but also to police the indigenous population and insure the colonists' safety. When natives arrive on the island, the boys watch, horrified, from their hiding place, while first two warring parties try to kill each other, and then the victors consume the bodies of the defeated. Martine Hennard Dutheil suggests that Ballantyne's "insistence on the veracity of the lurid descriptions of cannibalism acts evidences not only morbid fascination but also anxiety about their truth-value" (108). In this context, the act of mapping functions not only as the formulation of a blueprint leading to buried treasure, fame and fortune. It also separates the familiar from the unfamiliar, and the imperial state from its peripheralized regions. In addition, it distinguishes the civilized from the primitive, as the boys demonstrate when they chivalrously rescue a fair-skinned virgin who is about to be sacrificed by the victorious tribe of cannibals.

The functions of mapping in *The Coral Island* are echoed in *Treasure Island*. Stevenson states that he conceived of the novel as "'all about a map, and a treasure, and a mutiny, and a derelict ship'" (qtd. in Letley vii). The work's quest for treasure involves cut-throat competition sustained by imperialism and capitalist modes of production. Jim Hawkins, the now-adult narrator, informs the reader that he has been asked by "Squire Trelawney, Dr. Livesey, and the rest of these gentlemen [...] to write down the whole particulars about Treasure Island, from the beginning to the end, keeping nothing back but the bearings of the island" (1). Set in "the year of grace 17__," at the height of piracy on the high seas, Jim's refusal to reveal the location of the island reinforces a basic tenet of capitalism: the importance of protecting a valuable commodity – in this case, part of the still-buried treasure – against the predatory character of Jim's own culture.

In a capitalist society, the competition for goods creates a moral imperative regarding who has the right to the wealth promised by its imperial economy. The Victorian middle class assumed this right by defining itself through an ethos of gentility, subsumed into imperialist Englishness. Although Jim is not initially of this class, *Treasure Island* legitimizes his right to a share of the treasure through his association with Dr. Livesey and Squire Trelawney, both solid, middle-class figures who reflect public-school values of courage, friendship and sportsmanship. For example, when the pirate Billy Bones's cohorts lay siege to Jim's inn in order to retrieve the map to Treasure Island, it is Trelawney who generously offers Jim sanctuary in his home. It warrants emphasizing, however, that the squire is not necessarily altruistic here, since he knows that Jim owns the map containing the possibility of untold wealth. Jim further demonstrates his alignment with middle-class readers through his resourcefulness in single-handedly stealing the ship back from the pirates, as well as through his horror when he watches Long John Silver murder a cohort in order to prevent a mutiny and to keep a greater share of the treasure.

Stevenson's novel focuses on the opposition between the civilized and the savage, especially the Europeans' fears of degenerating into barbarism as the wealth of material treasure takes on a life of its own. These fears are shown as justified when the acquisitive hand of capitalism itself proves to be cannibalistic, as the European pirates essentially prey on each other and mutiny against legitimate authority, represented by Squire Trelawney and Captain Smollet. In *Treasure Island*, Otherness is thereby depicted as internalized within the market economy itself, the only "savage" on the island turning out to be a castaway, a former pirate and shipmate of Long John Silver, who has recovered the treasure (183). Until the treasure is unearthed, it is the map to the buried wealth that functions as the spectacle in the text's consumerist imagination. The map, in other words, is a blueprint for the imperial state's impetus for colonialism. As Fiona McCulloch argues, the state

> legitimises itself by claiming to civilize savage nations whilst concealing the insatiable appetite of Empire. [...] Like Ballantyne's *The Coral Island*, Stevenson's novel disrupts the fixed binarism of criminality and colonialism, identifying both as expressions of mercantile self-interest. (78-79)

Seemingly uninhabited by natives, Treasure Island's only value is mercantile – the buried treasure. The pirates, whose members range from gentlemen to deck-hands, embody one of the major characteristics of commodity culture, its criminality.

In *Treasure Island*, capitalism's alienating and dehumanizing influence on interpersonal relations further reinforces the assignment of value to commodities. Dr. Livesey, for example, calmly and callously steps over the murdered pirate Pew's body in order to retrieve the packet of papers that includes the map to Treasure Island. In this cut-throat competition for a finite product, an imperial ideology, characterized by the direct and brutal exercise of power, is asserted for the sake of the elaborate fantasies of consumption promised by the treasure. Stevenson's novel exposes the consequences of a free-trade ideology in which the value of human life is reduced to currency, and the self is defined by desire, and reduced to a commodity. As Jim notes, "for my companions, it was the knowledge that seven hundred thousand pounds in gold lay somewhere buried below its [the tree's] spreading shadow. The thought of the money, as they [the pirates] drew nearer, swallowed up their previous terrors" (179). The middle-class characters displace naked greed and the terrors of distrust, betrayal and death onto criminals, pirates and the lower classes.

Meanwhile, they depict themselves as earning the right to the treasure because of their loyalty, friendship and courage – virtues that are part of an imperialism in which the "aristocratic code of chivalry was strategically assimilated to fit the needs of a rising class in an expanding empire" (Krishnaswamy 54).

At one point in Stevenson's novel, the squire arrogantly assumes the right to the treasure while dismissing the rights of the pirates, a move that he justifies because they lack the gentleman's code of conduct: "'What were these villains after but money? What do they care for but money? For what would they risk their rascal carcasses but money? [...] [I]f we have the clue you talk about, I fit out a ship in Bristol dock, and take you and Hawkins here along, and I'll have that treasure if I search a year'" (32). In this passage, Squire Trelawney converts greed into survival, a matter of life and death, which he in turn bases on discovering the treasure and its untold riches. Wolfgang Haug suggests that "money steps between all commodities and mediates their exchange. [...] It grants to whomever controls it a power limited only in quantity over all the particular qualities; as money achieves omnipotence, all former qualitative powers are overthrown" (105). Implicated within this consumerist economy, the omnipotence of the novel's treasure overwhelms individual subjectivity. This is why Long John Silver can betray his fellow mutineers to save Jim and his companions, and then escape with "one of the sacks of coin worth, perhaps, three or four hundred guineas" (190). Although the territorial possession of foreign land has historically been rationalized as patriotism, marked by the prestige of coloring more blank spaces on the map with red ink, the map of Treasure Island – and maps in most Victorian adventure novels – essentially embody *terra nullis* (empty land), the only agenda of the adventurers being to lay claim to treasure, a claim justified only by a premise of "finders keepers," rather than to develop the land and administer its native inhabitants.

Despite its focus on adults, the grand narrative of imperialism promised by *King Solomon's Mines* also begins with the childish delight of a map, a blueprint for a treasure-hunt, disguised as a search for Sir Henry Curtis's brother. But while Ballantyne and Stevenson take the greed and criminality inherent in Britain's domination of overseas territories and displace them onto pirates, Haggard shifts these negative qualities onto the usurping king of Kukuanaland and his followers. By wearing an enormous diamond on his forehead, this native monarch displays both his primitiveness and his ignorance of the jewel's real economic value. Greed, the traditional impetus behind a quest for treasure, is rationalized in this novel by ideals of service, honor, duty and love of family. When Curtis finances the venture, he promises the hero, Quatermain, that, should he die during the quest, his son in medical school "shall be suitably provided for" (33). This is a novel of imperial manners, played out in a masculine world from which women are almost entirely absent. These manners are endorsed by a genealogy of violence and adventurous militarism, and they are transfused with the chivalric code of colonialist Englishness. Discussing Rudyard Kipling's novel, *Kim* (1901), Edward Said argues that, in the imperial adventure novel, "the common romance of fiction, and the enduring institution of marriage have been circumvented, avoided, all but ignored" (12). The happily-ever-after ending is defined in such novels by their heroes' financial security and male-to-male companionship, suggesting not only the implicit homosocial world of the empire and its servants, but also the idealized world of the Victorian boy's public school ethos (as yet uncontaminated by females).

An intrinsic part of the adventure, the map in Haggard's novel serves as the key guide for Quatermain, Sir Henry Curtis and his friend Captain Good, as they attempt to retrace the footsteps of Sir Henry's brother, who went missing during his search for the fabled King Solomon's Mines. A dying Portuguese adventurer who had failed to reach the mines bequeathed the map to Quatermain many years before. That adventurer had himself inherited the map from a sixteenth-century Portuguese explorer, José da Silvestra. Quatermain's map is an outline of the *terra incognita* that he has dreamt of exploring but never dared to enter on account of the land's inhospitable nature. Anne McClintock proposes that Haggard's map is

> explicitly sexualized. The land, which is also the female, is literally mapped in male body fluids [blood], and da Silvestre's [*sic*] phallic cleft bone [pen] becomes the organ through which he bequeaths the patrimony of surplus capital to his white heirs, investing them with the authority and power befitting the keepers of sacred treasure. (3)

In this sense, Quatermain's map is a malleable text, charting dreams of adventure for the intrepid, and offering adult and young readers a sensuous, albeit vicarious, experience of imagined acquisition; the reader's imagination becomes the fetishized commodity, embedded in a colonial discourse legitimizing domination. At the same time, however, for an imperial state such as Britain, possessing territories it cannot directly control or administer, the "map occupies a position of privilege. Its fiction remains the one most seductive to the imperial state: the fiction of fixity, of ordered, visible, and bounded space" (Baucom 94).[11] In *King Solomon's Mines*, the adventurers map an idyllic imperial state in which the native king, Ignosi, is a westernized servant whom they had restored to the throne. Loyal to the empire, Ignosi supports the imperial state's goals, and willingly gives up his wealth for them. Some of the native women are even willing to form liaisons with the adventurers, as Foulata does with Captain Good, before sacrificing herself for him. The friendly king also informs the three adventurers of an easier, more hospitable route to the mines: the long, hazardous journey depicted on the European map was unnecessary, even if it ensured a grand narrative of imperial adventure.

Although cartography may seem an intrinsically adult practice, the idealized nature of maps, and their importance to the world of imaginative fantasy, "may provide a sense of empowerment and control to young audiences, but it also reterritorializes childhood for the adult author and reader" (Honeyman 63). In *Treasure Island*, Jim Hawkins cannot give readers an accurate map. Quatermain, however, is able to make his map public because the entrance to the treasure chamber is sealed off. This physical barrier makes the treasure of the African mines inaccessible to other explorers or prospectors, and precludes any "gold rush" to the mines. As Quatermain notes, "The millions of pounds' worth of gems that lie in the three stone coffers will never shine round the neck of an earthly beauty" (302).

---

11   In *The Imperial Archive*, Richards claims that, because Britain's territories were dominated informally, it was militarily and administratively over-extended in its colonies; "'belonging' to the British empire was thus very often a fictive affiliation" (1-2).

In *The Coral Island, Treasure Island* and *King Solomon's Mines*, the narrator-heroes ensure their young readers cannot hope to follow their maps. This move ensures narrative closure by severing the fantasy world of the adventures – shipwrecks, pirates, cannibalistic natives and treasure – and returning readers to the adult world of civilization. In all three novels, the full-grown narrators reconstruct an idealized childhood. It would seem that, in the adult world, heroes can attain some wealth, but not the untold wealth of an imaginative child.

Ballantyne, Stevenson and Haggard all depict concrete wealth transformed into emblems of credit. The schooner of *The Coral Island*, the gold on *Treasure Island* and the diamonds in *King Solomon's Mines* become assets that give the narrators loci of authority and the leisure to write their histories. The focus in the novels is on the hero-narrators, who earn their patrimonies through courage, baptism by fire, altruism, and generosity to both friends and deserving converted natives. All three tales legitimize their heroes' right to their treasures by situating the characters' rigid middle-class ethos in a typological universe of good and evil peopled by pirates or by heathen, cannibalistic natives. In *King Solomon's Mines*, following the death of the evil native witch Gagool, the three Englishmen emerge with part of the treasure, which, as McClintock summarizes, "give[s] birth to three orders – the male, *reproductive* order of patriarchal monogamy; the white *economic* order of mining capital; and the global, *political* order of empire" (1, italics in original). The descriptions of the treasure troves in both *King Solomon's Mines* and *Treasure Island* read like a list of the contents of Aladdin's cave. When diamonds and gold were actually discovered in South Africa, these commodities glutted the market and caused their own devaluation; notably, however, at the end of both *Treasure Island* and *King Solomon's Mines*, part of the treasures remain buried. The authors thereby ensure that Britain's economy is not flooded with an excess of resources that will undermine their own monetary and symbolic value. Indeed, at the end of *King Solomon's Mines*, the London jewelers actually urge Sir Henry Curtis "to sell [the diamonds] by degrees, for fear we should flood the market" (319). Quatermain gives his readers the explicit value of his treasure, and his generosity of dividing it between himself, Captain Good and Sir Henry's brother reveals that upper-class culture is fashioned not through commodities, but by the chivalric code of gentility. This cultural fashioning stands in marked contrast to the lower-class, greedy, murderous pirates that populate *The Coral Island* and *Treasure Island*. With Quatermain's diamonds being "of the finest water, and equal in every way to the best Brazilian stones" (318), not only is Britain assured of remaining a major imperial power, but it also becomes a major producer of commodities, able to compete with its two major imperial rivals, Spain and the emerging United States. Rather than distancing consumers from the goods they desire, the African treasure becomes a consumerist spectacle for both the book's fictional adventurers and its readers. As in the other two novels, the exchange value of wealth is transformed, in Haggard's text, into an increase in social status. Quatermain's third of the profits allows him to return to England, buy a country manor house near Sir Henry Curtis's home, Brayley Hall, and live the lifestyle of the gentry. Ultimately, land – not liquid assets, credit, commodities or commerce – confer on Haggard's hero a rise from the bourgeoisie to the landed gentry.

For imperial states such as that of nineteenth-century Britain, the possession of an empire brought with it the possession of domestic security. For the individual, however, financial security became a means of self-realization. Each of the novels I have discussed concludes with the conversion of the exploits of the hero-narrator and his companions into a standard of living beyond their previous means. The heroes find themselves with sufficient wealth to purchase enhanced social status. The stock devices in nineteenth-century boys' adventure fiction – maps, pirates and treasure – underscore this connection between imperialism, capitalism and the fashioning by individuals of their identities. By employing these devices, Ballantyne, Stevenson and Haggard articulated for their audiences – young and old alike – the place of adventure, tempered by the rhetoric and logic of imperialism, in an era increasingly invested in the commodification of the individual. More importantly, they reinforced an understanding of the self defined through material possessions and shaped by the public exchange and consumption of commodities.

Works Cited

Armstrong, Nancy. "Victorian Children's Literature as Political Foreplay." Preface. *The Fictional Role of Childhood in Victorian and Early Twentieth-Century Children's Literature.* By Fiona McColloch. Lewiston, NY: Edwin Mellen, 2004. xi-xviii.

Ballantyne, R. M. *The Coral Island.* 1857. Ed. J. S. Bratton. Oxford: Oxford UP, 1990.

Baucom, Ian. *Out of Place: Englishness, Empire, and the Locations of Identity.* Princeton: Princeton UP, 1999.

Brantlinger, Patrick. *Fictions of State: Culture and Credit in Britain, 1694-1994.* Ithaca: Cornell UP, 1996.

---. *Rule of Darkness: British Literature and Imperialism, 1830-1914.* Ithaca: Cornell UP, 1988.

Deleuze, Gilles and Félix Guattari. *A Thousand Plateaus: Capitalism and Schizophrenia.* Trans. Brian Massumi. Minneapolis: U of Minnesota P, 1987.

Dutheil, Martine Hennard. "The Representation of the Cannibal in Ballantyne's *The Coral Island*: Colonial Anxieties in Victorian Popular Fiction." *College Literature* 28 (2001): 105-22.

Gerassi-Navarro, Nina. *Pirate Novels: Fictions of Nation Building in Spanish America.* Durham: Duke UP, 1999.

Gikandi, Simon. *Maps of Englishness: Writing Identity in the Culture of Colonialism.* New York: Columbia UP, 1996.

Gosse, Philip. *The Pirates' Who's Who, Giving Particulars of the Lives & Deaths of the Pirates & Buccaneers.* London: Dulau, 1924.

Green, Martin. *The Robinson Crusoe Story.* University Park: Pennsylvania State UP, 1990.

Haggard, H. Rider. *King Solomon's Mines.* 1883. Ed. Dennis Butts. Oxford: Oxford UP, 1989.

Haug, Wolfgang Fritz. *Commodity Aesthetics, Ideology and Culture*. New York: International General, 1987.

Honeyman, Susan. *Elusive Childhood: Impossible Representations in Modern Fiction*. Columbus: Ohio State UP, 2005.

Hunt, Peter. *An Introduction to Children's Literature*. Oxford: Oxford UP, 1994.

Kincaid, James R. *Child-Loving: The Erotic Child and Victorian Culture*. London: Routledge, 1992.

Krishnaswamy, Revathi. *Effeminism: The Economy of Colonial Desire*. Ann Arbor: U of Michigan P, 1998.

Letley, Emma. Introduction. *Treasure Island*. By Robert Louis Stevenson. Ed. Emma Letley. Oxford: Oxford UP, 1985: vii-xxix.

Loxley, Diana. *Problematic Shores: The Literature of Islands*. New York: St. Martin's, 1990.

McClintock, Anne. *Imperial Leather: Race, Gender and Sexuality in the Colonial Context*. London: Routledge, 1995.

McCulloch, Fiona. *The Fictional Role of Childhood in Victorian and Early Twentieth-Century Children's Literature*. Lewiston, NY: Edwin Mellen, 2004.

Richards, Jeffrey. Introduction. *Imperialism and Juvenile Literature*. Ed. Jeffrey Richards. Manchester: Manchester UP, 1989: 1-11.

Richards, Thomas. *The Commodity Culture of Victorian England: Advertising and Spectacle, 1851-1914*. Stanford: Stanford UP, 1990.

---. *The Imperial Archive: Knowledge and Fantasy of Empire*. London: Verso, 1993.

Said, Edward W. Introduction. *Kim*. By Rudyard Kipling. Ed. Edward W. Said. New York: Penguin, 1987: 7-46.

Saposnik, Irving S. *Robert Louis Stevenson*. New York: Twayne, 1974.

Stevenson, Robert Louis. *Treasure Island*. 1881. Ed. Emma Letley. Oxford: Oxford UP, 1985.

Tilden, Freeman. *A World in Debt*. New York: Funk and Wagnalls, 1936.

PART 4
Children and the Terrors of
Cultural Consumption

Chapter 10

Toys and Terror: Lucy Clifford's *Anyhow Stories*

Patricia Demers

I sat many a long hour thinking how happy the children should be as they grew up, what merry days they should have to remember, to what bright ones they should look forward. It is a good thing to have a happy childhood: it keeps the heart green through all after troubles; it sends a little perpetual current of youth through a whole life. My children should have this at least. It seemed such a blessed thing to have these two little lives, and I used to think that if I brought them up to be good and true and pure and above all selfishness, it would be good work enough.

Lucy Clifford, *Mrs. Keith's Crime: A Record* (81)

"Perhaps he was my punishment for all I did in the past. I have thought that lately, and tried to bear it – only it is more than I can bear. It has humiliated me too much."

Lucy Clifford, *Aunt Anne* (387)

Lucy Clifford's two most successful and talked-about novels, *Mrs. Keith's Crime* (1885) and *Aunt Anne* (1892), appeared at approximately the same time as her two *Anyhow Stories* for children I want to discuss: "The New Mother" and "Wooden Tony." The apparent opposition between Mrs. Keith's serenity and Aunt Anne's mortification is a preparation of sorts for the mélange of placidity and terror in *Anyhow Stories; Moral and Otherwise* (1882, 1892).[1] But surfaces and protestations in Clifford's novels and stories can be deceiving. These two children's stories are anything but serene. In fact, by denying moments of understanding or illumination, they implicitly question the stability of such a moralizing project. "The New Mother" charts a problem-filled passage to subjectivity, amid the pervasive lures of consumerism and the marketplace. "Wooden Tony" relates, in dispiriting detail, the

---

1 The collection *Anyhow Stories; Moral and Otherwise*, containing "The New Mother," appeared in 1882 and was never reprinted. Having first appeared in the *English Illustrated Magazine* in 1891, "Wooden Tony, An Anyhow Story" was included as the final story in *The Last Touches and Other Stories* in 1892. *Anyhow Stories and Wooden Tony* appeared in a Garland facsimile reprint, with a preface by Alison Lurie, in 1977. Jonathan Cott included "Wooden Tony" in *Beyond the Looking Glass: Extraordinary Works of Fantasy and Fairy Tales* (1974), as did Jack Zipes in *Victorian Fairy Tales: The Revolt of the Fairies and Elves* (1987). "The New Mother" is among the selections in Jan Mark's *The Oxford Book of Children's Stories* (1993).

transformation of child to object, a tragic self-commodification also located within a culture of commercial transactions. The expected protection, or bonds, of the nuclear family disintegrate in ways that both parallel and mirror the turnabouts of Clifford's novels, and heighten curiosity about the author herself.

The rosy prognostics of Mrs. Keith, the recently widowed first-person narrator of Clifford's début novel, do not materialize. First, Mrs. Keith sees her young son die from scarlet fever; then, as her own health continues to fail, and she approaches death herself, she chloroforms her little daughter so that the child will not be left to the care of strangers. Meanwhile, the heroine of *Aunt Anne*, the widowed Mrs. Anne Baines, is an imperious woman in her sixties. She shocks her nephew and his wife by marrying a man more than three decades her junior, who turns out to be a fortune-hunter. Her remorseful realization that her "old lady's infatuation" (173) is a "most repugnant [...] pollution" (397) traces the distance she travels in her reflections.

Both characters wrestle with and express emotional turmoil. Most riveting is Mrs. Keith's final interior monologue. In anticipatory stream-of-consciousness mode, it conveys a mingling of love, fear and self-castigation in the image of "Molly – alone – alone, and calling for mother, for mother, who could not bear her pain and died; mother, whose love was not strong enough to master her weakness, and so she went, and had not the courage to take her little one with her" (397). Such a cluster of feelings recalls some aspects of the theory of "the general stream of Consciousness" of Clifford's friend, George Henry Lewes (2: 63). However, the limitations of human consciousness and the impossibility of attaining "a keen vision and feeling of all ordinary human life" preoccupied Lewes's life partner, Marian Evans (aka George Eliot). Her observation that "As it is, the quickest of us walk about well wadded with stupidity" (194) might also apply to Mrs. Keith's and Aunt Anne's fatal decisions. Resigning herself to the necessity of infanticide – "I must; I can't leave her" (402), Mrs. Keith yearns for peace and happiness as she remembers the drastic turn of her husband's death:

> It will be a good thing to rest. [...] I am thankful to go, and thankful that my little one is going with me. It has not been a bad world, and there was no sorrow in it for me till Arthur died. All my happiness went down to the sea with him and vanished, it has only been a sad make-believe since. (409)

Religion is absent in these narratives; no clergyman attends Mrs. Keith's or Aunt Anne's deathbed. Clifford's whole oeuvre reflects the committed atheism of her husband, W. K. Clifford.

Remarkable for its subject matter and narrative experimentation, *Mrs. Keith's Crime*, published anonymously in 1885 by Richard Bentley (following rejections from Macmillan and Blackwood), created a sensation. Praised by Robert Browning, Thomas Hardy and the founder of the Society of Authors, Sir Walter Besant, the novel ran to four editions before Clifford's authorship was revealed. The prefatory paragraph describes the author as the mere recipient of what "the wind swept into the heart of one who understood all the unspoken thoughts of that passionate life" (1). Seven years later, Clifford chose to have her name appear on the title page of *Aunt Anne*. A widow with two children, she adroitly presented herself as either the conveyor or creator of these bold narratives. Unlike the widely available imprints of the Religious Tract Society and the Society for the Promotion of Christian Knowledge, by contemporaries such as Maria Louisa Charlesworth, Charlotte Tucker, Hesba Stretton, Mrs. O. F. Walton and Charlotte Yonge, which regularly invoke Providential guidance, Clifford's texts are entirely free of any entreaties for divine or religious assistance. It is her women alone who, though vulnerable, combine deep feeling and steely resolve. Mrs. Keith's voice and present-tense narration and Aunt Anne's bullying affection and pathetic gullibility invite the reader into their states of sentience and awareness. Quite removed from a distancing stream of observations, these narratives forcefully underscore that consciousness or "qualitative subjectivity" is, indeed, "irreducibly subjective" (Searle 51).

Three years before the publication of *Mrs. Keith's Crime*, Clifford had announced her authorship on the title page of *Anyhow Stories; Moral and Otherwise*, a collection ostensibly, but not exclusively for children. A decade after this initial collection, and at the time of the appearance of *Aunt Anne*, she added another *Anyhow* Story, "Wooden Tony," at the close of her collection *The Last Touches and Other Stories*. The most sensational *Anyhow Stories* are "The New Mother" and "Wooden Tony." In the first, an attentive mother abandons her two daughters, and is replaced in the family cottage by a frightening new mother with glass eyes and a wooden tail. In the second, a young boy withdraws from society to the extent that he becomes a wooden figure in a clock mechanism. *Mrs. Keith's Crime*, with its idiosyncratic, potentially subversive characterization of motherhood, anchored in real familial misfortunes, appeared between these publications, while *Aunt Anne*, with its insights into the perversity of affections, coincided with the last *Anyhow* Story. It is important, therefore, to incorporate an awareness of these novels, along with the accompanying stories in *The Last Touches*, into a discussion of the two unforgettable *Anyhow Stories*. In addition, because Mrs. Clifford, who is not well-known today, actually contributed to misinformation about herself during her lifetime, some biographical context is also helpful.

A short-story writer, novelist and playwright, Sophia Lucy Jane (Lane) Clifford (1846-1929) is a figure of contrasts and contradictions, disguises and impersonations. In some ways, she seems more postmodern than Victorian. Born in Camden Town, and not on the island of Barbados, as she allowed many contemporaries to believe, Clifford promoted a connection with her paternal Barbadian grandfather as assiduously as she concealed the influence of her maternal grandfather, the writer and historian Thomas Gaspey, at whose home in the London suburb of Shooters Hill she spent her childhood. The fact that she lived with her grandfather suggests, according to the deduction of her biographer Monty Chisholm, "that a family break-up of some sort had taken place" (9). Yet even Chisholm admits puzzlement at some features of Clifford's story: it is unclear, for example, why she systematically misrepresented her age, shaving off two, then four, and finally ten years, ultimately prohibiting any mention of a birth date on her tombstone in Highgate Cemetery. Likewise, although her narratives pulse with the recurring instances of tormented women, who endure men's "pinchbeck devotion," and who could admit no more than "after all, he might be bumped and battered and worthless, but he was the man of her heart still" ("A Sorry Love-Affair," *The Last Touches* 107, 122), she herself cherished the memory of the man of her own heart, the mathematician William Clifford, throughout her long widowhood.

After his brilliant career at Cambridge, Clifford was appointed Professor of Applied Mathematics and Mechanics at University College, London. One of the youngest fellows elected to the Royal Society, he delivered public lectures on philosophy (posthumously printed as *Seeing and Thinking*). As well as admitting women to his classes, Clifford presented a series of "lectures on Geometry to women in South Kensington" (Chisholm 30). He and Lucy were married for only four years before his death in 1879 at the age of 33. Left with two daughters to raise, the widow took advantage of her experience of having published stories serially in *The Quiver* since 1871, and turned to writing as the mainstay of her family's finances. She was assisted by a fund established with the Royal Society's help and by the intervention of Marian Evans and Thomas Huxley, who secured a Royal Literary Fund grant for her.

Reflecting her sensitivity to the ways of the marketplace, Clifford's widowhood was exceptionally busy and productive. As well as reviewing for *The Standard* for 14 years, she published a steady stream of short stories, novels and, from the mid-1890s, plays.[2] Her plays were produced primarily in London, at St. James's Theatre, the Court Theatre, Kingsway Theatre and the Little Theatre, and also in Manchester at the Royal Court Theatre. Clifford also maintained the practice of the literary salon she and her husband had started. Her "at homes" promoted authors Frances Low and Mathilde Blind, introduced a young Bernard Shaw, and initiated friendships with Rudyard Kipling and Noel Coward. A successful hostess, who realized her own good fortune in claiming as friends Thomas Huxley, the President of the Royal Society, the man of letters Leslie Stephen, the publishers Gerald Duckworth and George and Frederick Macmillan, and the writers Somerset Maugham and Henry James, Clifford also "supported anyone who needed her" (Demoor 30).

James's letters to "Dearest Lucy C" (21 October 1900), "Beloved Girl!" (27 August 1902) and "Dearest old Friend" (26 August 1914), inquiring about her girls, and sharing information and gossip about domestic help, mutual friends, separate Continental travels and planned teas, reveal a level of cozy relaxation rarely associated with him (qtd. in Demoor and Chisholm 35, 50, 90). Virginia Woolf's experience of tea with Clifford was, by contrast, distressing. "An atmosphere of rancid cabbage and old clothes stirring in their old water" (qtd. in Chisholm 117) was the summation of the visit in her diary. Woolf did not share her father's affectionate concern for Clifford, a woman who, in the third decade of the twentieth century, continued to write in the fashion of the 1890s. Woolf's pen portrait is a devastating critique: "she remains otherwise the same – large codfish eyes – the whole figure of the nineties – black velvet – morbid – intense – jolly, vulgar – a hack to her finger-tips, with a dash of the stage –'dear' 'my dear boy'." A later letter to her sister Vanessa is full of cutting similes about Clifford: "wattled all down her neck like some Oriental turkey,

---

2   Clifford's novels include *Love Letters of a Worldly Woman* (1891), *Aunt Anne* (1892) and *A Flash of Summer* (1894). Her plays include *A Honeymoon Tragedy* (1896), *The Likeness of the Night* (1900), *The Searchlight* (1903), *Hamilton's Second Marriage* (1907), *The Latch* (1908) and *A Woman Alone* (1914).

and with a mouth opening and shutting like an old leather bag, [… and] lurching like a black beetle that's lost a front leg." Explaining to Vanessa her refusal to attend Clifford's funeral, Virginia admits, "All that remains of her in my mind is a cow's black blubbering cunt" (qtd. in Chisholm 117-19).

Views as polarized as those of James and Woolf contribute to Clifford's fascinating complexity – inspirer of both loyalty and antipathy. In many ways, her *Anyhow Stories* began this interlacing of opposites, this atmosphere of ambivalence. How might we approach this collection and title? Customarily either an adverb or a conjunction, "anyhow" is a rare adjective. Is the connotation ironically dismissive, implying that the stories can be read in any way or manner? Does the additional label "moral and otherwise" gesture toward a mixture that disappoints expectations of order and sequence, didacticism and improvement? Is the recently widowed, yet experienced, author stepping onto a public stage with authentic diffidence or mock humility? Might her child and adult characters reflect familial realities? Might Clifford's mingling of sweetness and dread, community and estrangement, be construed as a cultural commentary on the last decade of the nineteenth century?

"The New Mother" and "Wooden Tony" are the most unsettling and mysterious tales of their respective collections. With three texts in verse and ten in prose, *Anyhow Stories* is draped in philosophical gauze. Locations and geography are generalized, while preternaturally good and inquisitive children abound, asking questions about the route to the end of the world ("The Story of Willie and Fancy") and about the constituents of greatness ("In the Porch"). The thread of work done well in childhood, exemplified in a little table and a sampler, connects four stories: "The Cobbler's Children," "Round the Rabbit Holes," "The Beautiful Lady" and "In the Porch." For Clifford, it is productivity, rather than consumerism, that is associated with the virtuous subject, exemplified by the cobbler whose words combine individual subjectivity with collective responsibility. In "The Cobbler's Children," a dying cobbler's direction to his son and daughter – "'when one does well, one does some good to the whole world, for one helps to make it better'" (2) – and the struggling of the tendrils of a creeper at their garret window introduce motifs laced throughout the collection. In "Round the Rabbit Holes," the cobbler's son appears as a mystical sage, "a strange boy that had come to the carpenter's" (49). Meanwhile, the creeper grows up to meet the stars, touching "the garret window on its way" (56), and the little table is now displayed in a great lady's drawing room. The boy-philosopher counsels children who want to see real rabbits emerging from their holes that he actually can like the rabbits more for not having seen them. As he intones, "'the things one thinks about stay unless one sends them away, and they never change unless one's self changes first'" (55).

The connection between the table and the cobbler's son resurfaces in "The Beautiful Lady." The little table has traveled to India with the lady's son, who allows that "'it always seemed to him more like a living thing with a human voice than a bit of furniture'" (99). The lad's influence has been pervasive. A dreamer who has led others to realize that "some dreams are far better and sweeter than any waking" (100), he has prompted one girl "to love books and the histories of far-off lands, and all manner of strange stories" (96). The importance of the cobbler's daughter's sampler emerges in the last story, "In the Porch." Here we discover that its inscription, "'I have tried to work this well, for Daddy said *good work lives on for ever*'" (134), inspires a despairing artist to complete his finest work. The cobbler's influence, productive and resounding, underscores the truism that "what we are matters little, but what we do matters to all the world" (138). Unlike the scholar who is a mere collector, a "human cupboard" (142), the stranger insists that "'it is the simple-hearted folk, pure-lived and pure-thinking, who do well for love of doing well'" (140). In these threaded stories, Clifford foregrounds the fully realized, alert and responsible subjectivity of the child characters, in order to carry on a series of debates between pragmatic functionality and aesthetic idealism, between class privilege and productive labor, and between hoarded knowledge and genuine, influential altruism, as knowledge in action.

Although these childhood artifacts enjoy a fabled and somewhat prosaic passage through *Anyhow Stories,* the collection also glances at late-Victorian social satire, highlighting the value of true productivity, always socially responsible, as greater than the value of conspicuous, appearance-conscious consumption. The most successful story dealing with class disparity is "The Baby's Legs." Betsy, 11 years old, and the eldest of the widowed charwoman's five children, is a paragon. She minds the children, cooks and cleans, and has the good sense to bundle up the baby in her own shawl. In contrast, well-dressed Sarah Jones allows her youngest brother to dangle from her arm "while his legs h[a]ng in the morning air" (80). A more oblique view of disparities and industrious pluck makes less satisfying the account of the cheeky urchins in "The Three Ragamuffins," who cause Mary Lee to drop her pineapple slice, and then eagerly consume it. Not only is Mary Lee unjustly bewildered, but the boys, after being treated to some lugubrious moralizing from an old gentleman who attempts to impress them with a lesson about experience, are actually rewarded for their candor. "'Only a fool buys twice'" (59), he tells the lads and then, in an ironic gesture that equates commerce with moral actions, gives them sixpence.

Toys and playthings also reflect aspects of late-Victorian life, sometimes by being anthropomorphized and at others by being eerie emblems of the inanimate. In "The Imitation Fish," for example, a tin fish attached by a magnet to a pole fears for its child-owner "lest its falseness should be betrayed to the one heart that, knowing no falseness, thought it must be real" (87). By contrast, "The Paper Ship" relates a journey "to an unknown land" and a town of cardboard "where all the people were dolls" (74) who debate the existential conflict inherent in their own materiality:

> "What shall we do to be real?" they cried,
> "What shall we do to be real?
> We none of us feel, though we look so nice,
> And talk of the vague ideal." (74-75)

Their chatter mocks the "expenses and pretensions of London upper-class social life" (Lurie 70). The fact that they are cardboard, literally cut-out objects of stiff paper, emphasizes the loss of subjectivity in a locale devoted to talk and appearances. Their worries seem all the more inconsequential because they are without capacity to feel or act.

For many reasons, "The New Mother," the second piece in *Anyhow Stories*, stands apart from the rest of the collection. There is no palliating conclusion, no sententious moral, nor are there redemptive possibilities. The two little girls, Blue Eyes and the Turkey (the nicknames of Clifford's own daughters), are abandoned by their mother because they have been "naughty" (18). Their uncharacteristic behavior has been prompted by a "strange wild-looking girl" (12) with hair "uncombed and unfastened, just anyhow" (11). This stranger, whom the girls assume to be "about fifteen years old" (12), has a peardrum, which is a lute- or balalaika-shaped stringed instrument, played like a hurdy-gurdy "by turning a little handle cunningly hidden on one side" (15). The children, whose ages are not given, but who appear, from Dorothy Tennant's chiaroscuro illustrations, to be around seven and eight, initially think that the girl is hiding a baby. The instrument has the appeal of an unattainable toy, which, in this instance, is freighted with sexual connotations. A box affixed to the side of the peardrum contains a little man "dressed as a peasant" and a little woman "dressed in a red petticoat," who "dance most beautifully" (16) when the girl places them on the lid. "Anxious to see inside the box," though thinking "it might look curious to say so" (15), the children become obsessed with the box and the peardrum, "shaped very like a womb" (Lurie 71). Their lives change forever when the wild-looking girl insists that they be "naughty" as a condition of seeing the man and woman dance. The fact that the stranger's promises are broken while the mother's threat to leave is fulfilled makes "The New Mother" an acutely tragic story.

The temptation of the peardrum and of the hidden man and woman, to which both Blue Eyes and the Turkey succumb, suggests a comparison with the sisters Laura and Lizzie in Christina Rossetti's *Goblin Market* (1862). Two decades before Clifford, Rossetti explored the consumerist lure of "the wicked, quaint fruit-merchant men" (62) and "Their fruits like honey to the throat, / But poison in the blood" (62-63). Although Laura, who succumbs to the goblin brothers' temptation, is saved by Lizzie, who resists – "For there is no friend like a sister" (63) – no sisterly intervention can save the equally doomed and abandoned Blue Eyes and the Turkey.

Another suggestive parallel (or possible inspiration) concerns the New Mother herself and an earlier embodiment of punitive surveillance and retributive justice, Charles Kingsley's Mrs. Bedonebyasyoudid. In *The Water Babies; A Fairy Tale for a Land Baby* (1863), he describes the arrival of this bony, ugly, mechanistic, hook-nosed figure, wearing "a black bonnet, [...] a black shawl [...] and a pair of large green spectacles" (130). However, Mrs. Bedonebyasyoudid is less fearsome than the New Mother. She carries only "a great birch rod" (130) under her arm, and she lacks a wooden tail. Moreover, as a vocal and explicit instructor of Tom, the Water Baby, she is neither silent nor enigmatic. Her lessons contribute to the baptismal motifs of Kingsley's Christian moral narrative, features noticeably absent from Clifford's story.

From the outset, a gloomy foreboding hangs over "The New Mother." In the "lonely cottage at the edge of the forest" where the "big black arms" of the fir trees make "tangled shadows" in the moonlight, the clock always strikes "the wrong hour" (8-9). This incorrect or out-of-joint timing parallels inverted or extraordinary expectations throughout the piece. Blue Eyes and the Turkey, for example, arrive a day late for the village fair. Meanwhile, the stranger's strictly logical, word-playing replies to the girls' questions twist conventional expectations, in a manner reminiscent of Lewis Carroll's Humpty Dumpty. Not only does the stranger render shabbiness "respectable" (16), her decisive, self-possessed answers also make the little girls feel more and more uncomfortable and ignorant. When asked whether she is crying, she retorts, "'Oh dear, no! Quite the contrary. Are you?'" (13). When asked if she is lost, the stranger replies, "'Certainly not. Why, you have just found me'" (14). And she greets the girls' curiosity about the peardrum by declaring, "'Most people in good society have one'" (14), enhancing our sense of her consumerist superficiality by adding that she bought it with her own money because she is "'very rich'" (15). The condition the peardrum-player imposes for showing the hidden dancers to the girls both shocks and tempts them: "'the worse the children the better do the man and woman dance'" (18). The girls attempt to comply by breaking the clock and throwing the looking glass out the window. Their tempter, however, is inconsistent. True to her materialist practice of calculating a price for everything, she dismisses the reality of "'mothers with glass eyes and wooden tails'" as "'much too expensive to make'" (25). Yet, after informing the children that they have performed their naughtiness "'badly'" (37), she announces the advent of their new mother who "'walks slowly, for her tail is rather long and her spectacles are left behind'" (39). When this bony, ferocious figure arrives, cracking and splintering the door with her tail, the girls flee in terror. The final image of these babes in the wood foraging on berries and creeping up under cover of darkness to their once-snug home only to glimpse the "blinding flash" of glass eyes and hear the "strange muffled noise" of the wooden tail dragging along the floor, fulfills the pervasive childhood fear of abandonment. The traditionally inanimate objects of wood and glass have infiltrated the domestic sphere and taken over the emotional responsibilities embodied by it. The cosmos that is objectified in this panoptic, domestic site has become forbidding and pitiless. The conclusion is a bleak inversion of nuclear family norms, with the children banished to the periphery and the parent occupying the center in absolute and frighteningly speechless control.

Is "The New Mother" "the most extreme example of pointless cruelty in a century that abounded in terrifying stories for the young" (Avery and Bell 52)? Does it fall "within the Victorian genre of didactic fairy tales" (Silver 738)? If the aim was to warn against naughtiness, then this *Anyhow* Story is not pointless, but so sharply pointed as to seem inhuman. Moreover, the biographical accounts of Clifford's fond and protective mothering of her own daughters do not square with such a punitive moral. Some residual sense of abandonment from Clifford's childhood, however, might have contributed to the story's grimness. The tantalizing, opaque allusions to sexual knowledge that flit in and out of the narrative suggest that Clifford was experimenting with notions of curiosity and excitement – a stream of consciousness as chaotic and occasionally erroneous as Mrs. Keith's and Aunt Anne's – rather than offering a systematic illustration, by negative example, of either pre-adolescent inquisitiveness or threat-based parenting.

If the curiosity of Blue Eyes and the Turkey is at least recognizable and engaging, the singularity of Wooden Tony is genuinely distancing. This "idlest boy in Switzerland" (*The Last Touches* 247), the single child of poor, hard-working parents, yearns only to be "very little and far off" (249), to lose "all likeness of himself" (250) and to "let the days and nights slip by as one that swims with but just enough movement to keep himself from drowning" (252). Clifford here replaces the forest gloom and shadows of "The New Mother" with a cloud of unknowing over the title figure. In contrast to the tangible, empirical lure of the peardrum stands the mysterious listlessness of Tony, who himself becomes an object, a carved figure attached by wire strings in a clock mechanism. Wrapped round in a "great cobweb" (254) and living "among his dreams, which grew so tangled that even he could not tell the sleeping from the waking ones" (255), Tony is virtually a somnambulist.

Three years before Freud and Breuer's first book on psychoanalysis and eight years in advance of Freud's *The Interpretation of Dreams*, Clifford sketches "the inner world of a deeply disturbed child" (Ekstein 124). Although he perceives his father's woodcarving as a release of "little animals and men and women in prison" (256), and seems to see into the reality of objects waiting to be brought to life in wood, Tony himself follows a de-animating path. In a desire that chillingly captures the alienating depersonalization he aspires to, Tony longs to join the wooden figures his father carves:

> "If I were but like one of them," Tony used to think as he saw them wrapped in soft paper, "to be always little, to be handled tenderly and put to sleep in a drawer till the summer, and then to be warmed through and through by the sun. Why should they have legs that never ache and hands that never work?" (259)

Envisioning himself as a commodity, the young protagonist articulates the act of self-objectification, which might be understood as a foreshadowing of the dystopia of conspicuous consumption on a mass scale by the end of the century. As the dealer from Geneva fits Tony with wire strings, the boy sings "mechanically, as though he were a puppet of which the string had been pulled" (262). Despite his yearning to understand the trees, "to learn their language and ponder their secrets" (262), his awareness of his surroundings increasingly fades: "He was not tired, or warm, or cold, or glad, or sorry, but only in a dream" (263). Finally having become a wooden figure, Tony is joined to the little woman his father had carved, "who had on her face an expression of listening and waiting" (257), and "jerked into the darkness" (269). Tony's carelessness in his descent into sentient woodenness – "He knew that he was bound and a prisoner, but it did not matter, he did not care" (266) – is the most alarming and distressing aspect of the story's outcome.

Although Chisholm finds it "unlikely that Lucy consciously intended to chart the child's decline through depersonalisation and alienation to eventual dehumanisation" (138), this *Anyhow* Story is a graphic example of precisely that. In contrast to Chisholm's diffidence, psychoanalyst Rudolf Ekstein interprets "Wooden Tony" as a depiction of childhood autism. He goes as far as to label Tony's linkage to the female figure a marriage and a "psychotic oedipal victory," while he reads the character's final state as "a painful description of confinement in a hospital for the insane" (141, 143). There is no medical, and certainly no psychiatric intervention in this narrative. It is true that the parents lament the loss of their child, the mother possibly recalling her doting and defensive nurture, and the father at last tempering his bull-headed insistence that his son was "'only a fool'" who would "'not use his hands and feet'" (260). No textual evidence, however, suggests that the increasingly distanced Tony ever longed for any kind of human, interpersonal relationship. Modern gestures of self-objectification, Clifford implies, counter a sense of social investment or agency.

The twinning of peril and paralysis in "Wooden Tony" contrasts stunningly with the animation and transformation of a mere piece of wood, "un pezzo di legno" (1), in Carlo Collodi's *Le avventure di Pinocchio, storia di un burattino*. The first English translation of the piece, Mary Alice Murray's *The Story of a Puppet or The Adventures of Pinocchio*, appeared in 1892, the same year as Clifford's final *Anyhow* Story.[3] Against Tony's listless withdrawal is Pinocchio's kinetic, fearless energy. While Collodi's impish picaro learns through his mishaps and expresses real filial concern for Geppetto, whom he rescues and restores to health, "Wooden Tony" follows a distinctly different narrative trajectory. Collodi's jauntily clad young man, with a full head of curly hair and well-shaped limbs, looks in bemusement at the "large puppet propped against a chair, its head turned to one side, its arms dangling and its legs crossed and folded in the middle so that it was a wonder that it stood up at all" (Collodi, *Adventures* 461). In contrast, the wooden figure of Tony locked in the clock mechanism, in "the little room [where] all was darkness till another hour had passed" (268), is completely oblivious of the "weary faces" of his parents "pressed against the window" (268).

Just as "The New Mother" stands out in the earlier volume, the depersonalization and lassitude that characterize Tony's woodenness also contrast with the eight other works in Clifford's *Last Touches*. The other stories concern forgotten, deferred or martyred romantic love. The long-suffering characters are invariably women. Although Mary Robbins, the sewing-girl in "On the Way to the Sea" loves Dick Grantley, she forgives him for marrying an heiress. As she reasons to "Mr. Dick," "'I would like to be poor best, [...] then I could always serve you myself'" (83). In "The Last Scene of the Play," another story involving the connection between money and human attachment, Harford Wilson, who has murdered his first wife, is holed up in a chalet with his second wife, Charlotte. As the police surround them, Harford plans to kill himself after poisoning Charlotte, who discounts the need for forgiveness and addresses the man who holds a pistol to his own head as "'my life, my heaven, my eternity'" (244).

While it would be convenient to place Clifford's *Anyhow Stories* in the same melodramatic vein, it seems to me that "The New Mother" and "Wooden Tony" operate in a different register. Tony's enervated uninterest and the lively curiosity of Blue Eyes and the Turkey show an author experimenting with the boundaries of narratives for children by focusing on defining moments in the development of subjectivity. It is a distinctly modern, yet in some senses inchoate subjectivity she probes, one beyond the convictions or consolations of the nuclear family, and influenced by external macro-social pressures and exchanges. Blue Eyes and the Turkey, disappointed at missing the village fair, release their pent-up consumerist energy and excitement in

---

3   For an extensive discussion of variations in translation and interpretation, see my "'*Diventassi anch'io un uomo*': Pinocchio's Shared Humanity."

encounters with the strange girl and her exotic instrument. The older girl's presence is seductive, both materially and sexually. She proffers both a desirable object and an initiation into the non-monetary price of disobedience, of non-tractability – a lure the youngsters (under their mother's regime of order and docility) cannot refuse. As an object in a shop on whom consumers gaze, Tony becomes a literal embodiment of reification, while his impecunious parents are reduced to desiring but powerless customers. Conveyed in language of strong physiological, as well as psychological resonances, Clifford's two *Anyhow Stories* explore the complex, dynamic nature of subjectivity and, in these instances, its sad interruption or failure. At the moment when they have attempted some independence of the mother, Blue Eyes and the Turkey are left alone, without direction or assistance; the girls test the limits of maternal protection and endurance. For his part, Tony resists independence and growth, favoring retreat, regression and imprisoning dependence. Although the child figures are the main actors, and their passions and predilections are central in these stories, parents are absent or punitive monitors, or otherwise ineffective non-interventionists. Offering no excuses or warnings, Clifford consents neither to palliation nor to the imparting of instructive moralizing nuggets. In what impresses me as acts of immense authorial bravura, she sidesteps orderly, satisfying conclusions, instead presenting grim, terrifying scenes of total abandonment and estrangement. However, she does not neglect to make these final pictures heart-rending. Equipped with what appears to be insider knowledge, this late nineteenth-century writer and mother was not afraid of the dark side of contemporary childhood.

Works Cited

Avery, Gillian, and Angela Bell. *Heroes and Heroines in Children's Stories*. London: Hodder and Stoughton, 1965.

Chisholm, Monty. *Such Silver Currents: The Story of William and Lucy Clifford 1845-1929*. Cambridge: Lutterworth, 2002.

Clifford, Lucy. *Anyhow Stories Moral and Otherwise*. Illus. Dorothy Tennant. London: Macmillan, 1882.

---. *Aunt Anne*. London: Richard Bentley and Son, 1892.

---. *The Last Touches and Other Stories*. New York: Macmillan, 1892.

---. *Mrs. Keith's Crime: A Record*. London: Richard Bentley and Son, 1885.

Collodi, Carlo. *The Adventures of Pinocchio: Story of a Puppet*. Trans. Nicolas J. Perella. Berkeley: U of California P, 1986.

---. *Le avventure di Pinocchio, storia di un burattino*. Ill. Benito Jacovitti. Brescia: La scuola, 1945.

Demers, Patricia. "'*Diventassi anch'io un uomo*': Pinocchio's Shared Humanity." *Quaderni d'Italianistica* 25.1 (2004): 29-41.

Demoor, Marysa. *Their Fair Share: Women, Power and Criticism in the Athenaeum, from Millicent Garrett Fawcett to Katherine Mansfield, 1870-1920*. Aldershot, UK: Ashgate, 2000.

Demoor, Marysa and Monty Chisholm, eds. *"Bravest of women and finest of friends": Henry James's Letters to Lucy Clifford.* Victoria, BC: English Literary Studies, U of Victoria, 1999.

Ekstein, Rudolf. "Childhood Autism, Its Process, as Seen in a Victorian Fairy Tale." *American Imago* 35.1-2 (1978): 124-45.

Eliot, George. *Middlemarch.* Ed. Rosemary Ashton. London: Penguin, 1994.

Kingsley, Charles. *The Water Babies: A Fairy Tale for a Land Baby.* London: Blackie and Son, 1920.

Lewes, George Henry. *The Physiology of Common Life.* 2 vols. London: Blackwood, 1860.

Lurie, Alison. *Don't Tell the Grown-ups; Subversive Children's Literature.* Boston: Little, Brown, 1990.

Mark, Jan, ed. *The Oxford Book of Children's Stories.* New York: Oxford UP, 1993.

Murray, Mary Alice, trans. *The Story of a Puppet or the Adventures of Pinocchio.* London: T. Fisher Unwin, 1892.

Rossetti, Christina. *Goblin Market.* Illus. Laurence Housman. London: Macmillan, 1893.

Searle, John B. "Minding the Brain." *The New York Review of Books*, (2 Nov. 2006): 51-55.

Silver, Anna Krugovoy. "The Didactic Carnivalesque in Lucy Lane Clifford's 'The New Mother.'" *Studies in English Literature* 40.4 (2000): 727-43.

Zipes, Jack, ed. *Victorian Fairy Tales: The Revolt of the Fairies and Elves.* New York: Methuen, 1987.

Chapter 11

"We have orphans […] in stock": Crime and the Consumption of Sensational Children

Tamara S. Wagner

In Charles Dickens's *Our Mutual Friend* (1863-65), a pointed verbal altercation concerning the exchange of a child depicts orphans as commodities, articulating a double investment in the fiscal and the sentimental. Mr. Boffin, the "Golden Dustman," is a childless foreman who has unexpectedly come into a dust contractor's fortune. He and his wife now wish to find an heir to their dust mounds and a child to grace their new home. Aiming to please, the Reverend Frank Milvey creates a list of children available for adoption: "'We have orphans, I know,' pursued Mr Milvey, quite with the air as if he might have added, 'in stock,' and quite as anxiously as if there were great competition in the business and he were afraid of losing an order" (110). As if this business attitude toward orphans were not enough, "[c]ounterfeit stock" (195) of fake orphans enters the market. Mr. and Mrs. Boffin might be genuinely interested in raising an orphan child, but their sentimental investment in a potential replacement for the dust contractor's missing son – the real heir to the family fortune – is converted into a financial speculation that generates a "run" on orphans, and a rise and fall in "orphan stock" (195).

The Boffins' failure to obtain the infant they desire significantly complicates the very commodification of the victimized child on which *Our Mutual Friend* capitalizes. Yet their failure is also part and parcel of a much larger collapse of financial discourses into domestic space, a collapse that inflects the text's rich symbolism of waste disposal and accumulation, of salvaging and scavenging, and of appropriation and recycling. Dickens's last finished novel depicts a consumer culture that works through an urban landscape of human and other "dust" – a euphemism covering a multitude of sins. Across this disturbing landscape, vultures in high and low life are shown both to feed on and into the commodification of bodies, from amputated legs to the recollected, ghostly faces of lost children. *Our Mutual Friend*, published when the sensation genre was about to achieve market saturation, reinstates the sentimental value of a disinherited son thought to be lost or dead, but who returns to face his father's manipulative last will. In an intriguing reworking of popular inheritance-plots, Dickens's novel thereby invests in, even as it reveals, the book market's appropriation of the consumable orphan.

Instead of buying into the moral discourses that inform the stocking-up of victimized children in debates on social reform (including their fictionalization in earlier social-problem novels), fiction of the 1860s represents the consumption of children as a central issue. Mary Elizabeth Braddon's first novel, *The Trail of the Serpent* (1860), for example, includes not one but two illegitimate infants fished out of a river – without sentimentalizing either child. On the contrary, in a disconcertingly ambiguous audit of their sensational potential, Braddon poses the foundlings – father and son – as villain and anti-hero in an intricate narrative of crime and retribution. Sloshy, the son of a man retrieved from the same river a generation earlier, washes up at the town of Slopperton-on-the-Sloshy, and is named after the river, prefiguring the likewise unsentimentalized character of Sloppy, who, in *Our Mutual Friend*, is "found on a Sloppy night" (200). Both novels feed a presupposed appetite for depictions of victimized innocence. At the same time, they re-evaluate the exploitation of such victims in fictional representations, and question the process of making a market of children's vulnerability. Dickens's reuse of domestic sentimentality, however, is premised on a rebirth, or recycling, that undercuts the closure of Braddon's detective plot. This marks a reversal of the sensation genre's substitution of the sensationalized child for its sentimental precursors in domestic fiction of the mid-nineteenth century, and it does so by repackaging and profiting from both.

Braddon's and Dickens's piling up of orphans in these two books testifies to the massive consumption of sensationalized children in fiction during the 1860s. It is Ellen Wood's *Lord Oakburn's Daughters* (1864), however, and specifically the way it is peppered with mysteriously removed, dying and abandoned newborns, that best illuminates sensation fiction's anti-sentimental recycling. Precisely because Wood is the sensation novelist most inclined to indulge in melodrama and moralizing (Pykett 114), her failure – if failure it can be called – to take full advantage of the sentimentalism invited by a series of "poor little mite[s]" (Wood 20) underscores the priority of the murder mystery plot in her novel. Indeed, the tale rides somewhat roughly over the sensationalized deaths with which it is paved. By subordinating a young boy's demise to the work of detection, Wood's extensive use of a child who is missing (and hence primarily off-stage) illustrates a conversion of the sentimentalized child as a literary figure into a clue in a detective plot. This shift is so effective that the question of whether the boy is rediscovered dead or alive seems ultimately irrelevant. His sudden reappearance admittedly provides a vital lead to the mystery enveloping the suspicious circumstances of his mother's death (a missing daughter herself); it does so, however, only to underscore the divergence of the narrative of detection from the novel's initial interest in an impoverished aristocratic family's inheritance, and in children as potential heirs and objects of sentimental effusion.

Recycling the Sentimentalized Child

The first half of the nineteenth century can be credited with establishing the sentimentalized child as an iconic literary figure; novels of what came to be known as "the sensational sixties" were eager to convert it for sensationalized use. In the figure's most intriguing reworking, novelists used the suffering child's sentimental potential as a false lead in mystery and detection plots: presumed victims were revealed to be villains, or else they figured as instruments of revenge or justice.

Child criminals in sensation fiction were consequently neither as glamorous as the Artful Dodger, nor as incorruptible as Oliver Twist. Instead, the marketing of the criminalized child in social-problem novels (Dickens's *Oliver Twist* among them) was, despite occasional reinvestments in the sentimental, taken up as a familiar plotline to be worked into tongue-in-cheek narratives. Indeed, what could possibly generate a more startling effect than the exposure of a seemingly vulnerable child as the driving force of a sensational plot? Still, the desire to consume the young, although conducive to sensationalization, was already intrinsic to their earlier sentimental representation.

In *Child-Loving*, James Kincaid diagnoses child death as among the most easily eroticized and sentimentalized representations of the Victorian sickbed. As Kincaid pointedly puts it in a more recent essay on the Gothic, the cult of the child that emerged in the nineteenth century was, from its beginnings, implicated in an unsettling desire among adults to love children "so much they could, as we say, just eat them" ("Designing" 2). This appetite was not a disruption of the middle-class idealization of the child, but in fact central to the fictionalization, the mythologization even, of such an idealization. Sick or dying, abandoned or orphaned, children could be used for a good many things. As Laura Berry notes, their representations "cross generic boundaries with relative ease" (3). Nevertheless, by stockpiling children and reissuing them as new commodities – whether as criminals or as victims of crime – sensation fiction was immensely effective in capitalizing on the age's sentimentalization of childhood.

It is precisely this emphasis on the child's fictional value that propels the orphans' circulation in *Our Mutual Friend*. They are a speculation, and, as such, aligned with stock-market scams, advertised as if there were "great competition in the business," and made part of a market alternately "rigged" and swamped by a surfeit of "orphan scrip":

> The suddenness of an orphan's rise in the market was not to be paralleled by the maddest records of the Stock Exchange. He would be at five thousand per cent. discount out at nurse making a mud pie at nine in the morning, and (being inquired for) would go up to five thousand per cent. premium before noon. The market was "rigged" in various artful ways. Counterfeit stock got into circulation. Parents boldly represented themselves as dead, and brought their orphans with them. Genuine orphan stock was surreptitiously withdrawn from the market. (195)

The orphan's high selling point in Victorian culture impels a critique of consumerism in a novel that similarly satirizes the prevalent slogan that "traffic in Shares is the one thing to have to do with in this world. [...] Where does he come from? Shares. Where is he going to? Shares. What are his tastes? Shares. Has he any principles? Shares" (118). The credit economy's new fortune hunter "goes, in a condescending amateurish way, into the City, attends meetings of Directors, and has to do with traffic in Shares" (118). It is hardly surprising that a society that supported the fraudulent Man of Shares also generated counterfeit orphans: if their production was at the same time a sarcastic jab at the amorphousness of the nineteenth-century use of the term "orphanhood," it is ironic that Dickens's story invests just as much in the circulation of orphans as it does in the marketability of the novel's own critique of consumerism.

Peter Coveney suggests that the child figure in Victorian literature is "the symbol of sensitive feeling anywhere in a society maddened with the pursuit of material progress" (74). This is nowhere more pervasive than in nineteenth-century domestic fiction, making its reflections on the commercial value of orphan narratives especially notable. More recently, Baruch Hochman and Ilja Wachs have explored the prevalence of orphans in nineteenth-century literature as an articulation of social anxieties, as "a state of mind" (14). "Orphanhood" was not only a common euphemism for illegitimacy, but by extension, the term could also express a more general sense of dislocation and disorientation.[1] Moreover, as Michèle Mendelssohn argues in her contribution to this collection, children (especially girls) became increasingly subject to a form of sexual and commercial exposure that operated in a latent economic exchange within the home – a concealed domestication of child abuse and prostitution, explored by Henry James in several of his novels. But it was when sensation fiction's fascination with child abuse outgrew social-problem and domestic novels that the orphan's sensational potential first made it profitable to leave sentimentality behind or, more precisely, to harness it for plots in which the chase, the gathering of clues and the tracking down of criminals drive the narratives. Sensation fiction regularly features children as both victims and perpetrators of crime, as its domestic Gothic recycles desirable child figures.[2] It is Wood's *Lord Oakburn's Daughters* that shows, perhaps most poignantly, how detective plots reused dying children.

Running Away with Dying Children: Re-Plotting Deathbeds

Strictly speaking, *Lord Oakburn's Daughters* is not a detective novel, and its professional detectives – like the tellingly named Inspector Medler – meddle only in private affairs, but without yielding any results. Wood's novel, however, pivots on a murder mystery seemingly unrelated to the tale of Lord Oakburn's three daughters, partly because even the omniscient narrator fails to acknowledge the existence of a fourth, missing daughter, until her murder is exposed. Indeed, the murder mystery detracts from the mysterious fate of the newborn child, with which the novel opens. Prematurely born, the "wee, wee infant" (16), "a poor little mite" (20), is literally

---

1   As Catherine Waters argues, orphans became a particular source of fascination because of their utility in representing an anxious relationship to the past (29). Carolyn Dever links the symbolic potentials of orphanhood to an epistemological crisis of origins, articulated in and spawned by Darwin's *Origin of Species* (6).

2   The sensation novel's central trope of the "domestic Gothic" takes as its premise the exposure of essentially bourgeois ideals of domesticity. Lillian Nayder speaks of sensation novels' disclosure of "the private sphere as a place of Gothic strife and suffering rather than a healthy and harmonious refuge from the conflicts of public life" (72). Karen Chase and Michael Levenson similarly refer to the "antifamily of popular sensation" (7), and Renata Miller argues that infanticide became central to a competition between the novel and the theater.

bundled off by a Mrs. Smith, last seen at the railway station "with two bundles: one bundle containing the baby, the other the baby's clothes" (22). The same night, the mother, known in the town only under an assumed name, is poisoned. When, over eight years later, Mrs. Smith returns with a dying child, the boy's likeness, both to Mr. Carlton, the surgeon, and to Lord Oakburn's missing daughter, incites "doubt and speculation in more minds than one" (387). But the child's undersized body works all too well as an intentional cover-up. "If so, could this be the same child?" thinks Carlton. "He had asked the boy's age that morning, and Mrs Smith replied 'six;' and the boy did not in appearance look more than six. That other child, if alive, would be much older" (351). Carlton might take a touchingly paternal interest in the sick infant without knowing anything about the boy's paternity, and "the extraordinary delight that suddenly beamed from his eyes [does send] a thrill through the senses of the surgeon" (345), but the recognition is ill-omened. It identifies Carlton not simply as the child's father, but as the mother's murderer as well.

Carlton's wife Laura does not know that she has married her dead sister's husband, and this makes it the more striking that she sees his interest in the boy as part of a puzzle that is eventually completed by an incriminating letter. Laura's elder sister, meanwhile, discovers in the child's face a missing sister's "very self-same eyes" (347). Given that the clandestine marriage has ended in a concealed murder, the boy's likeness to both the missing sister and the suspected husband is ominous:

> "There never was, I believe, so great a [likeness] in the world," was Laura's answer. "Every feature is similar, except the eyes. That is not all. Your ears are a peculiar shape, unlike any one's I ever saw; so are the child's. The very feather here," touching the parting of her own hair in front, "the wave of the flaxen hair: it is all you in miniature." (359)

The boy's identification is further assisted by a birthmark. But before he can be claimed by anyone, or for any agenda, the child dies offstage, making room for the detective plot's closure: the murderer's capture and then "escape" from execution by his death from heart failure. In the words of Mr. Policeman Jones, "Mr. Carlton *has* escaped, gentlemen. In spite of us all and of the law" (481).

The child's funeral is only a minor recompense for the aborted murder trial: "Some slight compensation [...] was afforded by the funeral of the little boy. For the excitement attendant on that ceremony was so great as to operate as a sort of balm to the disappointed feelings of the people" (486). The fact that hard-featured, unsentimental Mrs. Smith retains her exclusive right to grieve over the child perhaps most compellingly dismantles any sentimentality. For this surrogate mother, the mysterious child has replaced her own dead baby – yet another in a pile of sickly children including Laura's short-lived newborn; a similarly doomed infant whose birth kills the previous Lady Oakburn at the beginning of the novel; and an heir born to the new Lady Oakburn.

This last child survives and gains strength; ultimately, he is held up as a contrast to Carlton's abandoned son, the child of the eldest Miss Oakburn, and the "mite" brought up by Mrs. Smith instead of her own. That the young heir is moreover introduced as "the one link to life left by [the Misses Oakburns'] father" (289), however, makes it only more noticeable that the inheritance plot has been pushed aside in order to make way for the disclosure of the murderer. The boy's inheritance "need not be touched upon," the narrator specifically emphasizes, "for it does not concern us" (300). By contrast, Lord Oakburn's eldest surviving daughter, an obnoxious epitome of self-righteousness, raises her right to the guardianship of her youngest sister at her father's very deathbed, with her whiny "tone, broken by suffering, by sorrow, by a sound of *injury*" (284), jarring to the point of comical absurdity. Uncharacteristically for Wood's fiction, in this novel the surrogate mothers and stepmothers turn out to be worthy wives, as well as responsible and affectionate, if not always sentimental, caretakers.[3]

Most significantly, despite the deaths of several young children and the delineation of their parents' punishment, *Lord Oakburn's Daughters* clearly leaves behind the moral didacticism of Wood's most popular novel, *East Lynne* (1861). The latter commodifies maternal loss in what Peter Coveney has diagnosed as "the one last, careful, twist of the knife of the sadist masquerading as moralist" (136), yet it also trembles on the borders of readers' desires for a sensational delineation of parental abduction. A child dies as his mother moans that, because she is a runaway and her identity must remain hidden, the boy could never call her "mother": "No; not even at that hour when the world was closing on him dared she say, I am your mother" (493). The Victorian cult of the child, Coveney argues, is reduced here to absurdity; the child's "real use" is "to increase sadistic tension" (138).

Notably, this death scene spawned numerous musical and theatrical adaptations, as well as fictional imitations that climaxed on the refrain of "Never Called Me Mother." Such scenes have been read as expressions of maternity that make nursing and motherhood interchangeable (Vrettos 42). In *East Lynne*, the divorced mother, resenting her displacement by the stepmother, a former rival in love, returns in disguise to be a governess to her own children. An outsider at her son's deathbed, she grieves more over the transfer of the child's affection to his stepmother than over his quiet release from a long illness, a release he embraces with eerie calm: "It is astonishing how very readily, where the right means are taken, [dying children] may be brought to look with pleasure, rather than fear, upon their unknown journey" (484). The mother's violent anguish is not only juxtaposed with the innocent child's tranquil death, but also topped by the narrative's startling dismissal of an illegitimate infant in a railway crash. Abandoned by her lover, the divorced woman gives birth to a child whose death proves convenient in releasing her to seek employment and return to her legitimate children. Hence, if the popular deathbed scene confirms, as at least one critic has argued, Wood's "penchant for the angelic, and preferably dying, child" (Brown 61), it does so by defining a sentimental domestication of death against the sensational riddance of the illegitimate infant. Moreover, the mother's illegal/illegitimate infiltration of the household disconcertingly hints at possibilities

---

3   Although the sensationalized stepmother is a recurring figure in the period's literature, her most gruesome appearance is in Wood's *St Martin's Eve* (1866), in which she shuts the door on her burning stepson in order to ensure her biological child's inheritance.

of child abduction. The novel makes it abundantly clear that the mother's redeeming quality is her resolution never to reveal her true identity to her dying son.[4]

In the 1860s, the conflicting legal and moral issues of parental abduction formed such a popular narrative that two of sensation fiction's most virulent critics drew on it, even as they capitalized on the genre's market potential. In Margaret Oliphant's *Salem Chapel* (1863), the protracted youthfulness of a "sort of grown-up baby" (156) is represented both as the result of a custody dispute *and* as a disturbingly desirable commodity. In *He Knew He Was Right* (1869), Anthony Trollope similarly features a legally sanctioned child abduction specifically in order to criticize emergent detective plots. In this novel, a jealous husband hires an ex-policeman as a private detective for the purpose of having his wife "reckoned up," which is "detective English for being watched" (188). Considering that the term "plagiarism" derives from the Latin *plagiarius*, which refers to one who abducts a child or slave, a kidnapper, a seducer, or a literary thief ("Plagiarism"), it is doubly appropriate that Trollope's own reworking of sensation fiction depicts a despicable detective committing an abduction. Similarly, when Dickens recycles plotlines in *Our Mutual Friend*, he reestablishes orphanhood's sentimental function. In such ways, sensational detective plots consume orphan narratives, their rewriting bringing back the sentimentality while still profiting from orphans' sensationalization.

Consuming Paternity, Regurgitating Detective Plots

Published first as the serial *Three Times Dead, or the Secret of the Heath* (starting in February 1860), Braddon's *The Trail of the Serpent* was more successful in its severely condensed novel form rewritten for a middle-class market. The fact that the story had originally been aimed at the penny public might explain its remarkable introduction of a successful working-class detective. Joseph Peters does not merely outwit a criminal aristocrat: the first central professional detective in British fiction, he is, moreover, a mute who turns his disability into a powerful tool. He communicates by means of his "dirty alphabet" behind villains' backs, even profiting from their assumption that "deaf-and-dumb" is a single diagnosable category: "I signified to him that I was dumb, and he took it for granted that I was deaf as well – which was one of those stupid mistakes your clever chaps sometimes fall into – so he went on a-talking" (246). Because of this easy conflation, the villain, in front of the detective, openly discusses his desertion of the woman he seduced, and the child she bore him. Such professional eavesdropping is a strategy Peters uses more than once.

What makes Peters such an attractive, as well as unusual character, however, is that he is a bachelor who takes an interest in an abandoned child as a paternal and

---

4 Wood regularly used child abduction in her fiction. Her first serial publication, "Seven Years in the Wedded Life of a Roman Catholic" (1851), is a lurid anti-Catholic tale that includes child-snatching by Jesuits (Riley 168-69). Child abduction likewise features centrally in the first of the *Johnny Ludlow* series of 1868. In 1885, however, in "Tod's Repentance," part of her third series, Wood put a different spin on the topos: a boy goes missing, and a ne'er-do-well relative is suspected of abducting him, but it turns out the child has only been accidentally locked in a barn.

professional investment. The young victim of attempted infanticide is found shortly after a murder has been committed. The reader knows (and the detective suspects) that it is the son of the murderer. That he has ineffectively attempted to pay off the child's mother with coins taken from his victim ultimately leads to his exposure. These coins, brought into the country from India, and therefore easily recognizable, are later traced back to the killer. Like his discarded offspring, they are the fruits of his crime, and both are eventually converted into clues to his identity. However, just as the infant is abandoned for financial reasons – prompted by the ambition of his father and the despair of a single mother – the adoptive father is motivated in part by professional interest. Taking up the muddy baby, Peters thinks "of adoptin' him, and bringin' of him up," specifically, it is important to note, "to try the power of cultivation in the way of business, and bring a child up from the very cradle to the police detective line" (247). As it turns out, the baby's descent from criminals renders him instrumental in tracking down his own father.

The son's professionalism dispels Peters's doubts that the child's origins might disturb his commitment to his work. There is no "soft-heartedness" in the clever sleuth he has raised:

> "I thought perhaps you might let family interests interfere with business, you know." "Not a bit of it," said the youthful enthusiast. "I'd hang my grandmother for a sovering [sic], and the pride of catching her, if she was a downy one." "Chips of old blocks is of the same wood, and it's only reasonable there should be a similarity in the grain [. . .]. I thought I'd make him a genius, but I didn't know there was such a [sic] undercurrent of his father. It'll make him the glory of his profession. Soft-heartedness has been the ruin of many a detective as has had the brains to work out a deep-laid game, but not the heart to carry it through." (267)

Just as there is no attempt either to soften the detective's Cockney accent or to disguise the fact that "a murder and bread-and-cheese are inseparable things in his mind" (108), there is nothing sentimental about the foundling. Sloshy, the victim of attempted infanticide, is "found in the mud of the river" at three months old (197), shortly after a murder has been committed in Slopperton. As the son of a suicide and a murderer guilty of a spectrum of additional crimes (ranging from theft and check fraud to large-scale financial scams), Sloshy is an appropriate foil to the new master criminal. Made "preternaturally elderly and superhumanly sharp [by] his police-office experiences" (266-67), he is "wizen," while also displaying aristocratic features that have "nothing in common with the ordinary features of a boy of his age and his class" (196). A potential threat, he is turned by the detective's supervision, or surveillance, into a criminological instrument of detection.

Much has been written on the construction of the intelligent criminal, from Count Fosco in Wilkie Collins's *The Woman in White* to Sherlock Holmes's adversary Professor Moriarty.[5] What sets Braddon's novel apart is both its contribution of the

---

5   As John Sutherland has discussed, from the middle of the nineteenth century onwards, certain criminals began to be accorded a growing degree of intelligence. In fiction, "this founded a line of anti-heroes which begins with Fosco – who converses with scientists on equal terms – and led to that strange contradiction, the academically distinguished arch-

clever *professional* detective and its harnessing of inherited criminal tendencies in order to counteract criminals. Like Fosco, that "Italian virtuoso of crime" (Sutherland 87), Braddon's Marquis de Cevennes (Sloshy's father) is aristocratic and foreign. In *The Trail of the Serpent*, however, the imported danger is compounded by an ambition nurtured by English "charity." This combination helps bring to light an intricately plotted intrigue that spans several continents and three generations. There are two instances of abandonment in the child's family history, and this marks a compounding effect of criminal tendencies, or abilities, which eventually become a redirected cold-blooded interest in crime.

The marquis's crime is, after all, "only" the abandonment of the woman he married while a refugee in England. Once political circumstances allow his return to France, his mother-in-law is left with "a golden secret" (294): the truth of his identity and hence the potential exchange value of the twin sons he abandoned. But with "the river on one side, and a life of misery, perhaps starvation, perhaps worse, on the other" (84), the mother-in-law reaches the conclusion that she must throw the younger twin into the Sloshy. Living in abject squalor, she can afford to keep only one child, and so she literally disposes of, like so much household rubbish, what she considers excess supply.

Official charity retrieves the discarded twin in order to educate him into becoming the "Good Schoolmaster," a figure ominously introduced in the first chapter: "Slopperton believed in Jabez North. Partly because Slopperton had in a manner created, clothed, and fed him, set him on his feet; patted him on his head, and reared him under the shadow of Sloppertonian wings, to be the good and worthy individual he was" (7). But the parish has raised a monster: once Jabez becomes aware of the "golden secret," he murders his sickly twin, engages in elaborate deceptions to marry an heiress, absconds to South America, and then returns as an eminent banker with an aristocratic title. But in encountering his father, he "has found his match" (321). There is neither a sentimental reunion nor a melodramatic exposure scene. The father, in short, outdoes the son in cold-blooded calculations: "Truly father and son – all the world over, father and son" (317).

In *The Trail of the Serpent,* the revision of the traditional inheritance plot as a narrative of mystery and detection is twofold. First, there is no *deus-ex-machina* legacy for the aristocrat's rediscovered heir. Sloshy remains the working-class detective's adopted son, and any potential claims to his father's patrimony or parentage are simply irrelevant. Second, in a much more provocative re-plotting of the child's relation to crime and criminology, Sloshy assists in tracking down his biological father. As Peters raises the abandoned baby to be the heir to his work, the classic narrative of the orphan's fortuitous inheritance is changed into one of the first full-fledged detective plots.

---

criminal, like 'Professor' Moriarty and 'Doctor' Nikola." (76). Ever since Winifred Hughes's seminal study of the sensation genre's interest in exploring the motives that drive villains, Fosco has been seen as "one of the most delightful villains in literature" (143). Compare Ronald Thomas's study of the simultaneous emergence of criminology and detective fiction.

Shares in Dust: The Orphan's Will Reconsidered

In *Our Mutual Friend*, Dickens rewrites the legacies of Braddon's "Good Schoolmaster" by focusing on the villain's home-bred brutality. *The Trail of the Serpent* attempts to explain away the aberrations of the seemingly respectable result of a charity project as the child of a foreign aristocrat. Dickens's novel, however, introduces an obsessive stalker, Bradley Headstone, who causes a revaluation of the most vexed issues of physical inheritance.

At its most sentimental, child death in *Our Mutual Friend* operates within a fascinating array of consumable orphans. The comically generic "The Orphan" makes his will by leaving his toys to another sick child, and a kiss to a would-be wife "willed away" by the deceased dust contractor, Old Harmon. The boy's death functions as the climax of a critique of both the workhouse system and the administration and distribution of charity in mid-Victorian Britain. Yet the chapter "In which the Orphan Makes his Will" marks the closure of the orphan market, and parallels the ongoing rereading and retracing of Old Harmon's will in the main plot. Consumerism's wasteland, "a hilly country entirely composed of Dust" (24), the dust contractor's legacy might parody inheritance plots, but it also generates a speculation mania that links together a vast social panorama. With the heir apparently missing, everyone tries for shares in the dust, with several characters literally wading and digging through it in the course of their quests.

Mary Poovey points out the way in which John Harmon, Old Harmon's runaway son, attempts to alter the external parameters of his father's will by substituting a woman for stocks. By means of this scenario, *Our Mutual Friend* rewrites value by "[c]onverting the abstraction of commodification into a metaphorics of worth and the tyranny of a parent's will into permission to have what one wants" (Poovey 167). However, because John Harmon's revaluation of commercialism's penetration of the domestic sphere takes place in the cultural terrain of gender, it fails to go much beyond his attainment of impenetrable familial space (165). In addition, it no more than touches upon the most disconcerting commercialization of all: that of the purchasable child. Anticipating the aborted adoption of the generic orphan Mrs. Boffin wishes to obtain after her husband becomes the Golden Dustman, Old Harmon has commodified John's future wife by leaving her to him "in a will, like a dozen spoons" (45), knowing her, at the time, only as a randomly spotted screaming child, "a promising girl" (50) to be invested in the marriage market.

When John Harmon fakes his death, so that he can assess his "inherited" wife's true worth without revealing either his own identity or his own value as the miser's heir – what Poovey terms "the John Harmon deceit" (165) – the Boffins temporarily succeed to his fortune, and decide to set up a new John Harmon. This orphan is intended to take the place of the dead youth, so that at least some good might come out of the hoarded dust mounds. The Boffins's motivation might be restitution, but it is not easily purchased. When the couple ventures into the orphan market, they pay into a system that commodifies children as consumable and replaceable bodies. Well may the original John Harmon balk at Mrs. Boffin's promise to his future wife, Bella Wilfer, who at that point believes him drowned, to "have my little John Harmon to show" (116) to her. It is a startling as well as ominous remark to the real, live

John Harmon, an unsuspected bystander: "How can you show her the Dead? [... I]t sounded like an omen, that you should speak of showing the Dead to one so young and blooming" (116).

For fear of impairing the orphan's desirability, his illness is only belatedly reported to the Boffins, making the adoption process itself partly responsible for the orphan's eventual death. With his demise, Mrs. Boffin becomes "timid of reviving John Harmon's name," and looks instead for "a creature to be helped for its own sake," instead of a pretty infant expected to "be a pet and a plaything" (330-31). She chooses Sloppy, one of the most unattractive orphans of nineteenth-century fiction:

> Of an ungainly make was Sloppy. Too much of him longwise, too little of him broadwise, and too many sharp angles of him angle-wise. [...] A considerable capital of knee and elbow and wrist and ankle, had Sloppy, and he didn't know how to dispose of it to the best advantage, but was always investing it in wrong securities, and so getting himself into embarrassed circumstances. (200-01)

A "long boy" (198) who has literally outgrown the sentimentalized orphan's role, Sloppy contrasts sharply with the now dead little Johnny: distinguished by a crisply curling auburn head," "a bluff countenance" and an altogether "chubby conformation" (196). What is more, while Braddon's Sloshy is dangerously sharp, Dickens's Sloppy is described through a flood of commercial metaphors that suggest he has invested his own sharpness in the wrong securities.

Dickens, of course, used anti-sentimental representations of overgrown orphans in his earlier fiction, often in order to substantiate the social criticism that runs through his novels. It is particularly emphatic, for example, in his exposure of the underlying hypocrisy of what, in *Bleak House* (serialized in 1852 and 1853), he terms "telescopic philanthropy." Dirty, illiterate and spreading diseases that refuse to acknowledge class boundaries, the street-child Jo is an uninteresting, home-grown savage, who munches dirty bread on the door-step of the Society for the Propagation of the Gospel in Foreign Parts, having "no idea, poor wretch, of the spiritual destitution of a coral reef in the Pacific" (221). Jo's disease-carrying body is itself anticipated in *Nicholas Nickleby* (1839) by the elongated, emaciated form of Smike, an abandoned son doomed to die shortly after his rescue from Dotheboys Hall, a school for unwanted children that forms the novel's main point of critique. Smike ultimately dies in the arms of the cousin who has retrieved him from the school and brought him to his own old home, where the orphan is "quite contented" (762). "I almost think," he muses, "that if I could rise from this bed quite well, I would not wish to do so now." Much more pointedly, Jonas Chuzzlewit, one of the most ruthless businessmen in *Martin Chuzzlewit* (1844), is termed "that amiable and worthy orphan" (505), after he has done away with his father. Sharply calculative Jonas and long-suffering Smike are two sides of the same coin – versions of orphans who lack the capital of tender youth.

Sloppy's largely comic role in the detection of the "Harmon deceit" parodies Sloshy's function in *The Trail of the Serpent*, while Headstone – perhaps the most dreadful grown-up orphan of nineteenth-century fiction – constitutes a reworking of Sloshy's father. The chapter entitled "Of an Educational Character" introduces him as a "highly certificated stipendiary schoolmaster" (216-17) dressed for respect. This character's origins, however, are uncertain, and he is driven by "suppression" (218):

> Yet there was enough of what was animal, and of what was fiery (though smouldering) still visible in him, to suggest that if young Bradley Headstone, when a pauper lad, had chanced to be told off for the sea, he would not have been the last man in a ship's crew. Regarding that origin of his, he was proud, moody, and sullen, desiring it to be forgotten. (218)

Braddon's depiction, in *The Trail of the Serpent*, of a washed-up twin and his son is multiplied in Dickens's novel. The mystery surrounding the man whom Mr. Boffin jocularly calls "Our Mutual Friend" (115) is given away with deliberate urgency. Early in the novel, one of John Harmon's false identities is evoked as his first alias's potential "twin brother" (51). Their accidental likeness facilitates his scheme to observe his potential wife in secret. When the heir to the dust mounds is proclaimed dead, John – after he is saved from drowning – can investigate his future wife's real interests under the guise of a false identity.

It is nearly impossible to do justice to the proliferation of material the Thames washes up in *Our Mutual Friend*. Examples range from human "birds of prey" that literally fish their living out of the river to various combative doubles: John Harmon and the man mistaken for him; Headstone and Eugene ("well-born") Wrayburn, rivals in love and enemies in class status; and Headstone and Rogue Riderhood, whose final altercation flushes both villains down the river.[6] Thus, *Our Mutual Friend* might criticize consumer society and, specifically, the detritus it produces, but the waste disposal system appears to be working after all. The dust mounds yield the valuable wills they conceal, and, despite the emphasis on the high pollution levels of the Thames, the river operates well in flushing out villains. With their undesirable doubles dead, the deserving characters are paired off with suitable partners and tucked into safe pockets of domesticity, refuges from urban spread. Harmon can return from the dead to reclaim his true identity, inherit his fortune, and marry a duly re-evaluated wife, with their expected baby resuscitating the child-figure's sentimental value. Even Sloppy is matched with someone who is an expert in making a living out of waste by fashioning best-selling dolls' dresses out of discarded scraps. These miniature ball and wedding gowns constitute a tongue-in-cheek tribute to the smooth working of an industry in which waste is "done up," reused to cater to society's growing demand for luxury products. The dolls' outfits represent the ultimate commodification of marriages and children with which *Our Mutual Friend* concludes.

---

6 By failing to instigate any moral rebirth, Rogue Riderhood's resuscitation parodies John Harmon's transformation. Wrayburn, by contrast, is pulled out of the water by the woman he loves (a scavengers' daughter), an event that accomplishes his moral rebirth and her restitution (Wagner 149-50). If this episode rewrites the upper-class seducer, it becomes doubly significant that Headstone's monstrosity is neither foreign nor aristocratic.

Braddon's adaptation of a penny dreadful, in order to satisfy the growing middle-class appetite for sensation, provides a revealing point of entry into the nineteenth-century sensationalization of children and childhood. Dickens's *Our Mutual Friend*, however, readapts the sensation genre's recycled orphans, first by evoking their exchange value as a commercial venture through the novel form itself, and then by reinstating the value of a domestic refuge beyond the marketplace. Although no evidence has been found that Dickens deliberately drew on Braddon's fiction, the parallels between their two novels are compelling and testify to the pervasiveness of popular plotlines throughout the period. Braddon's references to Dickens were always simultaneously dedicatory and self-ironic about plagiarism. To note one example, her fictional defense of sensation fiction in her 1864 *The Doctor's Wife* (itself a rewriting of Gustave Flaubert's *Madam Bovary*) depicts an avid female reader feeding upon "the highest blossoms in the flower-garden of fiction" (28) – the works of Dickens and Edward Bulwer, the latter having influenced both Braddon and Dickens. The woman recites "long sentimental passages" to a fictitious male sensation writer, who then regurgitates them; "I am sorry to say," the narrator comments, "that the young man, going to work at Colonel Montefiasco next morning, would put neat paraphrases of Bulwer, or Dickens, or Thackeray into that gentleman's mouth" (28). The sensation writer is presented as living on the saleability of "highly-spiced fictions," produced specifically for readers who like "their literature as they like their tobacco – very strong," and prefer to purchase it "in the same manner as [their] pudding – in penny slices"; at the same time, however, he also works on a *"magnum opus"* that seeks to transcend, while building on, these pieces them (11-12). Recent interest in nineteenth-century disputes about copyright and plagiarism shows that there was much more to sensation fiction's fascination with intertextuality than consumer demand for recycled plotlines.[7] Nonetheless, as the novels ran away with sellable narratives of infanticide, child abduction and counterfeit orphans, they increasingly retained a firm grasp on the commercial use of the literary child, especially when they took it up as a marketable issue itself.

Works Cited

Berry, Laura. *The Child, the State, and the Victorian Novel*. Charlottesville: UP of Virginia, 1999.

Braddon, Mary Elizabeth. *The Trail of the Serpent*. 1860. Ed. Chris Willis. New York: Random House, 2003.

---. *The Doctor's Wife*. 1864. Ed. Lyn Pykett. Oxford: Oxford UP, 1998.

---. *The Lady's Mile*. 1866. London: Simpkin, Marshall, Hamilton, Kent & Co, 1892.

---

7   On Braddon's rewriting of Dickens and Collins, see Calovini. On intellectual property, see Pettitt. Significantly Smith, the plagiarizing hack writer of *The Doctor's Wife*, returns in Braddon's later *The Lady's Mile* (1866) as "Sigismund Smythe, the novelist, who had abandoned the penny public to court the favour of circulating-library subscribers, and had sublimated the vulgar Smith into the aristocratic Smythe" (3).

Brown, Penny. *The Captured World: The Child and Childhood in Nineteenth-Century Women's Writing in England*. Hemel Hempstead, UK: Harvester Wheatsheaf, 1993.

Calovini, Susan. "A 'Secret' Novel of Her Own: Mary Elizabeth Braddon's Rewriting of Dickens and Collins." *Tennessee Philological Bulletin* 38 (2001): 19-29.

Chase, Karen, and Michael Levenson. *The Spectacle of Intimacy: A Public Life for the Victorian Family*. Princeton: Princeton UP, 2000.

Coveney, Peter. *Poor Monkey: The Child in Literature*. London: Richard Clay, 1957.

Dever, Carolyn. *Death and the Mother from Dickens to Freud: Victorian Fiction and the Anxiety of Origins*. Cambridge: Cambridge UP, 1998.

Dickens, Charles. *Nicholas Nickleby*. 1839. Ed. Sybil Thorndike. London: Oxford UP, 1957.

---. *Martin Chuzzlewit*. 1844. Ed. Margaret Cardwell. London: Penguin, 1982.

---. *Bleak House*. 1852. Ed. Osbert Sitwell. Oxford: Oxford UP, 1959.

---. *Our Mutual Friend*. 1865. Ed. Adrian Poole. London: Penguin, 1997.

Hochman, Baruch, and Ilja Wachs. *Dickens: The Orphan Condition*. Madison, WI: Fairleigh Dickinson UP, 1999.

Hughes, Winifred. *The Maniac in the Cellar*. Princeton: Princeton UP, 1980.

Kincaid, James. *Child-Loving: The Erotic Child and Victorian Culture*. London: Routledge, 1992.

---. "Designing Gourmet Children or, KIDS FOR DINNER!" *Victorian Gothic: Literary and Cultural Manifestations in the Nineteenth Century*. Ed. Ruth Robbins and Julian Wolfreys. Houndmills, UK: Palgrave, 2000. 1-11.

Miller, Renata Kobetts. "Child-Killers and the Competition between Late Victorian Theater and the Novel." *Modern Language Quarterly* 66.2 (2005): 197-226.

Nayder, Lillian. *Wilkie Collins*. London: Prentice Hall, 1997.

Oliphant, Margaret. *Salem Chapel*. 1863. Ed. Penelope Fitzgerald. New York: Virago, 1986.

Pettitt, Clare. *Patent Inventions: Intellectual Property and the Victorian Novel*. Oxford: Oxford UP, 2004.

"Plagiarism." *The Oxford English Dictionary*. 2nd ed. 1989. *OED Online*. Oxford University Press. 20 Oct. 2005 <http://dictionary.oed.com>.

Poovey, Mary. *Making a Social Body: British Cultural Formation, 1830-1864*. Chicago: U of Chicago P, 1995.

Pykett, Lyn. *The "Improper" Feminine: The Women's Sensation Novel and the New Woman Writing*. London: Routledge, 1992.

Riley, Marie. "Writing for the Million: The Enterprising Fiction of Ellen Wood." *Popular Victorian Women Writers*. Eds. Kay Boardman and Shirley Jones. Manchester: Manchester UP, 2004. 165-85.

Sutherland, John. "Wilkie Collins and the Origins of the Sensation Novel." *Wilkie Collins to the Forefront: Some Reassessments*. Ed. Nelson Smith and R. Terry. New York: AMS, 1995. 75-90.

Thomas, Ronald R. *Detective Fiction and the Rise of Forensic Science*. Cambridge: Cambridge UP, 1999.

Trollope, Anthony. *He Knew He Was Right*. 1869. Ed. Robertson Davies. London: Penguin. 1994.

Vrettos, Athena, *Somatic Fictions: Imagining Illness in Victorian Culture*. Stanford: Stanford UP, 1995.

Wagner, Tamara S. *Longing: Narratives of Nostalgia in the British Novel, 1740-1890*. Lewisburg, PA: Bucknell UP, 2004.

Waters, Catherine. *Dickens and the Politics of the Family*. Cambridge: Cambridge UP, 1997.

Wood, Ellen. *East Lynne*. 1861. Ed. Sally Mitchell. New Brunswick, NJ: Rutgers UP, 1984.

---. *Lord Oakburn's Daughters*. 1864. London: Richard Bentley and Son, 1889.

Chapter 12

"And now Tom being killed, and all spent and eaten": Children, Consumption and Commerce in Nineteenth-Century Child-Protection Discourse

Monica Flegel

In *Past and Present* (1843), Thomas Carlyle tells of a Stockport mother and father "found guilty of poisoning three of their children, to defraud a 'burial-society' of some 3*l.* 8*s.* due on the death of each child" (4). Carlyle suggests that such a crime meets only with the public's disgust – "'Brutal savages, degraded Irish,' mutters the idle reader of Newspapers; hardly lingering on this incident" (4) – but argues that, instead, the crime should be seen as a sign of the condition of England: as an act to which the parents were "driven" by poverty and starvation. Rather than dismissing the parents as mere "savages," Carlyle imagines the "committee of ways and means" by which those parents came to their fateful decision:

> Our poor little starveling Tom, who cries all day for victuals, who will see only evil and not good in this world: if he were out of misery at once; he well dead, and the rest of us perhaps kept alive? It is thought, and hinted; at last it is done. And now Tom being killed, and all spent and eaten, Is it poor little starveling Jack that must go, or poor little starveling Will? (4)

Although the family's wretched preoccupation with starvation and "victuals" translates into a kind of cannibalism, in which the child who cries for food is murdered so that others might be fed, Carlyle's depiction of little Tom's death dues "all spent and eaten" also suggests a gruesome form of commerce: a child is converted into funds that then become food; once that child is "eaten," the rest soon follow.

More than forty years later, Carlyle's cannibalistic parents were still a subject of worry, particularly in the propaganda of the National Society for the Prevention for Cruelty to Children (NSPCC). At that time the primary organization in England concerned with the emergent crime of cruelty to children, the NSPCC mounted campaigns throughout the 1890s against insuring children, a practice that, the NSPCC feared, involved the transformation of a murdered child into funds – and from that, into alcohol and food for the murdering parents. But where Carlyle made room in his depiction of the family's starvation for feelings of sympathy toward the murderous Stockport parents, even while he "hovers between blaming working-class degeneracy and the utilitarian policies of a morally bankrupt government"

(McDonagh 114), the NSPCC sought to evoke only horror in its narratives of children "done in" for money.

The NSPCC conceived of child abuse as a classless crime, as an act motivated by flaws in the character of abusers rather than by social circumstance. However, in its attacks against child-life insurance (a primarily working-class scheme), the NSPCC found itself negotiating highly class-inflected territory, a position that called into question the Society's "careful separation of child abuse from economic conditions" (Behlmer 95). In this chapter, I argue that the NSPCC, in an effort to maintain the Society's classless stance, sought to reframe the debate surrounding child-life insurance by conflating stories of poverty and starvation with horrific narratives of parental savagery. In articles such as "Child-Life Insurance" and "Children as Articles of Commerce," Benjamin Waugh (the NSPCC's first director) created a world in which children are the raw materials – endlessly and cheaply produced – for commercial ventures that fatten lower- and working-class parents, middle-class middlemen and England's great insurance companies. Invoking images of children reduced to commodities, Waugh severed starved offspring from their starving families, making children's hunger separate from the appetites of their abusive parents. An analysis of Waugh's discourse, however, reveals the fissures within the NSPCC's representation of child abuse as a classless crime, fissures that Waugh attempted to overwrite through his recourse to a critique of money, power and commerce in England. In his anxieties about the "English savage," and about the openness of that savage's home to commerce, rather than to charitable or government intervention, Waugh illuminated the extent to which class-based fears and representations were in fact central to the NSPCC's understanding of child abuse as a pathology, and of child protection as its cure.

Child-Life Insurance in Nineteenth-Century England

Questions about the interrelationship of home and work, of family and commerce, continually occupied the nineteenth-century British imagination, particularly in the many debates surrounding the practice of child-life insurance. Such insurance allowed parents to receive money on the death of a child, ostensibly for the purpose of providing a decent burial. This arrangement, however, met with criticism on two major counts: the first was the belief that the poor "spent far too much on their funerals" (Behlmer 120). Such a criticism speaks both to the desire of middle-class commentators to impose models of frugality and respectability onto working-class families, and to the failure of these same commentators to recognize the motivation behind such a seemingly wasteful practice as the decent burial of a child.

Stories such as that of Carlyle's Stockport parents suggest, however, that child-life insurance aroused a second, even greater concern than that of excessively expensive child funerals. As George K. Behlmer notes,

> The notorious financial instability of these clubs encouraged parents to buy multiple policies, particularly on the young, for whom insurance premiums might run as low as a penny a week. To Edwin Chadwick and many social critics after him, it seemed that

duplicate policies on the lives of children earned reimbursements that were greater than the actual cost of a funeral, thereby sweetening the "temptation for evil." (121)

Concerns such as this were raised throughout the 1840s and 1850s. The national government undertook a variety of measures in response to these concerns.[1] But there was a lack of evidence that burial clubs were in fact tempting parents to murder their children: a select committee formed in 1854, for example, found "that the murder of children was not demonstrably linked with burial insurance" (Behlmer 124). This meant that no serious legal restrictions were put in place. Regardless, the burial society remained "the focus of middle-class anxieties about working-class demoralization and degeneracy" (113).

Furthermore, the issue of child-life insurance continued to resurface, particularly after the emergence of large life-insurance companies such as the Prudential. Earlier burial clubs had often been managed by community-based working-men's associations, but larger insurance companies had no ties outside of a business relationship to the parents they represented. Concerns about the influence of profit in a field in which financial benefits accrued on the death of a child led to the appointment of a Royal Commission on Friendly Societies in 1870. In their findings, the commissioners urged the prohibition of insuring children;[2] however, "largely because of renewed pressure from burial societies, this guideline emerged in the Friendly Societies Act of 1875 [...] as ceilings of £10 and £6 on the lives of children under ten and five respectively" (Behlmer 126). Many people, however, believed these limits were insufficient to protect the lives of poor children, and, throughout the late 1870s and 1880s, child-life insurance continued to draw their fire. And with the emergence of child protection in the 1880s, a new way of attacking the practice presented itself: depicting child-life insurance as a form of child abuse.

Child-Life Insurance and Child Protection

The London Society for the Prevention of Cruelty to Children was formed in 1884. As William Clarke Hall wrote in 1897,[3] "there was no such offence known to English Law as the mere ill-treatment, no such offence as the mere neglect of a child. The Society resolved to create these offences" (159-60). Pivotal to the "creation" of child

---

1   In August 1850, "Parliament passed legislation (13 & 14 Vic., c.115) that prohibited burial insurance in excess of £3 on any child under the age of ten" and mandated that "all death benefits be paid directly to the undertaker" (Behlmer 124).

2   The commissioners were especially troubled by the fact that the mortality rate for Liverpool children in their second year (when they were eligible for full benefits) was higher than in their first. The commissioners considered this finding "strong circumstantial evidence against such policies" (Behlmer 126).

3   According to the records manager at the NSPCC's archives, Hall's "connection with the London SPCC and the NSPCC was that he provided free legal policy advice (termed as 'legal opinions') to the Society. He was a personal friend of Benjamin Waugh, and became his son-in-law when he married Waugh's daughter Edna" (Malton). Hall wrote *The Queen's Reign for Children* and *The Law Relating to Children* (1905), which outlined the acts passed in the United Kingdom on behalf of children.

abuse as a crime were the many essays written by Benjamin Waugh, and the London SPCC's case studies printed in the Society's journal, *The Child's Guardian* (founded in 1887). In essays such as "The Child of the English Savage" (1886), for example, written by Cardinal Henry Manning and Benjamin Waugh, the London SPCC depicted abuse as the result of a "peculiarity of spirit in the adult abuser of the child" (696), and, as such, a crime that could best be addressed through the intervention of the Society and through legislative change. Manning and Waugh identify the "real root of persistent savagery" (696) as "a sullen, ill-conditioned disposition" and "a cowardice which limits its gratification to unresisting and helpless things" (696).

Such an understanding of cruelty is similar to Frances Power Cobbe's concept of "heteropathy," which "consists in anger and cruelty, excited by the signs of pain. [... T]he more the tyrant causes the victim to suffer, the more he hates him, and desires to heap on him fresh suffering" (119). The London SPCC, however, represented cruelty to children as unique, in that it was, in part, a crime entirely connected to the singular nature of the victimized child. As Waugh later argues in "Prevention of Cruelty to Children" (1892), "it is almost universally true that the more innocent and simple the child is – the better looking-glass does it make for its haters to see their own black villainy in" (143-44). A child might not be the cause of the abuse through any actions of its own, but Waugh suggested that childhood itself, and in particular its contrast with the savagery and violence of the abuser, is both what incites child abuse and what makes it particularly heinous.

Josephine McDonagh links the emergence of child-protection groups like the NSPCC to nineteenth-century concerns about infanticide (156), a crime that was feared to reveal, among other things, the "primitive core of Englishness" (154). But where McDonagh connects the late-Victorian version of the infanticidal mother to the growth of social Darwinism and its "corollary concern," a "theory of pathological hereditary decline – or degeneration" (158), Manning and Waugh referred to this kind of Darwinism as a *cause* of abuse rather than as an explanation for it: "The duty society owes to the lives of unwanted children is greatly increased by the waking-up of evil men to the modern ideas that population is a nuisance, and that God and future judgement are 'superstitions'" (693). According to Manning and Waugh, the "new ideas" of the value of human life, separated as they were from concepts of man's consanguinity with God, inspired abusive parents to reject the sanctity of the home, and fall away from their sacred duty of caring for their offspring. Thus, Waugh concluded, in order to make children a worthy object of protection, the NSPCC had to do battle with the "increasing tendency to regard human beings as protoplasm; to shake off the idea of Jesus as the living God, the Father of us all, and to account for human life by molecules," for "Child life and happiness are bound up with the Kingship of God" ("Some Conditions" 3).

The extent to which the NSPCC's depiction of abuse drew upon current ideas of degeneration, insanity and decline, while also rejecting these scientific excuses for cruelty and infanticide, speaks to the problems the Society faced in explaining behavior so far outside the Victorian ideological construction of the family. Drawing on moral depictions of a character flaw, rather than on scientific depictions of degeneration, the NSPCC sought to place its understanding of abuse primarily within religious rhetoric, rather than within social-scientific discourse. However, the Society's initial focus on the abuser's "peculiarity of spirit" suggests that the organization did not entirely avoid biological or psychological explanations for cruelty. The contradictions in the NSPCC's discourse of abuse illuminates the difficulty the Society faced in mapping its depiction of cruelty onto pre-existing and divergent narratives.

Because the London SPCC located cruelty in individuals rather than in their environments, it could argue that child abuse was a crime transcending class. An "ill-conditioned disposition" could be found, presumably, in individuals from every level of society and, while Waugh and Manning acknowledge that cruelty to children is generally accepted "as the accompaniment of great poverty, squalor, and social misfortune," they argue instead that "against the poor, the terribly poor, [the Society] can bring hardly a complaint" (691). Abusers, they claim, exist "anywhere and everywhere" (699). The Society's own work, however, classified such things as starvation, neglect, begging and exposure as acts of cruelty to children, actions of which a lower- or working-class parent was far more likely to be found guilty than his or her higher-class counterparts. Nevertheless, Waugh persists that the Society's work was "no class work" ("Notes" [1889] 224) – doubtless because the higher-class parent whose child was made to beg was equally liable to criticism.

The NSPCC did not remain committed to construing child abuse as a kind of character flaw. By the end of the nineteenth century, cases of neglect far outnumbered cases of assault in the NSPCC's work, and the Society's discourse began to focus on the role of alcoholism in the neglect of children.[4] Harry Hendrick counters Behlmer's attribution of the change in the NSPCC's emphasis, from cruelty to neglect, to the Society's "increasing professionalism," by suggesting that it might also be explained by the fact that "neglect was easier to 'treat' as a social problem than was cruelty" (30). Hendrick states that "The Society came to feel that neglect […] could best be dealt with through the inculcation of a sense of personal responsibility on the part of the parents" (30). In shifting its focus from cruelty to neglect, the NSPCC was therefore representative of a broad-based transformation in social welfare strategy, from criminalization and punishment to reform and rehabilitation (Hendrick 32). Under this logic, abusive parents were considered "temporarily deviant and subject to the 'rehabilitative' ideal" (Hendrick 32).

Hendrick's explanation accounts for the move in the NSPCC's discourse away from a pathological model to one focused on the role of social factors, such as poverty, addiction and inadequate living conditions. I would argue, however, that the "character flaw" model remained (and remains today) a residual narrative. Even with an increased focus on social factors, narratives such as those published in Walter Payne's memoir, *The Cruelty Man* (1912), still clearly distinguish between the respectable poor and the shiftless – between those who acknowledge their responsibilities as parents and those who "choose" not to do so. The failure to be a "proper" parent, although exacerbated by drink, was nevertheless still seen as a kind of moral failing.

---

4   Walter Payne's *The Cruelty Man: Actual Experiences of an N.S.P.C.C. Inspector, Graphically Told by Himself* provides numerous examples of neglect.

Child-life insurance was one of the areas in which the London SPCC wished to see greater government involvement and restriction. The London SPCC felt, like others before it, that this type of insurance encouraged unprincipled parents to neglect, or even to murder their offspring, and therefore made a point of mentioning, in *The Child's Guardian*, those cases in which abused children were also insured children. Although insuring a child was not a crime, claims made in *The Child's Guardian*, such as "fourteen of these 100 suffocated children were admittedly insured" ("Insurance and Suffocation in Liverpool" 93), sought to make the practice seem so. Furthermore, the Society was "sufficiently impressed with the strength of public sentiment that it announced in October 1888 its commitment to the total abolition of insurance on young lives" (Behlmer 128). The London SPCC did succeed in helping to bring about new legislation protecting children, and, just prior to the passage of the "Children's Charter" in 1889 (the first law making cruelty to children a crime), the London Society reconstituted itself as the National Society for the Prevention of Cruelty to Children. As a result, the Society seemed poised to take on what it perceived to be a grave threat to children throughout the nation. By 1890, the NSPCC had prepared a bill for Parliament, proposing to restrict the size of insurance payments for dead children, and to make all monies payable only to undertakers rather than to parents (Behlmer 129).

The NSPCC's involvement in the debate over child-life insurance, however, damaged the Society's claim that its work did not target lower- and working-class families. Child-life insurance was purchased primarily by those who had neither savings nor insufficient income to pay for a funeral. Accordingly, many people perceived attacks on the child-life insurance to be an attack on the lower and working classes. Waugh became, if his many "Notes" and articles on the subject are any indication, extraordinarily frustrated with such perceptions. In "The Rights of the Working Man" (1890), Waugh argues that the suggestion that the NSPCC's bill was an assault on the lower and working classes was "false in sentiment and in fact," because "A right to do wrongs belongs to no man, whether conferred by Parliament or custom or brute force" (81). According to Waugh, therefore, the NSPCC's attacks on child-life insurance were nothing less than positive evidence of the NSPCC's classless stance. Wrongs against children, regardless of who perpetrated them, and whatever custom they represented, could not be tolerated.

In articles such as "Child-Life Insurance" (1890), Waugh therefore disputes the charge that "to lay responsibility for the death of so many children at the door of child-life insurance societies is a slander on the working class" (40), arguing that "the class that is charged is all who worship a pound they have not got but want, more than a child they have got and do not want" (41). In order to defend himself and the Society against accusations of class bias, Waugh reconfigures class as a moral, rather than an economic category. The "class" of parents the NSPCC sought to prosecute for abuse was not that of the lower or working classes, but instead that of a particular kind of parent, one distinguished by immorality and the failure to feel proper affection for children. Such a "class," of course, might include the rich as well as the poor, and in articles such as "Cruelty to the High Born" (1889), Waugh is careful to accuse those in the upper classes who were willing to trade children for sterling:

Long flowing hair combed and crisped, and elegant dress of children, may conceal fatal constitutional mischiefs being deliberately wrought by those who have custody of the little wearers. If disease will but play its part, monies left to them by a father's will [...] will fall into their guardians' hands. (131)

When he writes in "Child-Life Insurance," then, of parents to whom "a child presents greater attractions dead than alive, especially if alive it costs sixpence and dead it is worth six shillings" (53), Waugh could argue that such parents "exist in every rank" (53).

The NSPCC's published case studies from the 1890s suggest that Waugh's desire to assert the NSPCC's classless stance may have had much to do with anxiety about the fact that class had become a significant issue in the NSPCC's work. Cases of "Neglect and Starvation" significantly outnumbered cases of "Assault" or "General Ill-Treatment" in those examined or prosecuted by the NSPCC.[5] While deliberate "Neglect and Starvation" could certainly be understood to be as savage and pathological a crime as "Assault," it is also true that it was a crime that lower-class families were more likely to commit. In articles such as "Cannibalism in England" (1891), Waugh therefore recasts starvation as a moral failing, rather than as an economic problem. He directly addresses the issue of hunger, acknowledging that "From infancy to death it is not possible for any of us to escape the need of something to eat" (9). However, Waugh suggests that hunger is to be met according to the "general conditions of child and adult life," in which the child's needs are supplied by the parent, and the adult's hunger is assuaged by his or her "own labour" (9). But while these are the "general conditions" of life, Waugh argues that they have not always been met. Prior to the passage of the Children's Charter, he suggests, children were allowed to support their parents. Because of this reversal, "These [toiling] children were regarded as the pantry, yielding the necessaries of adult life. They stood between the idle man and the gnawings of hunger. Their starving bodies were slowly transmuted into the muscles with which he got about" (9). The cannibalism Waugh describes is, obviously, very much akin to that reported by Carlyle. Rather than understanding such starvation as a symptom of economic conditions, however, Waugh instead reads it as a deliberate choice. Child labor and "the gnawings of hunger" among the lower and working classes represent, in his words, the moral flaw of idleness.

Although Waugh's focus on the "general conditions" of life suggests a failure to recognize the extent to which applying universal standards of child-rearing (based on middle-class values and standards of living) might be a form of class bias, there is much in his writings to suggest that his opposition to child-life insurance went beyond a middle-class inability to respect lower- and working-class realities and customs. When Waugh states in "Child-Life Insurance," for example, that the class he is referring to does not include the "respectable poor" but, instead, "that inglorious

---

5   The NSPCC devised various categories, such as "General Ill-Treatment," "Assault" and "Neglect and Starvation," to demonstrate the kinds of cases in which it was involved. For representative categories and annual statistics, see the NSPCC's "Quarterly Return of the Society's Cases" (1891, 1892), "Two Months' Return of the Society's Cases" (1893) and "Court Cases Proved True During Last Recorded Month" (1894).

herd of people who are everywhere the perplexity of our police" (52), he is utilizing language that works within late-nineteenth-century class-inflected discourses of criminality and the "lower orders." As Marie-Christine Leps observes, such rhetoric depicts "the 'laboring and dangerous classes' as a separate race, primitive, animal-like and threatening," and as an "atavistic resurgence of 'prehistoric man'" (5). In this discourse, representations of the criminal dovetail with that of the pauper, who is constructed as "defective, lazy, and unintelligent" (4). Waugh's depictions of abusive parents throughout his writings share these qualities: they are "big-limbed, arbitrary" ("Street Children" 827), "reckless" (Manning and Waugh 699), "impecunious, idle people" ("Child-Life Insurance" 41) who are "lazy as sloths, lustful as monkeys, crafty as serpents, savage as tigers" (53) and mere "she-things" ("Baby Farming" 705). Such representations of abusive parents emphasize the separation between them and the "genuine British mother and father" ("Child-Life Insurance" 52), and, consequently, mark these brutal parents as a distinct social class, one whose ills are "considered signs of moral weakness rather than economic struggles" (Leps 26). In his desire to assert that the class he was accusing of murdering children for profit is distinguished by its immorality rather than by its poverty, Waugh did not challenge class-based rhetoric; instead, he operated firmly within it.

Furthermore, Waugh's focus on the "gnawings of hunger" in the lower- and working-class home betrays anxiety about the presence of hungry, starving adult bodies, a worry that is particularly evident in his writings on child-life insurance. Certainly, Waugh's focus on the child as the subject of concern worked within a nineteenth-century discourse that sought to "transform, or try to transform, the dangerous hungers of powerful adults into the blameless and pitiable needs of infant victims" (Berry 10). The NSPCC's depiction of abused children as innocent and helpless might suggest that Waugh expressed his fear of English savages on behalf of their offspring; however, his rhetoric suggests instead that it was the ability of this class of parents to reproduce that was of gravest concern – that those "pitiable" infants were themselves the end result of adult hungers. What appears to have been particularly frightening to Waugh about the English savage was the reproductive power of this "herd of reckless married and unmarried creatures with maternal organism," and with "males to match them" ("Child-Life Insurance" 53). The "inglorious herd" (52), according to Waugh, is made up of strong "hardy folks" (50) of the "stolid Amazon type" (51), and they give birth to children who "are hardy themselves, and therefore hard to kill" (50). Despite the fear, therefore, that child-life insurance might lead to countless deaths of insured children, the central anxiety these images express is that this group has the capacity to replicate itself. London at the end of the nineteenth century "was a city of children, and its poor districts contained the greatest number of them" (Ross 13). Furthermore, the slums in which these children were often found were perceived to be "symptoms of a physical and moral deterioration of society" (Leps 23). Given these physical and discursive contexts, it becomes clear that Waugh's images of savage fertility tapped into common fears about the growth of the lower and working classes. Rather than sparking pity, England's hungry and starving evoked fear in rhetoric such as Waugh's, because of the perceived strength of those who sought to satisfy that hunger.

Waugh's "Child-Life Insurance" article connects those hungry bodies, able to reproduce, to the growth of corrupt business practices in the insurance industry. Waugh argues that the incentive of the insurance agent to sell as many policies as possible is occasioned by the business imperative that "Offices must have increase" (54). In Waugh's mind, the necessity – and capacity – of insurance business to "increase" is a source of concern, because those businesses, like their clients, tended to spread contamination and death while doing so. Waugh focuses particularly on the touts – the paid agents of insurance companies who sold policies from door to door (Behlmer 125) – who, he argues, were "silently teaching strong lessons on a vast scale" ("Child-Life Insurance" 52). Those lessons, Waugh believes, result in child murder in "vast numbers" (42). Waugh therefore directly connects the growth of the insurance industry to a perceived increase in the starvation of children, of whom there is an endless supply.

The perceived alliance between the insurance industry and the savage (lower- and working-class) parent appalled Waugh, because it showed parents how to be the wrong kind of "productive" members of society. That is, the lessons those touts taught the parents of the dangerous classes was how to put their productive powers to work for them – how to transform their children into food and drink. The business in which insurance companies and abusive parents engaged was "the making of 30s. on starved [children] for the churchyard" (Waugh, "Children as Articles" 122), money that could then be spent by "the drinking, gambling, impure" and "idle" as they saw fit ("Notes" [1890] 91). This system of money-benefit, according to Waugh, "incites such to change the child for the pound" ("Child-Life Insurance" 41), a system of exchange that perverts the proper parental role of caring for and of nurturing children. Instead, the "effect of a policy on the matter of which the child is composed tends not to the preservation but to the waste of it, and to the rate and certainty with which infantile disease becomes fatal to it" (58). Child-life insurance here represents, again, a form of economic cannibalism, as parents reaped financial benefits through a process that consumed their children's flesh and blood. Furthermore, the appetites fed by this process of altering "the matter of which the child is composed" went beyond those of mere physical hunger, as may be seen in Waugh's example of insuring parents who feel "a strong animal affection for one another" (49). The waste and starvation of children produced further reproduction, reproduction that supported the "impure" pursuits of parents and the increase of insurance offices.

While Waugh's depiction of child-life insurance seems to suggest a closed circuit in which savage parents satisfied their appetites through the continual production of offspring for the graveyards, he carefully points out the ways in which such production would inevitably infect the body of the nation itself. According to Waugh, insurance companies and their agents, working toward the goal of increased benefit, undertook the education of their clients. The system of money-benefit, Waugh asserts, seeks to convert "impecunious, idle people into crafty murderers. It teaches the drunkard that to face his son's death is the way to drown his raging thirst" ("Child-Life Insurance" 41). For Waugh, in order to do these things, the "idle" and the "impecunious" must be taught how to cheat the legal system. He suggests that insurance agents (by their action, if not their words) instruct their clients as follows:

You may go to the inquest, and because two of you were in the room, neither of you being able to give evidence against the other; you may escape by the skin of your teeth; you may be called by the court "a disgrace to humanity;" only pay me your pennies, and when denounced you leave the court, I will give you my pounds. (52)

The touts persuade avaricious parents, Waugh argues, that denunciation by those in authority means nothing, and that money – however gained – means everything. With this instruction, a parent goes on to dupe those in power, and Waugh marvels at "the crafty practices whereby child-killing is accomplished and yet inquests are escaped," and he laments that "defrauding the coroner of his case is the rule, not the exception" (43). The fear elicited by the alliance between a money-loving parent and a money-loving tout is, therefore, not just on behalf of the child, but also on behalf of the rule of law. The failure of certain parents to respect the natural order – that is, to feel "natural affection" for their child (Waugh, "Doing Children" 85), or to obey "the general conditions of child and adult life" by providing for their children (Waugh, "Cannibalism" 9) – threatens English society itself.

What might appear to have been a domestic scandal became, in Waugh's mind, a national shame that needed to be addressed "for the sake of England's children and the morals and interests of their homes" ("Child-Life Insurance" 63). For Waugh, because the alliance between the lower and the working classes and the insurance industry perverted the home itself, it degraded the community (53). In other words, the "moral sense of the nation" (63) depended on "the convenience of commerce" being made "to bend to the comfort and safety of our children" (63) for, as Waugh argues, "A child dishonoured is a nation's bane" (59). These pronouncements underline a perceived connection between home and nation, wherein the failure to uphold the natural order within one leads to the destruction of the other. These sentiments do not, of course, displace responsibility for a child's suffering from his or her abusive, neglectful parents, but they do place the imperative to address that suffering on the national level. The failure to intercede on behalf of a child is a failure not only to protect that child, but also to uphold the laws of England. Child-life insurance, then, "Whether it be by the societies, their agents, the undertakers, or the parents [...] must be treated as a serious crime, against both the bodies of children and the welfare of the State" (63).

Waugh and the NSPCC believed the only way to address the threat pose by child-life insurance was its complete abolition (Waugh, "Child-Life Insurance" 62). Such an aim, however, was never achieved. Although the NSPCC published a special issue of *The Child's Guardian* in August 1890 including condemnations of child-life insurance from physicians, the police and coroners, such testimony "offered impressions rather than facts" (Behlmer 132). Even the NSPCC's case studies failed to offer conclusive evidence that parents were "Doing children to death for money," as the title of the August 1890 opening editorial of *The Child's Guardian* proclaimed. Although the NSPCC gave these narratives sensationalist titles such as "The Way to £20" and "A £5 Prize for Killing a Baby," the cases themselves contain the same stories of neglect and abuse that can be found in any of the NSPCC's cases. In one case entitled "£17 7s. 0d.: Bonuses on Neglect," for example, the description of the family and their home simply underscores their desperate poverty. The house is described as being:

> in a shockingly neglected condition, very filthy. The bed-room in which the prisoners and their family slept measured 14ft. by 12ft., the height being 9ft. [...] The heads of the [six] children were covered with sores, and full of vermin; in fact, they were generally in a disgraceful condition. (88)

Although this case is indicative of the kinds of situations the NSPCC investigated and prosecuted under the Children's Charter, it does not provide any solid evidence that these children were, in fact, neglected for their insurance money. Its similarity to the many other cases of neglect published in *The Child's Guardian* therefore calls into question any causal connection between the condition of the home and the insuring of the children.

The NSPCC's rhetoric on the subject could not be matched by actual evidence. The Society itself therefore gave the insurance industry its strongest defense, as attacks on child-life insurance could be read as signs of the extent to which Waugh "overestimated the ease with which working-class mothers and fathers might be tempted to barbarism" (Behlmer 136). As a result of a lack of factual evidence, the NSPCC's bill to abolish child-life insurance failed, as did every measure against the practice brought before parliament in the following years (135).

The lack of any persuasive support for his attacks is a point on which Waugh expressed great frustration. As he complains in "Child-Life Insurance,"

> I am at a loss to understand the state of mind which excludes all the merely probable, however highly probable, from consideration, where all that happens happens to a little invalid in the sole charge of a drunken nurse, who has £6 coming at that little invalid's death; where, whatever moral certainty there may be in the doctor and amongst the neighbours, based on however many outside facts, as to what happened in the sickroom, is of no assize value; where, the child once dead, neither of its parents can give evidence as to what the other did. (60)

The problem Waugh identified was the lack of access to lower- and working-class homes in order to ascertain what was going on inside them. The gap between the "moral certainty" of commentators such as Waugh and any actual evidence of wrongdoing in lower- and working-class homes reveals the extent to which ideological constructions of the lower and working classes provided the primary impetus behind attacks upon child-life insurance. For Waugh, however, this gap merely signified the need for greater intervention. As he argues, until child-protection workers can move beyond simply asserting the "highly probable," the problem itself "cannot be approached" (60).

To be more precise, it could not be approached by the right people. Waugh laments that "It is miserable to a patriot to think how many of these collectors of premiums upon child death policies openly, week by week, call at doors within which, the neighbours believe, a child is being slowly neglected to death" (49). The home might be closed to those – such as neighbors, physicians and coroners – who are most invested in a child's well-being, but it is open to those who are not. In Waugh's view, the lower- and working-class home is permeable only by those who will have no positive effect on it – people who will not support or instruct parents in their proper responsibilities and duties, but will instead teach lessons that will lead to the degradation of their homes. Although, Waugh argues, the tout might have "eyes in his head to see what he [is] doing" (49) to the children in the home, he has "orders" (49) to continue with his work. Under the system of child-life insurance, those who are privileged to see what others can only believe to be happening are bound, by their love of money and the demands of commerce, not to intervene. As long as those who have no investment in supporting proper parental care and affection in the home have the most access to it, Waugh suggests, the children of the poor will be at risk, and, as Waugh's appeal to "patriots" makes apparent, so too will the nation itself. Waugh's battle against child-life insurance, then, was as much a battle for influence within the lower- and working-class home as it was an attack on the practice itself.

The implicit contrast to the influence of the insurance company on the lower- and working-class home was, of course, that of the NSPCC, which claimed that its sole interest in that home was in its reform, its sole desire to transform "parents, who are absolutely indifferent to their children's necessities and welfare, who even hate their children and see in their helplessness inducement to tyranny," into parents who "treat them with care, with even affection" (Waugh, "Emancipation" 33). Where the bad influence of commerce degrades the home, the NSPCC's influence restores its proper order:

> By the Society's treatment, and in a way little short of amazing to the ordinary mind, in ten thousand bad parents' conduct care has taken the place of indifference, and in thousands love has taken the place of hate. Under the means the Society employs, natural feelings have proven to be hidden, and those feelings have had the opportunity given to them to arise, have of themselves arisen, have been cultivated and strengthened, and have become in the strictest sense the feelings generally operating between the human race and its offspring. (33)

Again, Waugh asserts here the existence of universal laws governing the parent–child relationship. In the home of the English savage, these laws have been overthrown; through the NSPCC's intercession, such laws could once again take hold. The insurance agent, conversely, might have "eyes in his head," but he has neither the will nor the desire to see the true potential of lower- and working-class parents. The NSPCC, however, *could* see that potential and, if given more influence over the home than that of commerce, would bring about a reformation within it, by attacking "unnatural habits and tastes which prevent natural parental feeling arising" (33). Necessity and starvation were not, therefore, the primary threats to lower- and working-class children and their families; instead, it was the fact that the "old kindly affections of our race for its young have lapsed" (33). Those kindly feelings could be rekindled, but only through proper guidance and education. In order for England's homes to be saved, according to Waugh, they needed to be open not to commerce, but to intervention; not to the tout, but to the inspector.

Waugh's focus on production and commercial exchange allowed him and the NSPCC to avoid accusations of class bias, and to answer charges that the Society's work criminalized poor and starving parents. His representation of the problem of child-life insurance, however, reveals the extent to which the practice did, in fact, tap into deep-rooted fears about the lower and working classes, and, for that matter, about commerce. What ostensibly originated in a concern for abused and starving children expanded into a critique of the role of lower- and working-class families and their children in England's commercial economy, and of the role of commerce within those families. While it might be difficult to comprehend how the purchase of life insurance could have been perceived as a business venture – and a corruptive one at that – the fact that Waugh constructed it as such suggests that the possibility of a kind of alliance between the lower and working classes and commerce was a significant source of anxiety. Such a fear might speak, in part, to a more widespread recognition that the growth of England's economy had significantly altered the relationship between the higher and the lower classes, displacing an earlier paternalism that the NSPCC sought to reassert. I believe it also speaks, however, to a fear of lower- and working-class children. For while Waugh represented those children as objects of pity, his many images of productivity and consumption suggested a fear that the children, as yet powerless commodities, might in the future become producers and consumers in their own right. The attack on child-life insurance might have been on behalf of children, but it was also, in the end, on behalf of an entire nation that felt itself threatened by those children, and by what they might become.

Works Cited

"£17 7s. 0d.: Bonuses on Neglect." *The Child's Guardian* (Aug. 1890): 88.

Behlmer, George. *Child Abuse and Moral Reform in England, 1870-1914*. Stanford: Stanford UP, 1982.

Berry, Laura. *The Child, the State, and the Victorian Novel*. Charlottesville: University Press of Virginia, 1999.

Carlyle, Thomas. *Past and Present*. 1843. London: J. M. Dent & Sons, 1960.

Cobbe, Frances Power. "Wife-Torture in England." *Criminals, Idiots, Women, and Minors: Victorian Writing by Women on Women*. Ed. Susan Hamilton. Peterborough, ON: Broadview, 2004: 111-144.

Hall, William Clarke. *The Queen's Reign for Children*. London: T. Fisher Unwin, 1897.

"Insurance and Suffocation in Liverpool." *The Child's Guardian* (Oct. 1888): 93.

Hendrick, Harry. *Child Welfare: England, 1872-1989*. London: Routledge, 1994.

Leps, Marie-Christine. *Apprehending the Criminal: The Production of Deviance in Nineteenth-Century Discourse*. Durham: Duke UP, 1992.

Malton, Nicholas. "RE: Photo Copyright." E-mail to Monica Flegel. 30 June 2006.

Manning, Henry Edward and Benjamin Waugh. "The Child of the English Savage." *Contemporary Review* (May 1886): 687-700.

McDonagh, Josephine. *Child Murder and British Culture, 1720-1900*. Cambridge: Cambridge UP, 2003.

National Society for the Prevention of Cruelty to Children. "Court Cases Proved True During Last Recorded Month." *The Child's Guardian* (Jan. 1894): 4.

---. "Quarterly Return of the Society's Cases." *The Child's Guardian* (Nov. 1891): 116.

---. "Quarterly Return of the Society's Cases." *The Child's Guardian* (Feb. 1892): 18.

---. "Two Months' Return of the Society's Cases." *The Child's Guardian* (Jan. 1893): 4.

Payne, Walter. *The Cruelty Man: Actual Experiences of an N.S.P.C.C. Inspector, Graphically Told by Himself.* London: The National Society for the Prevention of Cruelty to Children, 1912.

Ross, Ellen. *Motherhood in Outcast London, 1870-1918.* Oxford: Oxford UP, 1993.

Waugh, Benjamin. "Baby Farming." *Contemporary Review* (July 1890): 700-714.

---. "Cannibalism in England." *The Child's Guardian* (Feb. 1891): 9-10.

---. "Child-Life Insurance." *Contemporary Review* (July 1890): 40-63.

---. "Children as Articles of Commerce." *The Child's Guardian* (Oct. 1890): 122.

---. "Cruelty to the High Born." *The Child's Guardian* (Jan. 1889): 131.

---. "Doing Children to Death for Money." *The Child's Guardian* (August 1890): 85-86.

---. "Emancipation – Child and Parent; or, Can Bad Homes be Reformed?" *The Child's Guardian* (Mar. 1896): 33-34.

---. "Notes." *The Child's Guardian* (Dec. 1889): 224.

---. "Notes." *The Child Guardian* (Aug. 1890): 91.

---. "Prevention of Cruelty to Children." *Dublin Review* (Jan. 1892): 140-151.

---. *Some Conditions of Child Life in England.* London: National Society for the Prevention of Cruelty to Children, 1889.

---. "Street Children." *Contemporary Review* (June 1888): 825-35.

---. "The Rights of the Working Man." *The Child's Guardian* (July 1890): 81.

Index